W9-ABD-454

*Understanding the
New Sailing
Technology*

Other books by Sven Donaldson
A SAILOR'S GUIDE TO SAILS

Understanding the
New Sailing
Technology
A BASIC GUIDE FOR SAILORS

Sven Donaldson

G. P. Putnam's Sons • New York

G. P. Putnam's Sons
Publishers Since 1838
200 Madison Avenue
New York, NY 10016

Copyright © 1990 by Sven Donaldson
All rights reserved. This book, or parts thereof, may not be
reproduced in any form without permission. Published simultaneously
in Canada

Designed by Rhea Braunstein

Library of Congress Cataloging-in-Publication Data
Donaldson, Sven.
    Understanding the new sailing technology/by Sven Donaldson.
        p.   cm.
    Bibliography: p.
    Includes index.
    1. Yachts and yachting—Design and construction. 2. Sailboats—
Design and construction. I. Title.
VM331.D66 1990   89-10341 CIP
623.8′223-dc20
ISBN 0-399-13506-5

Printed in the United States of America
1 2 3 4 5 6 7 8 9 10

This book has been printed on acid-free paper.

$ 24.95

To my son, Scott, age four,
who loves brief rides
in small, fast sailboats.

Contents

The accelerated pace of technological advancement in sailing today is viewed by most amateur sailors as either exciting or alarming, but few are genuinely indifferent to the rapid changes in our once-traditional recreational pursuit. There is little doubt that those who deplore these changes will eventually have to reconcile themselves to them. The escalating political and economic importance of major transoceanic races, Olympic competition, the America's Cup, and the recent emergence of full-fledged professional racing serve notice that the pace of sailboat development is certain to continue fast and furious.

This book is intended to help the casual recreational sailor come to grips with (and, I hope, appreciate a bit more) the leading edge of sailing technology. It undertakes to show how recent developments fit into a framework of fundamental principles and how the latest innovations build upon the best technology of an earlier era. It is not intended as an encyclopedic guide to everything that's new in sailing, but rather as an introduction for those who would like to know a little more about how contemporary boats really work.

Aficionados of automobile racing like to point out that many major improvements in automotive engineering originated on the track. The same argument when applied to sailing is equally compelling. Over the past thirty years a majority of the advances in sailing hull design, construction, rigging, spars, and sails were pioneered on the race-course. In a remarkable number of cases, the inventions inspired by competition have ended up being used on many, if not most, recreational sailboats. For this reason alone, no one with a genuine interest in sailing can ignore the progress currently being made by serious racing sailors, designers, boatbuilders, and sailmakers. If history shows any inclination to repeat itself, the cruising and daysailing boats of the next decade will incorporate many of the ideas being tested and refined by today's racing sailors, particularly those who compete offshore and shorthanded. Thus, while this is not a book about sail-boat racing, racing is indirectly responsible for much of its content. I make no apologies for this, and sincerely hope that even those of you who consider yourselves dyed-in-the-wool cruisers will elect to read on . . .

1

The Essentials of Sailing

You really don't need to know how a sailboat works in order to sail one, even to sail it well. On the other hand, to understand the latest developments in sailing technology, some knowledge of sailing theory is indispensible. This chapter provides a commonsense presentation of the essentials of sailboat function. It sets the stage for the remainder of the book, which will focus upon exciting advances in hull design and construction, keels and rudders, rigs and sails, deck gear, and electronics.

In the context of modern transportation, even high-performance sailboats are very slow vehicles. Their appeal stems not so much from absolute speed as from their ability to progress in any direction using only the natural forces associated with moving wind and water. Sailing craft that glide along smartly in light as well as strong breezes, accelerate powerfully in puffs, and provide a lively, responsive "feel" are regarded more favorably than either skittish or sluggish ones. After all, present-day sailing is a recreational activity, and the enjoyment it provides is largely sensual—a combination of sounds, sights, and movements that together provide an overall impression of effortless speed on the water. In a stiff breeze, a good sailboat feels like it's going considerably faster than it really is.

Sailing speed is limited on the one hand by the amount of energy that can be extracted from the air flowing past the sails, and on the other by the inevitable drag or resistance associated with moving the sailboat through the air and water. Improved performance can be achieved either by converting more of the kinetic energy from the wind into forward force, or by minimizing resistance so that whatever forward force is available will result in a higher speed.

Naturally, satisfactory sailboats must usually meet a number of other criteria which, by and large, are at odds with the goal of all-out sailing performance. Essential features like weight-carrying ability, ease of handling, seaworthiness, and below-decks living space all take a toll on ultimate speed. Aesthetic standards and cost limitations further reduce the speed potential of most designs—which is probably just as well.

The Feat of Upwind Sailing

Sailboats may be slow, but because they are the only transportation devices that operate simultaneously in two different fluid media—air and water—they are arguably the most complicated vehicles in existence. Everyone intuitively understands how a boat can be blown downwind. However, even some experienced sailors are not quite certain how the same sailboat can slice obliquely into the wind, often at an angle no greater than 40 degrees from the true upwind direction.

The flow of air past the wings of a fast-moving airplane creates a force called **lift** that acts upward, approximately at right angles to the flow direction, and literally keeps the airplane aloft by counteracting the downward pull of gravity. A popular analogy likens a sailboat to an airplane that has been tipped on its side so that one lift-producing surface—the sail—protrudes into the air, while the other—the keel—extends down into the water (fig. 1-1). Of course, a sailboat cannot move directly into the wind like a self-propelled aircraft. Therefore, our airplane/sailboat must be oriented so that the wind angles in from one side with its upper wing (sail) rotated or trimmed so that its lift becomes, in part, a forward propulsive force (fig. 1-1 left). To make the upended airplane even more like a sailboat, its upper and lower "wings" should be made very different in size and shape to allow for the substantial differences in density, viscosity, and flow speed between the air above and the water below (fig. 1-1 right).

Because the lift forces produced by the sails and the keel are predominantly sideways rather than forward when a sailboat is hard on

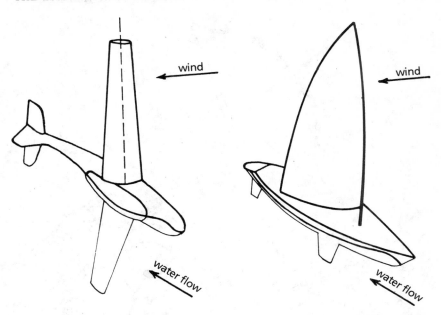

Fig. 1–1. In principle, a sailboat resembles an airplane turned on its side with one wing protruding beneath the surface and the other pivoted to face the wind at an advantageous angle. Wings, sails, keels, and rudders all function as lift-producing foils.

the wind, it may not be obvious why the boat nevertheless moves almost directly forward. A useful analogy is an arrow being shot from a bow. Think of the drawn bowstring as consisting of two separate segments, each attached to the end of the arrow and each leading to one tip of the bow or the other (fig. 1-2a). The pull in each string segment is aligned with the string itself—more sideways than forward. However, the side forces from each string segment cancel each other out, leaving only a net forward force to propel the arrow straight and true.

As viewed from above (fig. 1–2b), a sailboat conforms closely to this bow-and-arrow analogy. The sideways components of the largely opposing lift force created by the sails and keel cancel one another out, leaving only a net forward force to propel the boat almost (but not quite) directly ahead. It's much the same idea as shooting a slippery watermelon seed by squeezing it between thumb and forefinger, except that in the case of this popular analogy, the largely opposing forces work together to push the seed forward rather than to pull it along (fig. 1–2c).

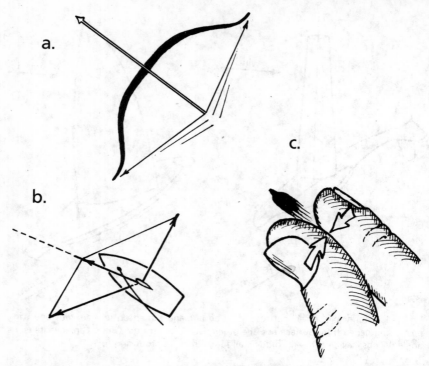

Fig. 1-2. On a closehauled or reaching course, the forces that propel a sailboat interact much like those that shoot an arrow from a bow or squirt a watermelon seed from between pinched fingers.

Where Does the Lift Come From?

Although air is a colorless, invisible fluid, it is still a real material like water, steel, or concrete. Moving air possesses energy in the same way a moving automobile possesses energy. If a stationary object is placed in the path of a moving car, some of the car's kinetic energy will be transferred to the object—usually with distressing results. Similarly, if the object is inserted into a stream of moving air, energy will again be transferred, producing a force that will tend to make the object move. The direction of this induced force depends upon the shape of the object. If it is symmetrically shaped (with respect to the flow) the resulting force will act directly downstream and is called **drag** or **resistance** (fig. 1-3a).

On the other hand, if the object is asymmetrical, the induced force

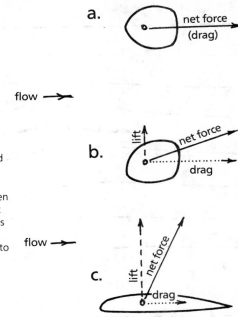

Fig. 1–3. The uniform-flow split created by a symmetrical object creates only a rearward drag force *(a)*. However, an asymmetrical object produces an uneven diversion of flow which results in a net force acting obliquely rearward *(b)*. This net force can be resolved into a lift component which acts at right angles to the flow and a downstream drag component. A foil is a special shape designed to produce high lift and minimal drag when properly oriented with respect to the flow *(c)*.

usually acts in a diagonal direction—partly downstream, but partly to one side. Just as in the bow-and-arrow analogy, what we have is a net force—in this case the diagonal force—that consists of a lateral or lift component superimposed on a downstream or drag component (fig. 1–3b).

Although an infinite number of different asymmetrical shapes are possible, only a few of these are capable of producing more lift than drag when placed in a stream of moving fluid. Shapes that have high (favorable) lift-to-drag ratios are called **foils** (fig. 1–3c)—either **airfoils** or **hydrofoils** depending upon the fluid in which they work.

The fabric sails used by most sailboats are surprisingly efficient airfoils at the low wind speeds experienced in most sailing. As air first begins to flow across a properly trimmed sail, its asymmetrical, curved shape deflects the flow and causes a small pressure imbalance to develop between one side of the sail and the other (fig. 1–4a). Approaching air reacts to this pressure imbalance by veering toward the high-pressure side and away from the low-pressure one. As a result, the air flow over the two faces of the sail becomes unevenly divided with more air passing over the convex, leeward face of the

a.

b.

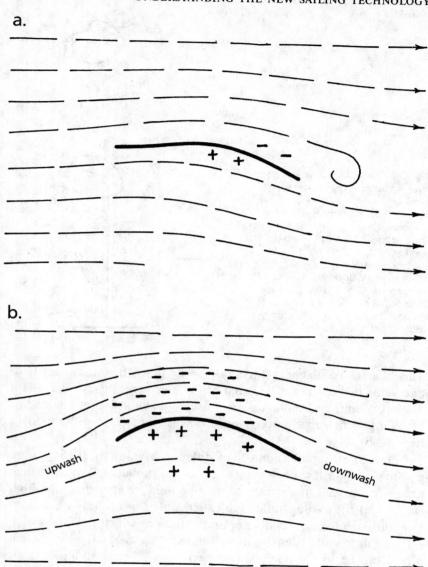

Fig. 1–4. When a sail is first sheeted in, a minor pressure differential is created between its windward and leeward sides *(a)*. Approaching air reacts to this imbalance by swerving toward the low-pressure area. This further increases the differential by boosting the volume and speed of the air passing over the leeward face of the sail. It ordinarily takes between 5 and 15 seconds for the upwash-downwash flow pattern to build to its maximum *(b)*.

sail than over the concave, windward face. The approaching air, being drawn toward the low-pressure region on the convex side of the sail, naturally picks up speed, while the somewhat smaller volume of air flowing into the high-pressure zone on the concave face of the sail tends to decelerate. It takes a few seconds after a sail is sheeted in for this asymmetrical flow pattern to become fully developed, and for the pressure differential across the sail to reach its maximum (fig. 1–4b).

For our purposes, the total energy content of a stream of moving air (or water) is the sum of its kinetic energy and its pressure (or potential energy). The two are interchangeable, so when flow speed or kinetic energy increases, then the potential energy or pressure must decrease. This effect, known as **Bernoulli's principle,** is the root cause of the pronounced decrease in air pressure on the leeward side of the sail. Likewise, it explains the more modest pressure increase on the opposite side of the sail where the flow speed has slowed. Together, these two localized pressure changes produce a force that acts laterally, from the high-pressure side of the sail toward the low. It's basically the same force that acts on a piston in an engine when gas pressure builds up within the cylinder. Despite that fact that this force acts more or less horizontally in the case of a sail, it is conventional to retain aircraft terminology and call it **lift.**

The underwater foils (keel or centerboard, and rudder) also generate lift (sometimes called **lateral resistance)** in much the same way that the sails do. Unlike most sails, the fins themselves are usually symmetrically shaped foils that are rendered asymmetrical with respect to the flow by being oriented at a small angle called the **angle of attack** (fig. 1–5). In practice, all boats seek out the proper angle of attack for their underwater foils automatically. The whole boat, fins and all, simply skids diagonally sidewise (makes **leeway**) until a combination of flow speed and angle of attack is reached where the lift generated beneath the surface exactly counterbalances the lateral component of the lift produced by the sails.

Stability: Resistance to Heeling Forces

Air flowing past the sails creates sideways and forward forces from the top of the rig down to deck level. The net effect of these forces can be regarded as identical to the effect that would be produced by a single force (of appropriate magnitude and direction) acting at a

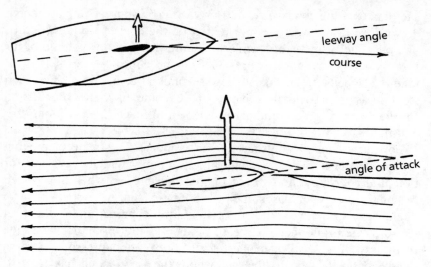

Fig. 1–5. The symmetrical foils used for most keels or centerboards produce lift only when oriented at an angle with respect to the flow. Because these foils are ordinarily aligned with the centerline of the hull, they cannot generate lift unless the hull itself makes leeway.

single point called the rig's **center of effort** (abbreviated CE). The CE is usually located between 30 to 40 percent of the distance from deck to masthead (fig. 1–6a). The CE for the opposing side force generated by water flow past the hull and fins is situated well below the waterline.

With two equal and opposite side forces acting at widely separated points, the boat experiences that well-known tendency to tip or heel. This would inevitably lead to immediate capsize if it were not for another pair of forces that tend to induce rotation in the opposite direction.

Just as all the sail forces can be regarded as having a cumulative effect identical to a single larger force acting at the CE, the force of gravity pulling individually on every part of the boat has the same effect as a single downward force equal to the weight of the boat acting at a discrete point called the **center of gravity,** or CG. Similarly, buoyant forces acting all over the wetted portions of the hull have an effect identical to that of a single force, equal in magnitude to the boat's weight, but upward, that acts at the **center of buoyancy,** or CB.

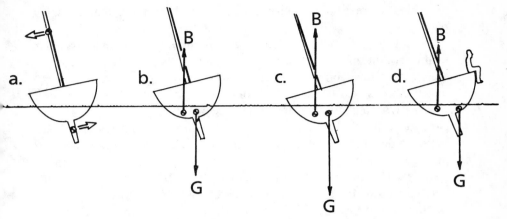

Fig. 1–6. Lateral sail force and keel lift acting in opposite directions at different heights *(diagram a)* create a **couple** that would capsize the boat were it not for an opposing couple created by buoyancy (B) and gravity (G). Lateral stability can be improved either by boosting displacement *(diagram c)* or by increasing the lateral distance between the CB and the CG *(diagram d)*.

When most sailboats heel or roll to leeward, the leeward side of the hull becomes more deeply immersed while the windward side lifts higher in the water. This causes the CB to shift somewhat to leeward while the CG remains fixed (fig. 1–6b). As the sites of action for downward and upward forces begin to separate, a rotational tendency that is opposite to the heeling tendency comes into play.

Increasing the displacement of the boat will generally yield an increase in lateral stability by simply causing the downward gravitational force and the corresponding buoyant force to grow larger (fig. 1–6c). This is usually the case even when the added weight does not lower the boat's center of gravity. Of course, shifting crew weight or ballast weight off-center to windward will further increase the lateral separation between the sites of action for buoyant and gravitational forces, thus providing additional stability for carrying sail (fig. 1–6d).

Why Sailboats Aren't Faster

In the absence of appreciable resistance, even the comparatively small net propulsive forces generated by air flow over sails would cause a sailboat to accelerate to very high speeds. Unfortunately, the bulk of the hull needed to float even a lightweight sailboat offers a great deal of resistance when moving at anything more than a snail's pace.

Whenever a sailboat reaches its maximum speed for the particular sailing conditions, it means that resistance has escalated to the point that it precisely counterbalances the propulsive forces generated by its sails. This resistance stems from a large number of separate drag sources with names like form drag, viscous drag, wave-making drag, parasitic drag, induced drag, and added drag. Yacht designers and builders devote a great deal of attention to reducing resistance, so many of these drag sources will come under scrutiny in the upcoming chapters. However, for the time being, it is only important to remember that improved speed under sail can only result through either a net increase in propulsive force or a decrease in overall resistance.

Sailing Theory in a Nutshell

In summary, all sailboats, no matter how simple or sophisticated, depend upon the shearing action of wind blowing over water to simultaneously generate flow over both the sails and the underwater fins. Lift generated by the sails acts forward and, on most points of sail, sideways as well. Lift generated by the fins acts predominantly sideways and serves to counterbalance the lateral component of the lift from the sails.

Because these opposing lift forces act at different levels, one above the water and the other below, they combine to produce a rotational or capsizing tendency. It must be counteracted by another pair of opposing forces that together create a rotational tendency in the opposite direction. This essential stabilizing effect is achieved by configuring the boat so that the net upward force acting at the center of buoyancy is offset some distance to leeward of the equal, but opposite, downward force acting through the center of gravity.

The final factor in the "sailing equation" is the resistance or drag associated with motion in water and air. The combined resistance increases as a boat accelerates until it exactly equals the propulsive force from the sails. This state of affairs usually lasts for only a moment, because wind and sea conditions are never entirely stable. However, while it persists, all forces acting upon the boat are in perfect balance, and it sails straight ahead at a constant speed.

2

Advances in Keelboat Design

The vast majority of yachts large enough to carry on-board accommodations are ballasted monohulls—a pattern that will almost certainly continue to hold true in the foreseeable future. Tangible advantages of the monohull configuration include simplicity of construction (and hence relatively low cost), a high proportion of accessible interior volume, a compact hull that is easily moored, and the safety of self-righting capabilities. Perceived advantages include a conventional and widely acceptable appearance together with familiar or "normal" sailing characteristics. These perceived advantages often translate into tangible ones when it comes to either joining a fleet of similar boats for racing or finding a buyer.

Ballasted monohulls have been evolving for hundreds of years, but this lengthy history has not inhibited a surge of new developments during the past two decades. The single most important performance advance is probably the emergence of self-righting sailboats with genuine planing capabilities. However, monohull upwind performance has also improved substantially, thanks to design refinements that reduce resistance without diminishing propulsive force. Because the struggle to minimize resistance is a critical part of yacht design, it makes sense to begin with a closer look at some of the more important sources of drag in sailing.

Form Drag, Skin Friction, and Wetted Surface

Form drag is resistance associated with a fluid being physically displaced to make room for a moving body and subsequently returning to fill the void that would otherwise be left after the body has passed on by. To some extent, the forces created by the displacing process are counteracted by forces generated during the "refilling" phase. Form drag results from imperfections in this out-and-back lateral-flow pattern. It shows up as a **turbulent wake** which trails away downstream of the moving body (fig. 2–1 top).

Experience with the friction of one solid object sliding over another makes it easy to appreciate how something similar can happen when a solid body like a boat moves with respect to water or air. With a fluid involved, energy losses occur, not merely in a single plane, but throughout an envelope of semiattached or slow-moving fluid called the **boundary layer** (fig. 2–1 bottom). However, on either land or at sea, the result is the same: a force that tends to resist motion. To minimize this skin friction (also known as viscous drag), the immersed portions of a boat must be very smooth.

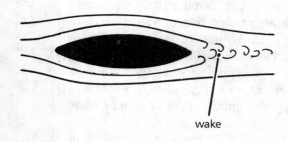

wake

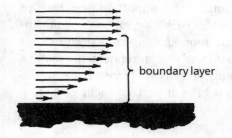

boundary layer

Fig. 2–1. *Top:* Form drag results when fluid displaced by a moving body fails to come together smoothly and quietly again once the body has passed on by. *Bottom:* Viscous drag is a consequence of friction between fluid molecules moving at a range of speeds within the boundary layer.

Because it must be buoyant enough to support the weight of crew, equipment, and often ballast, a boat's hull is a comparatively large and bulky object—something that is quite difficult to propel through the water except at very low speeds. For an indicator of how difficult, it's reasonable to start with **displacement** because a heavier boat must shoulder aside more water as it moves along. In fact, provided two boats of equal length are reasonably similar in other respects, the heavier one almost always offers greater resistance to motion. On the other hand, if the shapes of the two hulls are quite different, it is entirely possible that the heavier one may be easier to propel at certain speeds.

Wetted surface—the portion of a hull (plus underwater appendages) in direct contact with the water—is an excellent indicator of viscous drag, which is the dominant source of resistance at very low speeds. It can also be a fairly reliable indicator of form drag when comparing different hulls of similar length and displacement, because hulls with lower wetted surface, being narrower and rounder (fig. 2-2), will cause the passing water to deviate less from a straight-line path.

For light-wind, low-speed sailing where viscous drag and form drag are the dominant sources of resistance, minimum wetted surface is a top design priority. On the other hand, a circular hull section with the lowest possible surface-to-volume is not so satisfactory in stronger winds when the extra lateral stability associated with a wider, more flat bottomed hull shape becomes desirable (fig. 2-2). This is particularly true because additional sources of resistance that are almost entirely unrelated to wetted surface rise to the fore whenever sailing hulls are pushed to higher speeds.

Wave Drag and Theoretical Hull Speed

"Hull speed" is not an absolute speed limit, but an approximation of the top practical speed for a **displacement vessel,** a boat that continues to displace a weight of water equal to its own weight while under way. As a displacement boat advances and shoulders water aside, it creates a pattern of high and low pressure in the water nearby. Because these pressure variations are generated close to the water's surface, they induce local changes in water level—bulges in high-pressure regions and hollows in low-pressure ones. In this way, the moving boat creates its own system of surface waves.

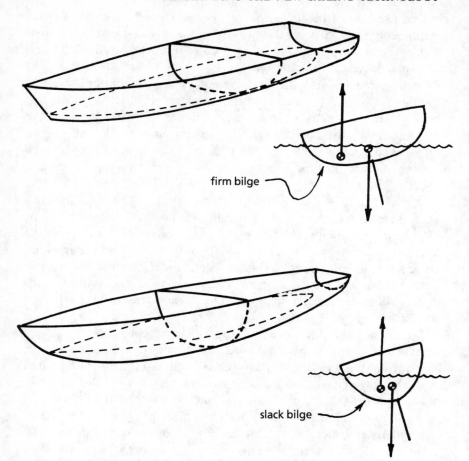

Fig. 2–2. A firm-bilged hull *(top)* has a relatively flat bottom, a wider waterline, and more wetted surface than a slack-bilged hull *(bottom)* of equal length and displacement. At moderate heel angles, the firm-bilged design is said to offer superior form stability because its shape ensures that the CB and CG will be separated more widely.

The speed of surface waves is proportional to wavelength. If the distance from one crest to the next in a wave system is greater, the wave system will advance faster because each rise-and-fall cycle covers more ground. It happens that the speed of water waves in knots is 1.34 times the square root of the wave length in feet. Because the speed of the wave system created by a moving hull is determined by the speed of the hull itself, when the hull goes faster, the wave length of its entrained wave system also increases (fig. 2–3).

When the **speed-to-length ratio** of a boat reaches about 1.3 and the natural wavelength of the driven wave system has grown to match the immersed length of the hull, the hull will have settled into the trough between its self-induced wave crests (fig. 2–3a). Resistance at

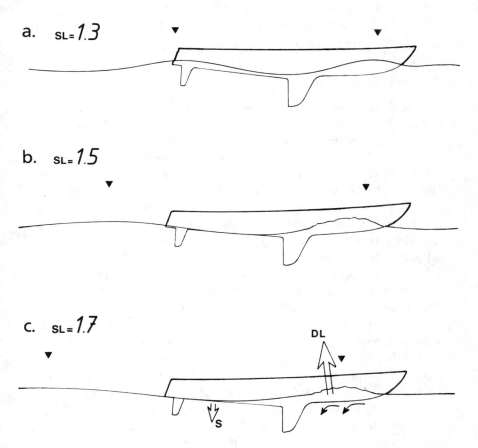

Fig. 2–3. As "hull speed" is approached, the crest of the quarter wave will have shifted aft away from the bow wave to coincide approximately with the boat's stern as shown in diagram a. Acceleration to a speed-to-length ratio of 1.5 (speed in knots ÷ √LWL) causes the crest of the stern wave to slide aft past the transom, which causes the stern to dip. If driven faster still, significant dynamic lift (DL) can be produced by water deflecting off the forward hull sections. Provided the downward suction forces created by water flowing over the convex stern sections are not too great, the boat will rise in the water and begin to plane.

this point will have reached quite a high level because the bow and stern must immerse quite deeply in order to displace a volume of water equal to the boat's weight.

However, if enough propulsive force is available to drive the boat faster yet, the wavelength of the induced wave system will automatically extend to exceed the immersed length of the hull. The bow wave still remains at the bow, but the crest of the quarter-wave slides aft beyond the stern itself (fig. 2–3b). In effect the boat is now positioned on a moving uphill slope of water—its own bow wave—balanced there by the propulsive force from its sails.

Planing in Sailboats

Whenever a boat moves ahead, its forward sections not only displace water sideways, but deflect some of it downward (fig. 2–3c). This creates an upward force called **dynamic lift**, which increases roughly as the square of the boat's speed. Therefore if the boat can get up enough speed, dynamic lift will cause it to ride somewhat higher in the water, causing its skin friction and form drag to be reduced (or at any rate to increase less rapidly with speed). A sailboat that loses a substantial fraction of its displacement when moving fast is said to be **planing**, although in almost all cases it is still partially supported by buoyancy.

Planing is nothing new for crew-stabilized, high-performance dinghies equipped with retractable centerboards to minimize drag for offwind legs. However, with most ballasted displacement yachts, the amount of dynamic lift obtained at hull speed—the speed at which wave drag tends to balloon to overwhelming proportions—is too small to significantly reduce displacement (and hence resistance). These boats are simply too heavy to lift appreciably as they plow through the water. A net propulsive force equal to roughly 10 percent of a boat's weight is needed to obtain any appreciable planing effect.

It has only been about fifteen years since the first true planing yachts with fixed-ballast keels and offshore capabilities made their appearance. Often called ULDBs (Ultra-Light Displacement Boats), these yachts are typically long, narrow, and low, with lots of sail area (fig. 2–4). Long sailing length provides a high theoretical hull speed, while the relatively powerful rig gives the propulsive force needed to approach this speed easily and often. As a ULDB nears "hull speed," dynamic lift gradually raises the light hull higher and higher in the

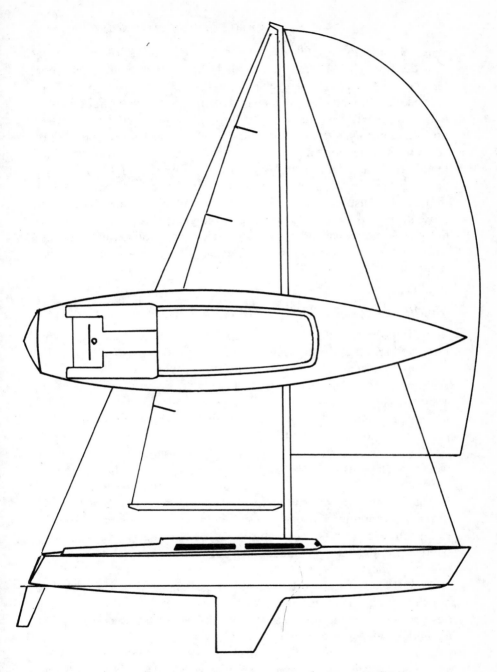

Fig. 2–4. Archetypal ULDBs are light, narrow boats with relatively large rigs. The Santa Cruz 50 shown here is 12 feet wide and weighs only 16,000 pounds, less than half the displacement of most 50-foot yachts.

water. Thanks to this shift to a planing mode, the ULDB can circumvent the wave-drag barrier that holds back sailboats with greater displacements relative to their lengths.

Since fast powerboats are usually beamy vessels, you might wonder why sailing ULDBs are typically long and slim. Certainly, there is no inherent reason why a wide-beam sailboat will not plane at least as well as a slender one, provided it has a similar displacement-to-length ratio and sufficient "sail power" for its weight. However, keeping the displacement of a wide boat low enough can be very difficult, because more beam means more hull surface area, and hence more structural weight. Nevertheless, the general trend in fast monohull development has been toward greater beam, not so much because it facilitates offwind planing, but because it can greatly improve upwind performance.

Stability for Windward Sailing

An important point to remember from the previous chapter is that improved speed under sail can result only when the ratio of propulsive force to resistance is somehow made more favorable.

When sailing upwind, a boat that heels excessively, even one with a slim, easily propelled hull, will experience a catastrophic increase in drag. As the rig, keel, and rudder incline, the lift force that each produces becomes less and less favorably oriented for either propelling the boat or counteracting leeway (fig. 2–5a). To make matters worse, most boats become badly "unbalanced" when allowed to heel too much (fig. 2–5b). What this means is that the boat can be kept in equilibrium and prevented from rounding up into the wind only through the application of excessive helm, which causes substantial rudder drag and costs speed (fig. 2–5c). Reducing sail or otherwise depowering the rig will reduce this heel and weather helm, but at the cost of propulsive force.

A better way to keep the resistance associated with heeling from mushrooming out of control is to improve lateral stability. Unless a designer opts for more displacement and accepts a reduction in light air and offwind performance, the only way to gain extra stability is to somehow increase the lateral distance between the center of buoyancy and the center of gravity. As mentioned in Chapter 1, shifting crew weight (or other weights) to windward is one common way to increase the righting tendencies of a sailboat. Another is to change

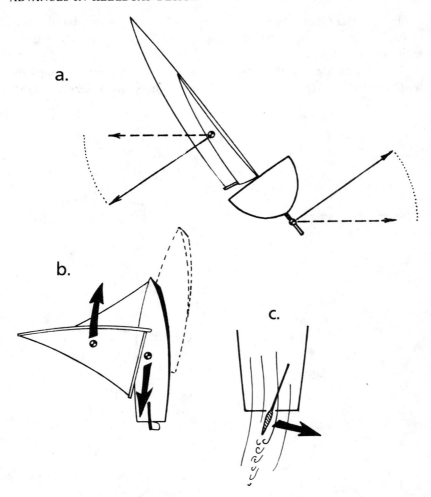

Fig. 2–5. Heeling reduces the useful horizontal components of both the sail and the keel forces *(a)*. It also causes the action center for propulsive sail forces to shift to leeward of the action center for drag forces. The resulting couple tends to pivot the boat into the wind *(b)* and must be counteracted by "weather helm." Note how the lift from the offset rudder retards the boat by acting obliquely backward *(c)*.

the cross-sectional shape of the hull. Contemporary designs with substantial waterline beam, relatively flat bottoms, and "firm" bilges are characterized by a CB that moves rapidly to leeward of the centerline as the hull begins to heel (fig. 2–6a). These boats are said to have greater **form stability** than narrower, more round-bilged designs (fig.

2–6b). On the other hand, too much emphasis on form stability will result in excessive wetted surface (see fig. 2–2), so most designers avoid extremes.

To compensate for their relative lack of form stability, narrow, traditional-style keelboats with rounded bilges must rely primarily

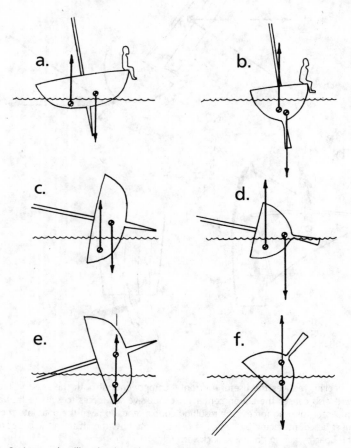

Fig. 2–6. At usual sailing heel angles, a modern flat-bottomed hull *(a)* provides superior sail-carrying power due to a combination of extra form stability and crew weight far to windward. With a narrow traditional hull *(b)*, crew on the weather rail have much less impact on the lateral position of the CG, while heel shifts the CB to leeward only slightly. However, in knockdown situations, the modern hull *(c)* is likely to exhibit less inclination to self-right than the traditional one *(d)* because the latter's narrow hull is deeper and typically has a lower CG. Likewise, the **limit of positive stability**, or heel angle at which the self-righting tendency becomes a capsizing tendency, will be smaller for the modern boat *(e)* than for the traditional design *(f)*.

upon heavy displacement (sometimes called **ballast stability**) for their sail-carrying power. As long as the ballast is positioned to give the whole boat a low CG, this approach is superior from the viewpoint of safety because it ensures reliable self-righting performance at high heel angles (fig. 2–6c, d).

Nevertheless, narrow, heavily ballasted keelboats are largely out of vogue because yacht designers have found that wide, modestly ballasted hulls have superior **initial stability** and can therefore carry more sail. With the addition of highly flaired topsides and exaggerated deck beam, crew weight on the weather rail becomes much more effective in further augmenting lateral stability (fig. 2–6a). For sailing downwind, the combination of light displacement and a big rig boosts surfing/planing performance. Unfortunately, there has been some tendency to push these design trends to extremes in recent years, causing **ultimate stability,** and hence seaworthiness, to suffer (fig. 2–6e, f).

Added Resistance in Rough Water

A sailboat beating to windward in stronger winds usually encounters head seas that cause it to heave and pitch. Besides making the crew uncomfortable, these motions slow the boat by dispersing a fraction of its kinetic energy into the surrounding water—a process called **damping**. Logically enough, this extra drag caused by sailing in disturbed seas is termed **added resistance**. In addition, pitching reduces the average propulsive forces produced by the sails, because the fore-and-aft movements of the rig cause abrupt fluctuations in the angle and velocity of air flow past the rig. In effect, the sails of a wildly pitching boat will be either overtrimmed or undertrimmed most of the time.

Weight near the ends of a hull, in the rig, and even in the keel tends to accentuate pitching by increasing the inertia of these peripheral parts of the boat. This extra inertia lengthens time needed for a pitching oscillation to die away while increasing the amount of kinetic energy lost in the process. For this reason, contemporary designers and builders often go to extraordinary pains to minimize rig weight, and to concentrate weight amidships.

Shaping the Hull Ends

The forms of the bow and stern are particularly important to performance, and tend to receive a disproportionate share of a designer's attention. At low speed, "fine" or highly tapered ends produce less form drag; but at higher speeds, full ends give better support to the hull as the self-induced wave system causes the water level to fall away amidships. A hull with its volume concentrated amidships is said to have a lower **prismatic coefficient** than one with somewhat fuller ends (fig. 2–7).

One might think that a high prismatic coefficient would ensure greater speed potential in a sailboat, but the situation is more complicated than that. For one thing, an overly blunt bow creates so much added resistance in head seas that performance-oriented designers today almost always opt for fine bows with entry angles (at the resting waterline) of 22 degrees or less. On the other hand, because the volume of a boat has to go somewhere, these fine-bowed, modern boats generally have considerably fuller sterns. A typical modern hull is, in effect, a low prismatic bow mated to a high prismatic stern (fig. 2–7d).

Full sterns provide extra buoyancy and form stability aft that minimizes squatting and increases sail-carrying power at higher speeds. On the other hand, a full stern combined with an overly fine bow will produce a boat that may well be very fast when sailed "flat," but which will round up uncontrollably if allowed to heel a little too much. The cause of this nasty behavior is a major rearward shift in the longitudinal center of buoyancy—radical bow-down trim—that takes place when this sort of hull begins to heel. Since speed is a powerful lure, there are currently quite a few boats around with this unpleasant, built-in characteristic. Recently, however, designers have been attacking the problem by designing hulls with more flare above the waterline in the bows and less toward the stern.

Contrary to popular belief, the dynamic lift that enables some boats to plane is generated over the forward half of the hull where the water impinges upon the bottom at a positive angle of attack (fig. 2–3c). The exceptionally fine or deep-V bows which produce only minimal added drag in rough water are at a disadvantage in this respect when compared to fuller ones that provide more "planing area."

Although flat **aft runs** are often associated with planing hulls, they assist planing more than promote it. Underbodies with convex shapes tend to create downward suction forces in much the same way that the convex face of a foil produces negative pressure and lift (see Chapter 1). A flat longitudinal bottom profile is better for planing

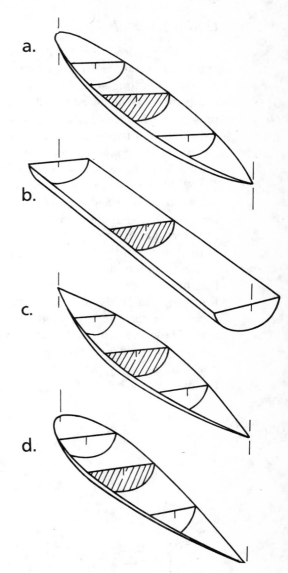

Fig. 2–7. Prismatic coefficient is the ratio between the actual displaced volume of a hull *(diagram a, c or d)* and the volume of an equal-length "prism" that has the same maximum cross-sectional area, but extending all the way from one end to the other *(diagram b)*. An exceptionally "full-ended" hull *(a)* might have a prismatic coefficient of 60 percent, while a fine-ended one *(c)* could be as low as 43 percent. Although many modern yachts have unbalanced ends *(d)*, the prismatic coefficients for these hulls when evaluated as a whole usually fall between 52 and 56 percent.

because it allows water to flow freely past without creating these adverse suction forces. On the other hand, the flatter bottom will typically hurt performance in nonplaning conditions due to its greater wetted surface.

Optimized Hull Designs

Coaxing more speed from ballasted monohulls of any particular length is an increasingly demanding task because all the "easy ground" has long since been gained. Much of the progress currently being made is being achieved with the aid of computers which are programmed to model the elaborate flow patterns around hulls as they move through the water at varying speeds and heel angles. With the aid of computers, it is potentially feasible to very quickly evaluate the costs and benefits associated with large numbers of design options (fig. 2–8). For this reason, computerized design offices can potentially afford to explore a great many more design avenues than was once the case, and may therefore stand a better chance of coming up with an optimal combination.

In all probability, however, even the very best keelboat hull shapes of the upcoming decade will be only marginal improvements over the best hulls of the past ten years. Much greater gains in monohull performance are likely to stem from increases in sail-carrying power; superior underwater foils and rigs; and lighter, yet stiffer construction. These are the main avenues of development being pursued by the designers of the most innovative and performance-oriented keelboats sailing today, which will be discussed further in the chapter that follows.

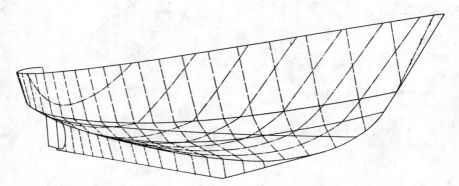

Fig. 2–8. Modern computer tools can greatly assist a yacht designer in developing an efficient, attractive hull shape in a reasonably short time. This twin-chined steel cruising hull was designed by Edward Fry of Houston, Texas, using AutoYacht™ software. A related computer program can specify the exact sizes and shapes of the individual flat panels needed to assemble the hull.

3

Coaxing More Speed from Self-righting Boats

To a sailboarder or multihull aficionado, the notion that any ballasted yacht can be a pure performance design may seem like a contradiction in terms. Nevertheless, within the restrictions of "single hull and self-righting" it has proven possible to build some "lead draggers" that come surprisingly close to the pace set by unballasted boats. For the serious cruising sailor, advances in "pure performance" are a great deal more interesting and potentially worthwhile than advances in the design of handicap racing yachts. With the latter, gains in speed relative to rating have too often resulted in either absolute speed losses or diminished seaworthiness. Fortunately, the recent proliferation of prestigious "adventure" races which regulate only overall length, general configuration (monohull vs. multihull), and equipment/safety standards is having a real and very positive impact on the design of fast cruising yachts. This chapter provides a glimpse at some of the more radical avenues of development currently being explored in the ongoing search for better performance from ballasted sailboats.

The Narrow Beam Approach: Its Virtues and Limitations

Transverse stability—the ability to carry sail—is perhaps the most difficult characteristic to achieve in a monohull design because it is

Fig. 3–1. A light, narrow boat taken to extremes, the Alan Adler–designed Fast 40 is just 8 feet wide and displaces 3600 pounds.

so much at odds with the need to minimize resistance in all conditions. Gentle winds yield only a tiny fraction of the propulsive and heeling forces provided by a stiff breeze because aerodynamic forces increase as the square of the wind velocity.* But bear in mind that a small propulsive force does not automatically mean slow sailing *pro-*

*Assuming sail and trim and camber remain unchanged, sail forces increase geometrically with wind speed because more air molecules, each with more velocity and kinetic energy, encounter the rig in a given time. For example, if the wind speed doubles, twice as many molecules, each with twice the energy, flow past the sail producing 2 squared or four times the aerodynamic force.

vided resistance can also be kept very low. A hypothetical monohull designed exclusively for light air speed would have plenty of sail area, minimal ballast, and an extremely slim, round-bilged hull—not unlike one hull of a catamaran. Narrow ULDB designs like the Santa Cruz 50 (fig. 2–6) or the less well known but even more radical Fast 40 (fig. 3–1) conform to this general description and tend to perform quite well in gentle breezes as well as offwind in surfing/planing conditions.

The Achilles' heel of most narrow, lightweight monohulls is windy upwind sailing. In theory, a slender, round-bilged hull is easily driven, even when heeled, but in practice, any sailboat that heels excessively when sailing upwind will experience the catastrophic increase in drag that was discussed in the preceeding chapter. On the other hand, the importance of sailing length as a speed-producing factor should not be underestimated. For a given displacement, a moderately slim hull (beam-to-length ratio near 1:4) will usually be faster and more pleasant to sail than the shorter, wider hulls which are currently in vogue. A slender boat is particularly attractive for short-handed sailing because it will not require as large a rig as a beamier boat, and because it will usually be less sensitive to crew weight and crew-weight positioning.

In fact, the principle reasons why monohull yachts have grown dramatically wider over the past two decades are primarily economic rather than performance-related. Skyrocketing moorage costs, paid by the foot, can make a long boat quite expensive to maintain, so designers are frequently encouraged to maximize below-decks space by increasing beam. Furthermore, boat buyers have become accustomed to comparing boats of similar overall length; and a wide 30-footer will usually show better than a narrow one because the former offers a more spacious cabin. In reality, this basis of comparison is largely invalid because the building cost of sailboats is primarily determined by displacement and onboard equipment, not by overall length.

Coaxing Speed from Beamy Hulls

Despite the advantages of length and slenderness, it is a fact that a high proportion of contemporary performance-oriented keelboats are exceptionally wide (fig. 3–2). The primary reason that beamy modern sports boats like the J-29 and Soverel 33 can leave many longer boats in the dust is because their substantial beams give them the stability

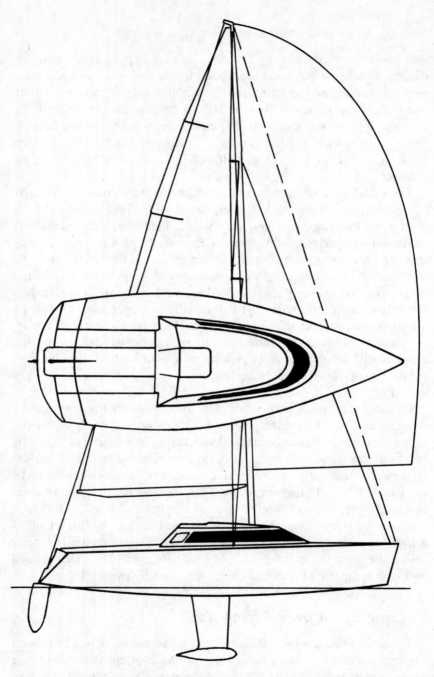

Fig. 3–2. The *Eureka*, designed by the late Ben Lexan of Australia, is a 5500-pound sports boat designed to sail fast without regard to rating rules. The 31-foot hull is over 12 feet wide on deck, while the huge fractional rig is stayed for masthead light-air headsails.

needed to carry enormous rigs. The end result is much the same as when a hotrodder mounts a big V-8 engine in a compact chassis—outstanding speed and acceleration, but a more lively and temperamental vehicle.

The acceleration and maneuverability of these beamy lightweights greatly enhance their racing performance in variable winds by permitting quick, frequent tacks and rapid course alterations. On the other hand, these boats tend to be less tolerant of heel, more difficult to manage shorthanded, and more uncomfortable in a seaway than slimmer boats of similar displacement.

If displacement is fixed, a greater waterline beam will be accompanied by reduced hull depth amidships, and indeed, most modern sports boats have nearly flat bottoms and sharply turned bilges (fig. 3–3). Righting forces for this sort of hull typically peak at heel angles of only 35 to 40 degrees, as illustrated by fig. 2–6 in the preceeding chapter. From the viewpoint of performance, this is almost optimal because these boats are best sailed "flat" (20 degrees heel or less) in order to minimize resistance associated with weather helm and to keep the rig and underwater foils close to vertical.

Fig. 3–3. Radical topsides flare and extreme form stability characterize this 22-foot "Pocket Rocket" designed by Gary Mull of San Francisco, California. The exceptionally wide transom is visible on a second hull in the background.

Movable Ballast

Many of the high-performance monohulls being raced today not only have substantial waterline beam, but a great deal of outward flare in the topsides amidships—so maximum beam may be as much as 40 percent of overall length.

Great beam at deck allows the crew to position their weight far to windward for a dramatic increase in stability. At the small heel angles favored for fast sailing, movable ballast disguised as crew weight is much more effective, pound for pound, than additional fixed ballast either in the bilges or the keel. Today, human ballasting has become *de rigueur* in most keelboat competitions, not only for day racing but also in offshore events conducted under the International Offshore Rule (see Chapter 6). Not surprisingly, most crews are less than enthusiastic about the prospect of spending almost twenty-four hours per day on the windward rail, sometimes for days on end. For this reason, many traditional overnight races and passage races are being replaced by shorter day races—a fundamental change in the character of big-boat racing. Blasting around the buoys in the 40- to 80-foot yachts is unquestionably an exciting sport that demands the utmost in teamwork and athletic ability, but it's a completely different game from traditional ocean racing.

On the other hand, there is one type of competition—single-handed and shorthanded "adventure" racing—that bucks this trend. For many of these events, the usual prohibitions against movable ballast are now being eliminated and the resulting performance gains have been dramatic. Competitors in the '86–'87 BOC Single-handed Round-the-World Race reported from 1.5 to 3 knots extra speed when windward ballast tanks holding from two or four tons of seawater were flooded under appropriate conditions. For safety reasons, BOC rules currently limit water ballast to an amount that would induce no more than 10 degrees heel in a calm, because more might lead to an extended knockdown or capsize if the yacht was accidentally caught aback. But even when used in moderation, water ballasting promises to be a real boon for cruising sailors, making it feasible for shorthanded cruising yachts to match the pace of all but the most radical of fully crewed contemporary racers.

The design of tackable water ballast systems for offshore sailing is still in its infancy, but a general format has emerged. Hulls are fitted with paired port and starboard tanks. In most installations there are

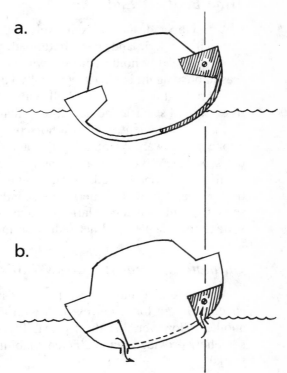

Fig. 3–4. Many water-ballast systems feature tanks near the sheerline with piping to shift the water to leeward just prior to a tack *(a)*. However, some recent designs have tanks situated below counter height which makes them easier to fill and empty using extensible scoops *(b)*. The lateral position of the ballast CG is identical with these two systems when the heel angle is 20 degrees as shown, but at higher heel angles the low-placed tanks provide more stability.

one or more large pipes, controlled by valves, that interconnect each pair of port and starboard tanks (fig. 3–4a). Before tacking, the crew uses this plumbing to drain the contents of the windward tank(s) into the previously empty leeward one(s), temporarily increasing heel, but avoiding any laborious pumping.

In some cases, a ram-action scoop can be used to fill a ballast tank initially without recourse to pumping. Likewise, aft-facing scoops function like the suction bailers of racing dinghies to rapidly empty tanks. Using this system, it is feasible to situate the ballast tanks below the resting waterline for better ultimate stability at high heel angles and, in some cases, a more livable interior arrangement (fig. 3–4b).

Wide Boats in Light Air

A fast boat designed exclusively for light air would probably be very narrow, light and round bottomed, yet many modern wide-beam boats can readily hold their own when the going gets light. The main reason once again is the exceptionally large rigs that these stable hulls can carry. Although a wide hull with a flat bottom has considerably more wetted surface and added drag than a narrower, rounder one of similar displacement, the extra horsepower from a really big rig goes a long way toward overcoming this additional resistance. In addition, the same crew weight that keeps a beamy sports boat upright on a windy beat can be moved forward and to leeward in light air. Altering trim in this way will immerse the rounded turn of the bilge and bow sections while raising a large portion of the flat aft run above the surface for a substantial net reduction in wetted surface.

Ultimate Solutions: Narrow Hulls with Great Stability

A wide, stable hull with a huge rig is one approach to monohull speed, while a long, narrow hull with a more modest rig represents another. However, the third possibility—a light, narrow hull that is somehow provided with sufficient stability to carry large sails—is potentially the fastest of all.

This combination was only recently achieved because in the past the only widely accepted way to give a narrow boat great stability was to load it down with an immensely heavy keel. This approach is exemplified by the International 12-Meter Rule which produces racing yachts 65 feet long, 12 feet wide, and carrying ballast up to 75 percent of their overall displacement. Obviously with this much lead aboard, a 12-meter is most reluctant to surf or plane; however, thanks to a great deal of refinement, they occasionally achieved speed-to-length ratios as high as 1.7 on windy reaches during the '87 America's Cup series in Perth, Australia.

On the other hand, there is now a new breed of radical keelboats that are not only slender but light, and at the same time stable enough to carry big rigs in brisk conditions. Naturally these boats depend primarily upon movable ballast, usually crew weight that can be positioned far to windward with trapezes, hiking extensions or both. Trapezes, now perfected through decades of small-boat racing, are cheap, light, and fun for a crew. Transferred to big boats they are, if anything, somewhat easier to use because the footing is more stable and dependable. However, woe to the trapezing sailor who does slip and go overboard on a 40-footer traveling at 20 knots plus. Unlike a dinghy or beach cat, which will inevitably stop (and usually capsize) within a length or two if the crew slips off, a big boat won't even pause while the hapless victim is dragged along and slammed against the hull.

Nevertheless, trapezing from larger boats has proven manageable in sheltered water, and in Europe a unique line of awesome keelboats has developed for the so-called lake racing circuit. A state-of-the-art Class Libre machine (fig. 3–5) is 46.5 feet long, the maximum allowable length, with a waterline beam of only 6 feet. However, for greater hiking leverage, the boat is equipped both with overhanging deck flanges and hiking racks made of aluminum tubing that together boost the beam to 21 feet—the maximum permitted by class rules. The lean, low freeboard hull has relatively little skin surface area and is carefully constructed using advanced materials and techniques to shave weight. Likewise, rig, sails, and gear are kept as light as possible, permitting a ready-to-sail weight (without crew) of around 3000 pounds! Sailing stability comes from the weight of up to ten men trapezing from the end of the windward hiking rack, while the deep, narrow bulb keel is barely heavy enough to right the boat from 90 degrees with the requisite 66-pound weight attached to the masthead. Sail-area-to-displacement ratios for these "monster boats" are well into the range for high-performance dinghies and multihulls, permitting upwind planing at 12 knots and routine sailing in excess of the true wind speed.

The risks associated with trapezing in rougher waters have lead some experimenters, mostly in North America, to develop radical sports boats with exaggerated deck beam for the purpose of getting crew weight farther outboard (fig. 3–6). Hiking platforms that are lateral extensions of the deck and topsides are usually called **wings** because they resemble the stubby wings of jet fighters. Most such boats to date have had relatively thick buoyant wings that contact the water at heel angles of 15 degrees or so. Although the boat slows considerably when this happens, the shift in the center of buoyancy to leeward adds extra stability when it is most needed and the additional drag on the leeward side of the hull reduces weather helm when the boat might otherwise round up out of control. On the other hand, high-volume wings have a major failing: they float the boat too high

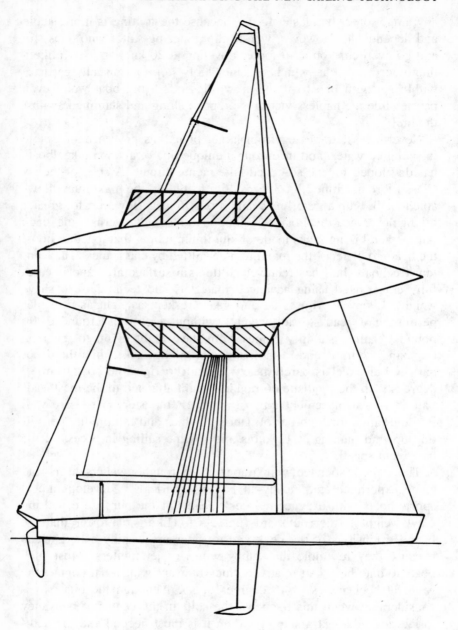

Fig. 3–5. Highly specialized Class Libre "monster boats" are 46-foot daysailers stabilized by up to ten crew trapezing from aluminum hiking racks. They are probably the world's fastest keelboats.

Fig. 3–6. The weight of an eight-man crew provides virtually all the righting momentum as this Moore 30 powers to windward. This radical boat has a 14-foot deck beam and weighs only 2000 pounds rigged.

in the water at large heel angles (fig. 3–7a). A knockdown of 90 degrees or more may expose so much of the undersides of hull and deck to a strong wind that the lightweight boat will be laid on its side for extended periods or even flipped bottom up. Hiking racks made of aluminum tubing and covered with fabric mesh don't add buoyancy or appreciable windage and are therefore much less of a liability in a knockdown situation (fig. 3–7b), although they lack the aesthetic appeal of sleek, faired-in wings and cannot be disguised as anything other than outboard hiking extensions.

Adequately Self-righting?

The narrow, heavily ballasted yachts of yesteryear may have been slower and less commodious than their modern counterparts, but their self-righting characteristics were by and large beyond reproach. Today, however, prolonged knockdowns and broaches are a routine (if

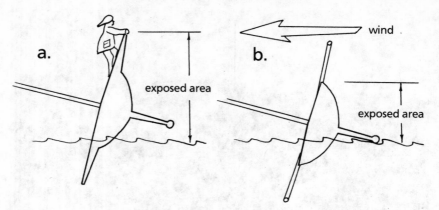

Fig. 3–7. The chief drawback of using solid wings as hiking extensions on a high-performance keelboat is that their buoyancy is likely to float the hull too high in the water during a knockdown *(a)*. When this happens, too much bottom area is exposed to the wind, inhibiting righting. Hiking frames covered with open netting are generally safer *(b)*.

unwelcome) part of big-boat racing. More alarmingly, quite a few contemporary keelboats have been flipped upside down by breaking waves, and in some cases lives have been lost as a result.

As discussed earlier, all keelboats, whether modern or "old-fashioned," must have sufficient displacement to provide the "stiffness" or sail-carrying ability needed for satisfactory upwind and reaching performance. However, with beamy, firm-bilged hulls that are best sailed at modest heel angles, it makes very little difference whether this weight is centered low in the hull or fairly high. Therefore, when a hull of this type is outfitted for cruising, there is always a temptation to devote a large proportion of the overall displacement to comfortable furnishings with relatively less left over for ballast. Similarly, for racing, extra crew weight on the windward rail does a great deal more to boost sail-carrying ability than an equal weight of fixed ballast in the bilge or keel. Under the circumstances, it is hardly surprising that some contemporary boats, although stiff and powerful at normal heel angles, have self-righting capabilities that are marginal or inadequate at unusually high heel angles.

The development of keelboats with this undesirable characteristic was a gradual evolution that might not have been recognized as a serious problem had it not been for the 1979 Fastnet Race off the south coast of Great Britain. During this prestigious international event, an intense, unforecasted storm produced extreme sea conditions that caused 180-degree capsizes or 360-degree rollovers in 18 boats out of a fleet of 303. Several of these were rolled repeatedly and some remained inverted for rather lengthy periods of time. Ultimately 24 yachts were abandoned, 5 sank and fifteen sailors died. In the wake of this calamity, a great deal of attention has been focused upon the phenomenon of wave-impact capsizes and determining how best to prevent them. Of course, only a minority of ballasted monohulls will ever sail in open ocean areas where large breaking waves might be encountered. Certainly the more radical sports boats and "speed machines" described earlier in this chapter are inshore designs intended only for day racing and perhaps some harbor hopping. Even the wildest broach or wind-induced knockdown is unlikely to progress past the point where the upper portion of the rig strikes the water, which for a beamy design will usually occur at a heel angle of 100 to 110 degrees. Unfortunately, the limit of positive stability for some modern keelboats is not much more than this (see fig. 2–6), which means that the self-righting forces during a severe wind-induced knockdown may be quite small. In actual knockdown situations, this small righting tendency may be overcome by a combination of wind drag on the exposed hull bottom, the weight of the water that floods into the mast, and the weight of the crew clinging to the rail or struggling to climb the near-vertical deck. When a dinghy dumps, the crew can usually swing over the windward rail and stand on the centerboard to right the boat. If a keelboat with a 15-foot maximum beam is flattened by a ferocious gust and pinned on its beam ends, a crew member hanging by his hands from the edge of the deck will be unable to reach the root of the keel with his feet!

Are the self-righting characteristics of future generations of inshore keelboats likely to deteriorate still further as the relentless quest for speed continues? On the whole, probably not, if only because quite a few existing designs are already borderline in this regard. In addition, most big-boat sailors are uncomfortable aboard a boat whose self-righting capabilities are suspect. One of the best things about keelboat sailing is that a gung-ho crew can confidently probe the outer limits of control knowing that the boat will quickly recover should someone make a mistake.

Wave-Impact Capsizes and Offshore Safety

Although many yacht designers have knowingly experimented with the lower practical limits for stability at high heel angles (for the reasons described earlier), designing a ballasted monohull that is capable of recovering promptly from any wind-induced knockdown is fundamentally a straightforward task. Designing a yacht that is immune to being capsized by huge breaking seas is a far more difficult undertaking, partly because of the tremendous forces involved, and partly because the circumstances surrounding such capsizes are highly complex. Nevertheless, thanks to a crash program of research and analysis that began soon after the 1979 Fastnet disaster, a good deal is now known about the behavior of various types of yachts in large, breaking seas. The bulk of this work was done in the United States under the joint auspices of the Cruising Club of America and the Society of Naval Architects and Marine Engineers. Key findings from this program are summarized here, but a much more extensive discussion is available in a 1987 reference book entitled *Desirable and Undesirable Characteristics of Offshore Yachts* (see the Further Reading section).

Huge waves capable of inverting yachts were once believed to be extremely rare ''freak'' events. Today, however, they are known to be associated with intense, fast-building storms known as **climatological bombs** which occur with some regularity in certain waters. Winds which rise quickly into the 60- to 70-knot range cause wave heights to build rapidly while wave lengths fail to stretch out proportionally. Especially large, steep waves created by the momentary coincidence of lesser waves will frequently break, and when this happens, a high-speed jet of water hurls down the wave flank. A yacht unfortunate enough to be situated beam-to on the flank of such a breaking wave will be violently struck by this mass of white water (fig. 3–8a, b).

Whether a particular yacht that is struck by a particular breaking wave will be flipped over or not will depend upon a large number of factors. In general terms, the size of the yacht is obviously important because a given sea will affect a small boat more violently than a larger one. However, there is no simple relationship between the dimensions of a boat and its susceptibility to wave-impact capsizes. Greater displacement helps because it increases the inertia of the boat which makes it slower to respond to large but short-lived forces. But much more important than displacement *per se* is the **rotational in-**

ertia of the yacht. Rotational inertia is determined by the distribution of all onboard weights with respect to the boat's roll axis. Weights that are positioned farthest from the axis of roll make disproportionately large contributions to the overall rotational inertia of the yacht, and hence to its ability to resist the impact of a breaking wave. Paradoxically, it's the weight of the rig which—due to its height—produces most of the rotational inertia in monohull sailing yachts. Of course rig weight also makes a boat more "tender" and less competent at self-righting, but the combination of a robust, relatively heavy rig and a deep, heavy keel is optimal from the viewpoint of offshore safety. Rig integrity is critically important, not only because a dismasting will render the boat uncontrollable and vulnerable to being caught broadside to the waves but because a yacht loses so much of its rotational inertia when the rig is lost.

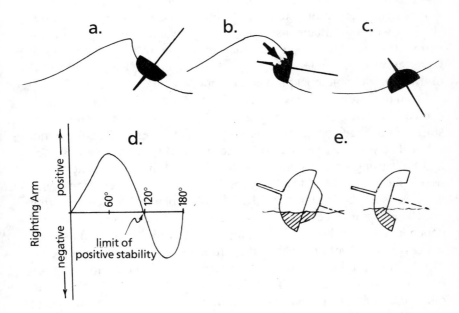

Fig. 3–8. Wave-impact capsizes can occur when a yacht is caught on the leeward side of a steep wave at the moment it breaks. As the wave approaches (a) the yacht rolls in response to the increasing slope of the water surface, ultimately exposing its topsides and underbody to the fast-moving jet of white water formed by the collapsing wave crest (b). Once inverted (c), a modern wide-beam boat is likely to have substantial inverted stability (d) and may float upside down for quite some time. Raised cabins tend to enhance positive stability at high heel angles (e) while cockpits reduce it.

Large beam, although a potent source of lateral stability for sail-carrying purposes, tends to increase susceptibility to wave-impact capsizes. The problem is twofold. First, a hull with generous beam exposes a greater surface area to the jet of fast-moving water that cascades down the flank of a breaking wave and consequently experiences greater capsizing forces. Second, a beamy hull will typically have a smaller range of positive stability (fig. 3–8d) and is therefore more likely to be heeled beyond the point of no return by wave impact.

Should a yacht be flipped bottom-up by a breaking wave, it is likely to sink or drown its crew unless it rights promptly. How long a yacht is likely to stick in a turtled position will be determined primarily by its range of positive stability. Boats with an excessive inverted stability may remain upside down for quite some time waiting for another wave to roll them far enough to start the self-righting process. Large beam and a relatively high CG—common characteristics of many contemporary performance-oriented yachts—will reduce the range of positive stability while simultaneously increasing unwanted stability in the inverted attitude. The added buoyancy of a large trunk cabin works to increase self-righting tendencies at high heel angles, while the volume of a large floodable cockpit has the opposite effect (fig. 3–8e).

From the foregoing, it is clear that some modern keelboats are risky choices for voyages or races that traverse areas where severe ocean storms and large, breaking seas may be encountered. This does not mean that very fast yet safe offshore monohulls cannot be designed and built using contemporary technology, and the remarkable yachts developed for the BOC Challenge and similar races are cases in point. To a considerable extent, the IOR can be blamed for encouraging wide beam, high freeboard, overly light rigs, high CGs and extensive dependence upon human ballasting (see Chapter 6 on handicapping systems). However, now that the problem has been widely recognized, steps are being taken to encourage more wholesome offshore designs through changes in the IOR formula. In general, thanks to our increased understanding of the dynamic behavior of yachts in severe wind and sea conditions, it has become quite feasible to design yachts which strike an appropriate balance between performance-enhancing factors and safety-related ones to suit the type of sailing that is contemplated.

4

Form and Function in Keels, Centerboards, and Rudders

Lateral resistance in most modern sailboats is furnished mainly by the centerboard, daggerboard, or keel; with the rudder and hull(s) making relatively minor contributions. The primary role of the rudder is, of course, to steer the boat, a task it performs by producing an additional lateral force that swings the stern either to port or starboard as the need arises.

In addition to its hydrodynamic function, the keel of most self-righting sailboats is a reservoir for ballast. To perform this task, it must have substantial volume—a requirement that is often at odds with its role as an efficient foil. Draft restrictions often lead to additional compromises, as does the need to balance high lift for upwind work against low drag for offwind sailing. All in all, the trade-offs involved in developing the fins of a modern sailboat are often among the most difficult and complex that the yacht designer must make.

Fins in Principle

In Chapter 1 it was noted that any keel or centerboard, no matter how primitive and inefficient, will automatically "seek out" that angle of attack at which the side force it generates exactly counterbalances the total side force produced by air flow over the sails and hull topsides. However, if a boat is moving slowly or if its underwater foils are crudely shaped, the angle of attack needed to obtain the necessary side force will be considerably larger than it would be if the boat was traveling faster or had superior foils. Of course, when the angle of attack is large, both the resistance produced by fins themselves and extra drag from cross flow beneath the hull tend to be higher. In practice, if the fins perform badly, it is usually preferable to point lower (i.e., steer at a larger angle with respect to the wind) so that the ratio of forward to side forces generated by the sails will become more favorable.

Sailboat fins produce resistance in two distinctly different ways. The first is the combination of form drag and skin friction that would be associated with moving almost anything through the water. A symmetrical foil like a sailboat fin experiences this kind of resistance even when its angle of attack is zero (as when running before the wind). Under these conditions, the amount of resistance produced at a given speed will depend primarily upon the length of the fin from root to tip—its **span**—along with its thickness and wetted surface.

A second, additional source of resistance called **induced drag** comes into play as soon as a fin is reoriented at a small angle to the flow so that it starts generating lift. A minor component of induced drag is the extra form drag caused by the presentation of a thicker shape to the flow whenever the angle of attack is greater than zero. However, much more induced drag results from cross flow beneath the tip of a fin (or around the end of any lifting foil). This cross flow reduces the pressure difference between the high-pressure side of the

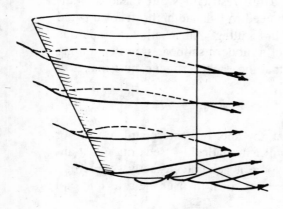

Fig. 4–1. A tip vortex is caused by flow around the end of a foil from the high-pressure side toward the low-pressure side. The resulting induced drag substantially reduces the upwind performance of most sailboats.

foil and the low-pressure side, degrading lift in much the same way that leaky piston rings reduce the power output of a car engine. Tip losses are manifested in the form of a spiral turbulence pattern called a **tip vortex** that streams away behind (fig. 4–1). The resulting drag is considerable, often 20 to 30 percent of the total resistance of a closehauled sailboat!

Centerboards and Daggerboards: Single-Function Fins

Foils whose sole purpose is to generate side force for upwind and crosswind sailing are called centerboards and daggerboards, a linguistic holdover from the days when flat plates of wood or metal were used to do this job. Today, carefully shaped foils are always preferred in these roles because they offer dramatically superior lift-to-drag ratios. Nevertheless, the old-fashioned names have stuck.

Centerboard and daggerboard installations, although straightforward in principle, can become mechanically involved and the very devil to integrate into the overall design of a boat. Some of these problems will be discussed at the end of this chapter, but for now, it is fair to regard these foils as the simplest of fins because they have no function other than to generate lateral force with the smallest possible drag penalty. In most cases it is not even important to worry about drag during downwind legs because these foils can ordinarily be retracted when side force is not needed.

Given such simplified requirements, it is no surprise that the best modern centerboards and daggerboards are the most efficient of all sailboat fins for upwind work. Interestingly enough, the cross-sectional shape that remains most popular is the most basic of the hundreds described in *The Theory of Wing Sections,* a widely used reference text published by the National Advisory Council for Aeronautics (NACA).

The NACA 00 series symmetrical foils are relatively blunt and rounded at the leading edge, with the thickest part of the section only 30 percent of the chord length behind the leading edge (fig. 4–2a). This makes these foils resistant to **stalling** (losing lift) at large angles of attack, and tolerant of the disturbed flow created by nearby surface waves. So-called laminar flow sections such as the NACA 64 and 65 series (fig. 4–2b) are sometimes specified for fast dinghies and multihulls because flow-tunnel test data suggest that they can deliver superior lift-to-drag ratios at small angles of attack. However, they are

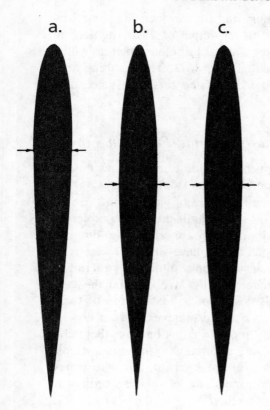

Fig. 4–2. A comparison of three NACA sections, all with thickness-to-chord ratios of 10 percent: *(a)* NACA 0010, *(b)* NACA 6310, and *(c)* a recent LS design. Position of maximum thickness is indicated in each case.

also more temperamental under suboptimal conditions and have yet to demonstrate a clearcut advantage when used on small sailboats.

A NACA foil designated 0010 (fig. 4–2a) refers to a symmetrical section from the 00 family whose maximum thickness is 10 percent of its **chord** or distance between the leading and trailing edges. The ratio of thickness to chord length for modern centerboards and daggerboards is frequently less than 1:10, usually between 6 and 8 percent. Thinner foils offer less resistance when used downwind and superior lift-to-drag ratios, although they are slightly more prone to stall when the angle of attack becomes exceptionally large (as when accelerating out of a tack). In practice, the minimum acceptable thickness for a centerboard is usually determined by the need for adequate strength and stiffness, rather than by hydrodynamic considerations.

As mentioned earlier, the main source of induced drag is the cross flow and vortex shedding that takes place at the tip (or tips) of a lifting foil. For this reason, and because the lion's share of the lift is generated only a short distance behind the leading edge of most foils, one of the surest ways to improve the lift-to-drag ratio of a foil is to increase its span and decrease its chord. Long, narrow foils are known as high-aspect foils—**aspect ratio** being the ratio of span to chord (fig. 4–3). Because a high-aspect centerboard will produce more lift per square foot than a low-aspect one, it can usually be designed with less lateral area, which in turn means less skin-surface friction (although not necessarily less form drag).

There is a practical upper limit for aspect ratio in centerboards. Exceptionally high aspect ratios yield diminishing returns in terms of additional efficiency, while at the same time are increasingly difficult to build. Furthermore, changing to a deeper, slimmer underwater foil shifts the foil's center of effort downward, causing the boat to heel more (fig. 4–3). Experience in a variety of boats has shown that

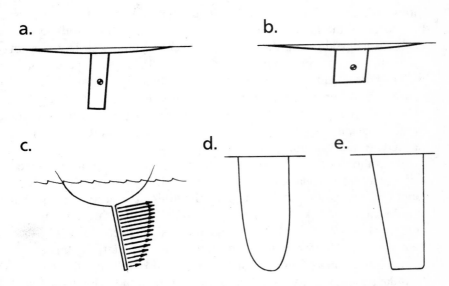

Fig. 4–3. Induced drag savings from a high-aspect centerboard (or keel) can be offset by a lower center of effort which increases heeling tendencies *(diagrams a and b)*. An elliptical lift distribution pattern as shown in sketch c provides the lowest possible induced drag. A foil with an elliptical planiform *(d)* is often regarded as the best way to approach this ideal, but a trapezoidal planiform *(e)* may perform virtually as well.

optimal aspect ratio for centerboards usually falls between 3:1 and 4:1.

Fluid dynamics investigators have learned that an elliptical pattern of pressure distribution, or "wing loading," (fig. 4-3c) gives rise to the lowest possible induced drag for any foil of limited span. This fact is often used as an argument for fins with an elliptical profile, or **planform,** as viewed from the side (fig. 4-3d). Unfortunately, this argument fails to recognize that pressure-pattern distributions will not necessarily conform to the distribution of area along the length of a foil. In practice, a trapezoidal profile (fig. 4-3e) is virtually as efficient as an elliptical planform, in most cases, and is far easier to build.

Keels: The Trapezoidal Norm and Elliptical Variants

As mentioned earlier, ballast keels present much more of a design problem than centerboards, because they must perform two conflicting roles. In most cases, the overall draft of fixed keel sailboats is sharply limited, either by the need to negotiate shallow waters or by rating rules. With this limited draft, the amount of ballast that must be housed in the keel to obtain adequate stability and/or self-righting characteristics almost always dictates a keel volume well in excess of the hydrodynamic optimum. In other words, ballast keels are usually wider, fatter, and more drag prone than than an optimized centerboard would be. The exceptions are yachts that carry much of their ballast internally with only a fraction housed within the fin—an approach that necessitates more ballast, but is often worthwhile under the IOR rating system.

When the draft limitations for a particular design are fairly relaxed and a keel span equal to at least 15 percent of the yacht's waterline length is acceptable, it is surprisingly difficult to improve upon a simple trapezoidal keel profile (fig. 4-4a). Keels of this general type are sometimes described as "Peterson keels" in recognition of Doug Peterson, the California-based designer who popularized this shape with a long string of successful IOR racing boats during the 1970s.

Today, the majority of modern yachts are fitted with trapezoidal keels. Many are tapered quite dramatically with a tip chord no greater than half the root chord. Under the IOR rule, which does not encourage a particularly low-ballast CG, sharply tapered foils make good sense, because the center of lateral resistance for the keel remains

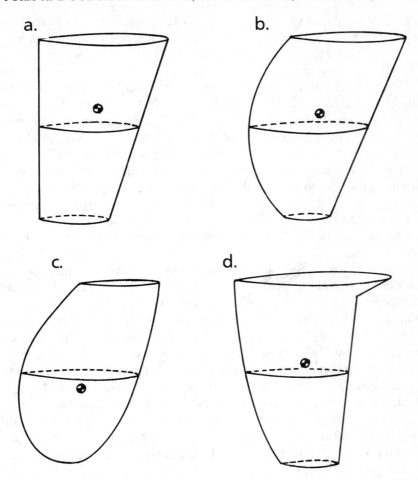

Fig. 4–4. Modern keel configurations: *(a)* trapezoidal—easily constructed and still the norm; *(b)* typical elliptical design provides a lower-ballast CG; *(c)* "Mickey Mouse Ear" shape with radically reduced root chord and very low ballast CG; *(d)* Vacanti design with "active fence" near root.

high to help minimize heeling. At the same time, the short chord near the tip reduces tip vortex formation and induced drag.

Taper in a trapezoidal keel can be achieved by raking either the leading edge or trailing edge, but experience has shown that an aft-raked leading edge and near-vertical trailing edge are generally most satisfactory. Although the vertical leading edges are clearly desirable for narrow centerboards, an aft-raked leading edge is progressively less detrimental as the aspect ratio of a foil goes down. Typical keels with aspect ratios around 2:1 lose little efficiency when the leading edge is raked as much as 25 degrees, while the tendency to collect weeds is greatly reduced.

The cross-sectional shapes used in almost all modern keels are again NACA symmetrical sections. Low drag "laminar flow" sections such as the 63, 64, and 66 series (fig. 4–2b) are often chosen because big-boat keels are more deeply submerged than dinghy centerboards and therefore are thought to experience more stable flow. Lately, however, some designers have opted for recently developed laminar-flow sections belonging to the NACA Low Speed or LS series (fig. 4–2c). These foils feature a relatively blunt leading edge for improved resistance to stalling, yet have their point of maximum thickness situated well aft to encourage laminar flow to persist over more of the keel's area.

For the same chord and thickness measurements, some sections can house slightly more lead than others. Nevertheless, to obtain the volume needed for sufficient ballast, most keels must be considerably thicker than centerboards, with average thickness-to-chord ratios ranging from 9 to 15 percent. This extra thickness invariably increases form drag, not only upwind, but downwind too.

Water flow across a keel is not uniform from top to bottom, in part because the pitching and rolling of the boat cause exaggerated variations in the angle of attack near the keel tip. For this reason it is accepted practice to select a thicker, more stall-resistant section for the keel tip that gradually gives way to a thinner, less drag-prone section near the root (fig. 4–4a). In addition, by making the tip proportionally thicker, the CG of the ballast within the keel will be lowered somewhat.

Since 1984, an increasing number of offshore racing keels have been designed with more or less elliptical profile shapes (fig. 4–4b). Because most keels have lower aspect ratios than centerboards, any reduction in tip loses and induced drag obtained by going to an elliptical profile should, in theory, be more worthwhile. In some cases, great pains have been taken to whittle away the chord and thickness of the keel where it joins the hull in an effort to reduce **interference drag**—a flow disturbance caused by the interaction of the separate flow patterns around the hull and keel respectively. Extreme "Mickey Mouse ear" keels (known as MMOs) are very hard to anchor securely to the hull (fig. 4–4c). While it is possible that they may offer a reduction in interference drag, it is equally likely that they suffer from an increase in induced drag due to tip losses at both ends, rather than just one.

Due to the elaborate compound curvature of their surfaces, building a fair, accurately shaped elliptical keel represents a major challenge. The best ones are machined out of billets of solid lead by computer-controlled milling machines. Although elliptical keels undoubtedly score some points in the psychological warfare that is an integral part of high-level racing, there is little hard evidence so far that they are significantly superior to trapezoidal keels. Indeed a good trapezoidal keel that is somewhat V-shaped on the bottom and/or slightly rounded at the "toe" may well be every bit as fast.

Reducing keel root area may not be the best way of minimizing interference drag even when possible increases in induced drag are disregarded. A promising keel configuration developed by aircraft engineer David Vacanti features sharp aft rake in the keel root area that switches abruptly to a near-vertical leading edge for most of the span (fig. 4–4d). The sloped leading edge near the keel root is intended to deflect flow downward and away from the hull for a reduction in both interference drag and induced drag. The enlarged keel root makes it relatively easy to build a strong keel-to-hull junction.

Practical Centerboard and Lifting Keel Installations

A **centerboard** swings back around a pivot pin and is housed in either a long trunk within the hull or a deep recess in the bottom of a shallow ballast keel. A **daggerboard** drops vertically through a close-fitting trunk. Because the former can swing back freely, a boat equipped with a centerboard is less likely to sustain damage during a grounding than one with a daggerboard. The swing-back capability of a centerboard can also be used to adjust helm balance without appreciably altering the upwind efficiency of the foil.

On the other hand, a long centerboard, if housed entirely within the hull, takes up more interior space than a compact daggerboard trunk. In addition, with a centerboard installation it is difficult to close off the long slot in the bottom of the hull (or keel) in order to avoid considerable turbulence and extra drag when the board is down. The usual solution, long overlapping gaskets made of a springy material, tends to be temperamental and short-lived.

The loss of interior space is not a problem in the case of a shoal-draft cruising yacht with a centerboard housed entirely within a low-aspect external keel (fig. 4–5a). This configuration continues to be popular because it permits a very deep, efficient foil for open-water upwind work, yet can be retracted for shallow water or offwind sailing. Provided the drag of an open centerboard slot is minimized by fitting flexible flaps, the keel-centerboard combination probability has better upwind performance potential than that more trendy solution—the winged keel of equal minimum draft. Its chief drawbacks are the added complexity associated with the lifting mechanism and a slot that is apt to plug up with marine growth.

Daggerboards are most often used on dinghies and small multi-hulls, but can be employed on larger, heavier craft if certain practical problems can be overcome. Side loading on a large daggerboard can make it very difficult to lift while under way, so a series of roller bearings lining the trunk may be required. Also, with a large or heavy yacht, some sort of "crash box" to absorb energy in the event of a grounding is critically important; otherwise the daggerboard could easily slice back through the bottom and sink the boat!

Lifting keels are mechanically similar to centerboards or daggerboards. However, because they are much heavier than their unballasted counterparts, they require stronger trunks, closer tolerances (to avoid slamming movements within the trunk), powerful lifting gear, and a secure locking mechanism to ensure that the keel cannot accidently (and violently) retract in a knockdown that exceeds 90 degrees. In addition, the designer must take into account the loss of stability that will occur when the keel is intentionally raised. For this reason, some lifting-keel sailboats are designed so that they can only be sailed with the keel in the "locked down" position.

Inside Ballast, Dry or Wet

Self-righting centerboard or daggerboard yachts often carry their ballast internally, generally in the form of lead castings secured in the lowest part of the bilge (fig. 4–5b). The shallow canoe bodies favored for most contemporary yachts are not well suited to internal ballasting, so a somewhat deep-bellied hull is usually selected. Even so, the righting power of an external fin keel can only be matched by using a substantially heavier weight of internal ballast. Nevertheless, internal ballasting makes good sense when the extreme shoal-draft capabilities of a fully retractable centerboard are desired.

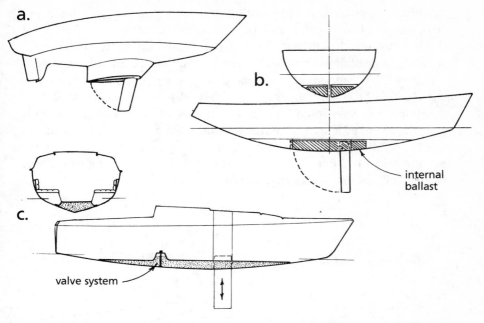

Fig. 4–5. Centerboard yachts can be ballasted either with a shallow external keel *(a)* or internally *(b)*. The use of a centerline water tank for internal ballasting is a good solution for trailerable sailboats such as the MacGregor 26 shown here *(c)*.

Water ballast carried in one or more tanks beneath the cabin sole on the yacht's centerline behaves almost exactly like an equal weight of other internal ballast in the same location (fig. 4–5c). Of course, being much less dense than steel or lead, a far larger volume of water must be used to provide equal righting abilities. On the other hand, water ballast is great for trailerable boats because it can be drained to lighten the trailering load. "Trailer sailers" with internal water ballast and an unweighted centerboard first gained popularity in Australia and New Zealand, but are now being accepted in other sailing areas including the United States.

Basic Rudder Alternatives

At one time, most sailboat rudders were movable flaps hinged to the trailing edge of a long keel. Today, it is more common to use a separate rudder positioned as far behind the keel or centerboard as possible, because this configuration permits a large turning force to be generated by a small, low-drag rudder blade.

Skeg-mounted rudders (fig. 4–6a) are used on many contemporary cruising designs, primarily because they are potentially stronger and hence less susceptible to being damaged by collisions with floating debris. At small rudder angles, they also have the potential for creating more side force for a given amount of drag, because whenever the blade of a skeg-mounted rudder is deflected from the centerline, the skeg-rudder combination becomes a highly efficient asymmetrical foil not unlike the asymmetrical foils used for propeller blades and aircraft wings (fig. 4–6b).

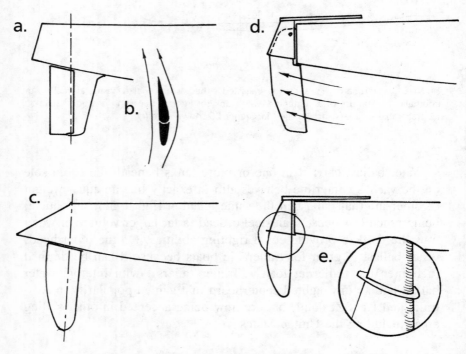

Fig. 4–6. Skeg rudders *(a)* are sturdy and efficient at small steering angles *(b)*. However, spade rudders *(c)* are preferred for most racing boats because they provide superior maneuverability. Ventilation with a transom-hung rudder can be countered by notching the blade and raking it forward to encourage flow to angle up the blade *(d)*. Another solution is a fence that physically blocks the downward flow of air along the low-pressure face of the rudder *(e)*.

Why then do almost all modern high-performance racing boats have one-piece **spade** rudders (fig. 4–6c)? The main reason is maneuverability; a spade rudder can continue to apply a large lateral force even after the stern is already skidding sidewise, and thus enable the boat to "turn on a dime." In contrast, when a skeg-rudder boat cranks into a hard turn, the flow in the vicinity of the rudder abruptly swings to meet the skeg at a negative angle of attack, which not only reduces turning force but creates a lot of extra drag. Other advantages of the spade rudder include simplicity, lighter weight and minimal resistance when the boat is "in balance" and the rudder angle very low. With a skeg-hung rudder, the joint between the two sections is a significant source of turbulence and drag even when flexible fairing strips are used to cover the gap.

High-Performance Rudder Design

Modern rudders are usually positioned either just forward of the counter or, on small boats, may be transom-hung. The former is slightly more efficient because, at normal heel angles, the hull acts as an end plate for the top of the rudder. The latter is simpler and much easier to raise or remove for shallow water use. However, it ordinarily surrenders some steering effectiveness because air from the water's surface can be sucked down air on its low-pressure side—a problem known as **ventilation.** The problem can be largely prevented either by notching the rudder and raking it forward slightly so that a portion of the blade extends beneath the hull (fig. 4–6d), or by fitting a horizontal fence just beneath the water's surface to physically block the downward flow of air along the low-pressure face (fig. 4–6e).

The angle of attack for a spade rudder varies over a much wider range than that of a keel or centerboard, not uncommonly going as high as 45 degrees when the helmsman is attempting to avert a broach or other crisis. No symmetrical foil can sustain such high angles of attack for more than a moment without stalling completely and losing most of its lift. However, choosing a relatively thick sectional shape with blunt leading edges can increase stall resistance considerably, although at the cost of some extra drag.

5

Radical Fin Developments: Wings, Slots, and Variable Camber

The now-famous winged keel had its origins in a much older configuration—the **bulb keel**—which ironically was virtually written off in the 1960s and 1970s as old-fashioned and inefficient. What a bulb keel design does accomplish, of course, is to position much of the ballast very low, in the most advantageous possible position. However, until recently, bulbs were widely regarded as hydrodynamic disasters—a source of extra resistance that would inevitably neutralize the benefits of a lower ballast CG.

Lately, many yacht designers have done an about-face and begun a return to bulb keels. This change has come about partly due to improvements in bulb design, but largely because of the new emphasis on light displacement. By taking advantage of the low-ballast CG of a bulb keel, less ballast weight is needed, permiting a reduction in overall displacement. The resulting reduction in the resistance of the hull itself may offset the extra resistance from the bulb, while the lower displacement relative to length increases its surfing/planing potential.

Another way that a bulb helps to make up for the extra resistance it causes is to partially block the cross flow of water beneath the keel tip. By functioning as a **fence** or **end plate** in this way, a bulb reduces tip vortex formation and induced drag on upwind legs. A shallow-draft, low-aspect keel experiences proportionally greater induced drag than a deep one with a short tip; hence the former stands to benefit much more if equipped with some sort of end plate.

Traditionally, a bulb shape was developed by rotating a NACA symmetrical section around its central axis to create a tapered, cylindrical "torpedo" (fig. 5–1a). There is, however, no reason to assume that a shape derived from a lift-generating foil section is going to be optimal for a keel tip appendage. Some variations, like the much-publicized Scheel keel (fig. 5–1b), are intended to make the bulb into a better end plate to reduce tip vortex formation. More recent design programs have focused upon minimizing the resistance caused by the bulb by optimizing its shape to conform to the local flow patterns once the effects of the nearby hull and keel fin are taken into account. Flow-tunnel tests and computer flow simulations suggest that slightly bowed shapes with drawn-out tails can often offer worthwhile drag savings (fig. 5–1c).

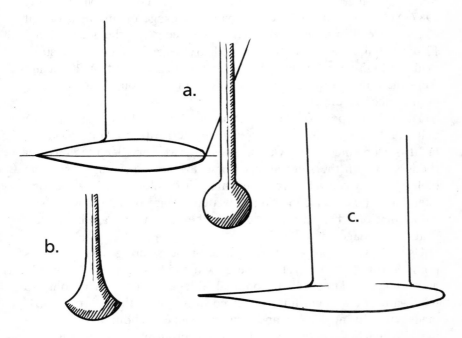

Fig. 5–1. Contemporary variations on the bulb-keel theme include: (a) compact streamlined shapes with circular cross sections for minimal wetted surface; (b) the Scheel keel intended to minimize cross flow beneath the tip; and (c) a sophisticated "low-drag" shape.

Of course, a bulb keel (or winged keel) that produces little drag in smooth water conditions may fare considerably worse in rough seas when the vertical and horizontal movements of the entire boat cause the bulb to meet the flow at constantly varying angles. When a bulb-keel yacht is bouncing around a great deal, the resulting added drag is quite likely to nullify the combined gains from reducing tip losses and a lower ballast position. Optimizing bulb-keel configurations for rough-water performance is, at present, a largely unexplored field.

Total Segregation of Keel Functions: The U.S.A. Experiment

While much developmental work with keels has been aimed at smoothly integrating the antagonistic roles of carrying ballast and providing upwind lift with a minimal drag penalty, it is also possible to use different appendages to provide lift and to house ballast. The best-known test of this concept to date was the 12-meter *U.S.A.* designed by Alberto Calderon, Heiner Meldner, and Gary Mull for the 1987 America's Cup. The entire ballast package of this boat (about 18 tons of lead) was suspended beneath the center of the deep-chested 12-meter hull by a slender foil-shaped strut (fig. 5–2, top). This strut, made of high-strength steel, has a lateral area of less than 10 square feet—the minimum feasible—and only a tiny fraction of the keel area of any other 12-meter.

The sole purpose of the strut was to support the massive ballast bulb (or "Geek," as it was irreverently termed). Lateral resistance or lift for upwind sailing was supplied by two very deep high-aspect rudders, one in the stern as usual and the other near the bow. The high efficiency of such narrow fins made it feasible to reduce the total lateral area (and hence the overall wetted surface of the yacht) to well below that of other 12-meters despite the presence of a third underwater appendage.

Using a very complex and trouble-prone steering system it was possible (in theory) to set up these twin rudders so that both would have angles of attack in the optimal 3-degree range when going to windward in a straight line. Balanced in this way, the hull of *U.S.A.* made virtually no leeway and thus experienced additional drag savings. In maneuvers, the variable ratio steering was expected to provide additional benefits ranging from a tighter turning radius to a reduction in weather distance lost during tacks.

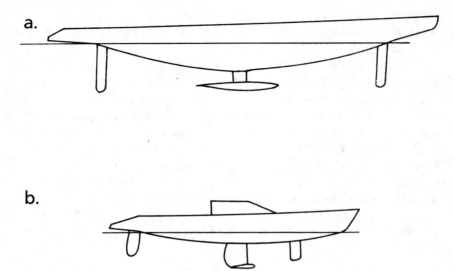

Fig. 5–2. The 12-meter yacht *U.S.A. (top diagram)* features spade rudders bow and stern together with a central "ballast package" suspended by a tiny strut. The one-tonner *Backlash* designed by Julian Everitt *(bottom)* has a forward daggerboard for upwind work, and looks somewhat similar in profile.

Unfortunately, time and budget constraints probably prevented *U.S.A.* from reaching its full potential, although it was obviously improving rapidly up to the point that it was eliminated in the Challengers' semifinal round. It currently appears quite unlikely that this strange configuration is likely to be used at all widely because of its great complexity and associated balance problems. However, bow-mounted daggerboards (fig. 5–2, bottom) and bow rudders will probably be developed further in years to come because both approaches permit the ballast keel to be situated farther aft. This makes it possible to design a hull with finer bow sections yet greater transverse stability.

Winged Keels

The celebrated winged keel is really nothing more than a special sort of bulb keel in which the bulb has been shaped to serve as a particularly efficient end plate. By widening the bulb into a pair of horizontal fins—foils in their own right—cross flow beneath the main keel can be reduced substantially. At the same time, the relatively bulky wings can lower the CG of the ballast even farther than a more compact bulb could.

If the keel is a low-aspect, restricted-draft type that would ordinarily have a high-ballast CG and shed a severe tip vortex, the presence of wings can definitely improve sail-carrying power and upwind efficiency. Winged keels work on 12-meter yachts largely because they are restricted-draft boats. Despite an overall length of about 65 feet, a 12-meter is limited to a draft of a little over 9 feet. Even worse, the bottom of the hull, where the keel itself begins, is itself almost 5 feet beneath the surface (fig. 5–3). In addition to this severe limitation on keel span, a 12-meter carries approximately 60 cubic feet of lead ballast, so the keel must be bulky, thick, and long. Clearly, 12-meters are ideally suited to winged keels and it is not difficult to understand

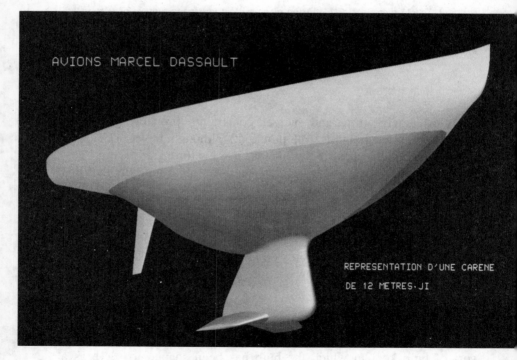

AVIONS MARCEL DASSAULT

REPRESENTATION D'UNE CARENE DE 12 METRES·JI

Fig. 5–3. An *Australia II*–style winged keel graphically depicted by a computerized imaging system developed by the aviation company Dassault-Breguet as part of the '77 *French Kiss* America's Cup program.

why *Australia II* represented a breakthrough design for this class.

Most 12-meter winged keels have the so-called "inverted" profile which features a longer chord at the tip than at the root. Advantages of this configuration are the reduction in interference drag in the area where the keel joins the hull and a lower-ballast CG. Thanks to the end plate effect of the wings, the very long tip chord of these inverted keels does not result in an unacceptable increase in induced drag while sailing upwind.

Following Australia's victory in the 1983 America's Cup, winged keels were fitted to almost every imaginable sort of sailboat, frequently with disappointing results. When wings are used on fins with substantially higher aspect ratios than those of 12-meters, the extra form drag and skin friction of the wings often overshadows the savings in induced drag provided by the end plate effect. Today it is generally recognized that winged keels are a simpler alternative to keel-centerboard installations for shoal-draft yachts, but are unlikely to match the upwind speed of a good, conventional deep keel. Some sailors do feel that a winged keel improves comfort in rough seas by damping vertical heaving motions, but it's difficult to imagine how this effect could be achieved without increased resistance.

Most cruising winged keels (fig. 5–4) have raked leading edges to minimize the problem of weed catching, and substantial root chords to help ensure a strong keel-hull junction. A minor problem stems from the fact that the draft of a winged keel will increase initially as the boat begins to heel and only starts to decrease at higher heel angles. This may make it difficult to free the boat after running aground in some cases.

Slotted Keels

The wings of many contemporary aircraft incorporate adjustable leading edge slots and separate trailing edge flaps to provide sufficient lift for low-speed takeoffs and landings. These slotted foils work by allowing some of the high-pressure air from the underside of the wing to bleed through to the top face of the wing where it invigorates stagnating flow and prevents stalling. A slotted wing can produce dramatically more lift for its area than one without slots because it can continue to operate without flow separation at much higher angles of attack. On the other hand, its lift-to-drag ratio will be less favorable than that of a less cambered wing (which is why the pilot of a jetliner

Fig. 5–4. Winged keels such as this Hydrokeel™ designed by Reijo Salminen are increasingly popular among production boatbuilders seeking good performance from their shoal draft models.

must open the throttles as the flaps are extended in preparation for landing).

Although experiments with slotted sailboat fins have been undertaken repeatedly, it appears probable that the configuration developed recently by British designer Warwick Collins is the first reasonably efficient version. The Collins Tandem Keel™ is an outlandish-looking device consisting of a small, aft-raking foil positioned directly ahead of a larger foil with an inverted trapezoid profile (fig. 5–5). The roots of both are joined to a massive delta-shaped end plate that contains most of the ballast. Consequently, the ballast CG is as low as that of a conventional fin keel with 40 to 50 percent more draft. The wetted surface of the two small vertical foils combined with the end plate is similar to that of the equivalent fin keel.

The slot between the front and rear foils of this unique keel is narrow near the bottom and wide near the top. This tapered configuration is intended to induce the flow through the slot to angle upward so that it will partially counteract the wasteful cross flow beneath the keel tip. With this ''active'' cross-flow barrier augmenting the passive

Fig. 5–5. The Collins Tandem Keel™ from Great Britain is compact and shallow, but its massive delta-shaped end plate ensures a low-ballast CG. *Photographs by Collins Yachts, Ltd.*

barrier created by the massive end plate itself, good efficiency from an exceptionally low aspect keel is theoretically possible. Because the twin foils are so small and slender, these keels must be cast from iron instead of denser but weaker lead. On the other hand, the keel-hull junction is exceptionally secure because both foils share a long, sturdy baseplate that is recessed flush with the bottom.

End Plates and Slots for Rudders?

Some designers (including Collins) are now experimenting with slots and/or end plates on rudders. On the one hand, the possibility of extracting more lift from an exceptionally small rudder is enticing, because it translates into lower rudder drag without giving up the ability to steer out of trouble. On the other hand, when a central stern-hung rudder is made too short, it will rise to the water or even lift out completely when the boat heels substantially (fig. 5–6a). For beamy monohulls with stern-mounted rudders, the practical lower limit for rudder span may have little to do with steering efficiency and ability to resist stalling. Furthermore, finding sufficient draft for adequate rudder span is rarely a major problem, because the rudder is ordinarily situated near the stern where the hull depth is modest.

This problem of rudder lift-out can be averted in a number of ways. One is to use two small rudders positioned somewhat to port and starboard instead of a much deeper central rudder (fig. 5–6b). This approach originated during the last century in the inland lake scow classes, and recently has been adapted by many BOC Round the World Race competitors. When heeled sufficiently, the windward rudder lifts largely or completely clear of the surface while the leeward one projects almost vertically into the water for maximum immersion and efficiency. At the time of this writing, only conventional spade and skeg-hung rudders have been employed in twin rudder installations. However, the configuration should be ideal for slotted foils, end plates, and even the variable contour foils described in the following section.

A less common but effective method of keeping a small rudder immersed at high heel angles is to cant it to leeward (fig. 5–6c). This approach necessitates a transom-hung rudder and involves obvious complications. Nevertheless, it has been used with good success, notably on *Thursday's Child,* the 60-foot monohull that recently broke the 154-year-old sailing speed record from New York to San Francisco.

Variable-Contour Foils and Bow Rudders

As mentioned in the preceeding chapter, a fixed, stationary skeg ahead of the rudder blade can improve the lift-to-drag ratio under some circumstances. Introducing a second articulating joint to allow both the center and the trailing segments of the fin to be angled with respect to the flow promises an even greater efficiency (fig. 5–7a). Once again, a good parallel is the wing of a modern jetliner, which deploys "droopy" leading edges and trailing edge flaps to change from a thin, low-drag foil suitable for economical cruising into a highly cambered foil that can support the weight of the airplane at low takeoff and landing speeds. To maintain maximum steering effi-

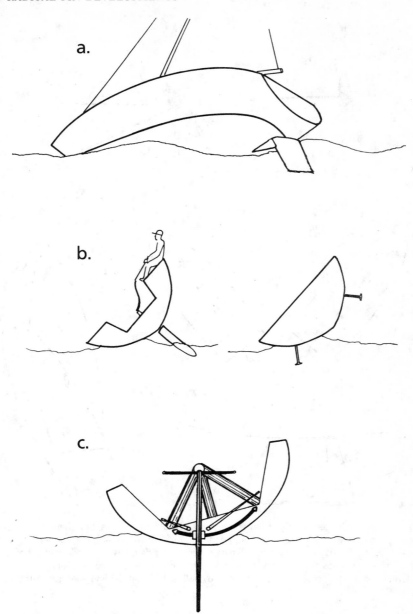

Fig. 5–6. At large heel angles, the rudder of a modern yacht with a full stern may lift out of the water causing loss of control *(a)*. Short twin rudders are often more effective than a single long one *(b)*. An ingenious rudder that can be canted to compensate for heel was designed by Lars Bergstrom for *Thursday's Child (c)*.

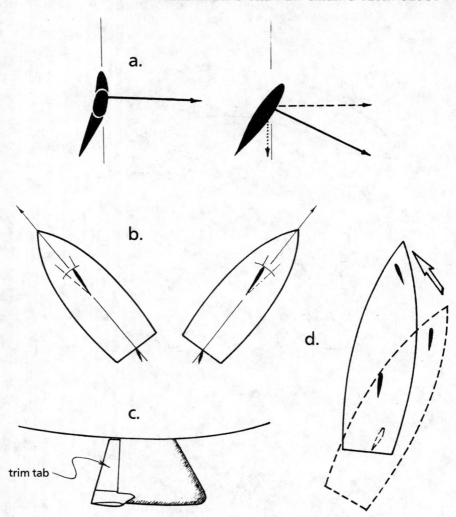

Fig. 5–7. An optimized variable-camber rudder *(a)* would be capable of generating large turning forces with a much smaller drag penalty than a conventional spade rudder incurs. Gybing centerboards can reduce (or eliminate) leeway in dinghies *(b)*, while meter boats often have trim tabs on the keel to achieve the same end *(c)*. Bow rudders have the potential for enhancing upwind performance by pulling the boat to windward during tacks.

ciency during sharp turns, the ideal variable-contour rudder would be capable of pivoting as a whole like a conventional spade design.

Variable-contour foils are promising, not only for rudders which need to be capable of generating very high steering forces to deal with the occasional crisis, but also for keels and centerboards. Trying to eliminate leeway by altering the attack angle of a symmetrical keel or centerboard has proven very troublesome, although some high-performance dinghy classes sometimes use "gybing" boards as diagrammed in figure 5-7b. The articulating **trim tab** used on many meter boats turns the keel into an asymmetrical foil and often provides a significant improvement in upwind performance (fig. 5-7c). A few big-boat designers have also experimented with dual, asymmetrical bilgeboards that are alternately extended and retracted each time the boat is tacked. With this setup a small, symmetrical centerline keel is also needed to carry ballast and make the boat controllable downwind, so the complications and redundancies involved are obvious. All in all, while variable-contour foils also pose significant engineering problems, the potential for efficiency gains is much greater.

Variable-contour rudders might work particularly well if mounted forward, ahead of the keel or centerboard. A major advantage of this unusual configuration is that the bows tend to immerse more deeply when the stern of a hard-pressed boat begins to lift, thereby ensuring good control with even a small rudder (so long as it's sufficiently powerful). A secondary advantage of the bow rudder is that it pulls the boat to windward during a tack (fig. 5-7d), while a conventional stern-mounted rudder has the opposite effect. Drawbacks include a potentially awkward steering linkage, increased risk of rudder damage, and possible difficulties with fore-and-aft ballast location.

6

Handicapping and Its Impact
upon Yacht Design

For sailors who do not race big boats, the subject of ratings and handicaps might appear to have little relevance. This is not the case, however, simply because handicapping rules have had such a profound influence upon the design of sailboats in general. Today's "performance cruisers" routinely incorporate features such as overlapping headsails, exaggerated beam amidships, and reverse-raked transoms—features that originated in handicap racing but are of questionable value on a true cruising yacht.

Although it is generally agreed that one-design sailors enjoy the fairest possible racing, handicapping is a virtual necessity for racing in a big-boat fleet. Numerous attempts to establish viable offshore one-design classes have seldom met with great success, partly because there are too many designs competing for a limited market, and partly because it is too difficult to transport big yachts to out-of-town regattas. In the future, the diversity of racing/cruising sailboats is quite likely to increase still further, because fiberglass sailboats, unlike automobiles, do not wear out or rust away within a decade or so.

In handicap racing, success is not so much a matter of out-and-out speed superiority as of achieving a more favorable ratio of actual speed to rated speed. Any relatively simple rating formula can (and will) be exploited by a new generation of purpose-built boats. To keep would-be rule beaters at bay, modern "scientific" handicapping systems have necessarily become extremely complex and quite expensive to administer. This, in turn, has created a niche for another sort of handicapping based not so much upon the physical characteristics of various boats as upon their observed performance over a number of races.

The Theory of Handicapping

To clarify some of the terms used in yacht handicapping, a **rating** is the resolution of a measurement formula that takes into account a boat's physical characteristics like length, beam, draft, displacement, sail area, and so forth. **Handicaps** are the actual **time allowances** awarded to the slower boats in a race. When a rating system is used, the time allowance for a particular boat is determined by a calculation using the boat's rating and either the length of the race course (time-on-distance handicapping) or the time needed by the boat to complete the course (time-on-time handicapping).

Key factors determining the speed potential of sailboats are discussed throughout this book. The most important are: effective sailing length, wetted beam and hull depth, wetted surface area, displacement, stability, sail area, and efficiency of the underwater fins. All these, except perhaps the last, vary with the size of the yacht, but not, for the most part, in direct proportion to its linear dimensions. For example, if a yacht was to be scaled up to double its original length, its sail area and wetted surface would be squared, its displacement cubed, and its stability increased to the fourth power. On the other hand, its hull speed, being a root function of sailing length, would only increase about 40 percent ($1.43 = \sqrt{2}$).

A good rating formula must take into account each of these speed-determining elements and assess the impact of each independently. To further complicate the problem, the importance of each factor can vary dramatically with the sailing conditions. For example, stability or sail-carrying ability is essential for upwind speed in windy weather, but unimportant in drifting conditions. Sail area and wetted surface are much the opposite—critically important in light air, but of reduced significance in a blow.

The International Offshore Rule (IOR)

With the rapid growth of yacht racing in the 1960s, the sailing community sought a new universal rule that would permit equitable competition among nations in offshore yachts. At the time, the only rating rule with intercontinental applicability was the International Rule that governed the meter boat classes. Unfortunately, the yachts it produces are day racers, ill-suited for either serious cruising or offshore use.* To rectify this shortcoming, a committee with representatives from Europe and North America set out to develop a new international rule for offshore racing.

The IOR is largely based upon two rating rules that were in widespread use in the 1960s: the Royal Ocean Racing Club rule and the Cruising Club of America rule. For the most part, IOR hull measurement procedures trace back to the RORC, while sail and rig assessment methods stem from the CCA. Like its predecessors, the IOR is a conservative rule that effectively excludes multihulls, unballasted yachts, very light boats, most adjustable or retractable underwater foils, full-length sail battens, rotating masts, and a lot of other potential innovations. However, despite its limited sphere of influence, the IOR has played a pivotal role in helping international offshore racing "come of age." Along the way it's generated plenty of controversy during its first two decades.

Under the IOR, displacement is not determined directly, because weighing large yachts accurately can be quite difficult. Instead, the probable resistance of the hull is estimated by deriving a **rated beam** and a **rated depth**. Both these components appear in the denominator of the IOR formula and therefore tend to reduce the rating as they grow larger. They are derived using a fairly small number of measurements taken at discrete points on the hull, first while ashore and later afloat.

Sail area and effective sailing length are the two speed-producing factors which appear in the numerator of the IOR formula. Sail area is derived from a straightforward series of rig measurements with correction factors thrown in to allow for the varying efficiencies of different types of rigs. Unfortunately, these corrections have not been

---

*To be fair to the meter boats and their many supporters, it should be mentioned that keen competition in the 6-, 8-, and 12-meter classes continues to this day. In addition, countless important advances in sailing technology have originated with these boats, particularly as a result of America's Cup programs in 12-meters.

revised to keep up with rig and sail developments. As a result, the only currently competitive rig type for most high-level IOR racing is the fractional sloop.

Sailing length under the IOR is estimated using a series of measurements and calculations that are aimed at establishing the "slope" of the bow and stern overhangs. Gently rising overhangs tend to immerse more length while sailing, thus increasing speed potential.

Because the measurements used in deriving an IOR rating are taken at a small number of discrete points on the hull, it is not surprising that designers have found ways to improve the ratio of rating to speed. Since the early 1970s, a new breed—the IOR yacht—has evolved and any experienced sailor anywhere in the world can instantly recognize one. An IOR hull (fig. 6–1) has "pinched" ends designed to position the forward and aft girth stations closer to one another. Exaggerated beam amidships indirectly accomplishes the same thing. In addition, it often yields a lower rating due to its effect on the rated beam, one of the key drag-estimating components mentioned earlier. Also characteristic of the IOR hull is a flat strip down the center of the forward and mid-portions of the bottom which provides a reduction in actual displacement by whittling away a part of the hull where no depth measurements are taken. This feature also permits slightly greater keel span without penalty.

IOR sheerlines are much straighter than those of earlier designs because a more traditional sheerline that dipped substantially amidships would translate into either a smaller measured beam or a greater waterline beam—both deleterious. Most IOR sterns have a "crease" or discontinuity in the aft run that induces the rule to overlook a portion of the stern overhang that in reality will contribute to effective sailing length. When all these design features (and a number of others) are taken together, the net result is a boat that under the IOR rule appears to be 5 to 10 percent heavier and shorter than it really is.

Between 1970, when the IOR was officially adopted as the international rating system for offshore racing, and 1975, the fledgling rule was subjected to an incredible assault from an army of professional designers, sailmakers, and technically minded racing sailors. Compact computers were just becoming available, and everyone, it seems, was dissecting the IOR, looking for "loopholes" that could lead to improved speed relative to rating. The Offshore Racing Council that administered the IOR was equally astute and persevering in plugging

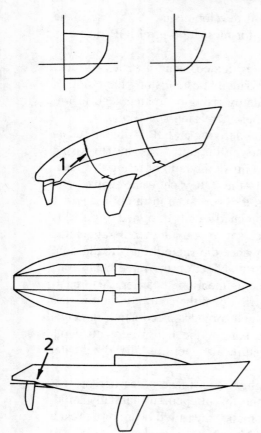

Fig. 6-1. An IOR hull is characterized by flattened midsections inside the depth measurement points and a "creased" stern *(arrow 2)*. Many also have subtle "bumps" *(arrow 1)* that artificially boost the critical rated-beam measurement.

these loopholes—issuing Mark II and Mark III versions of the new rule in rapid succession.

Not surprisingly, there was widespread unhappiness over the "instability" of the new rule during those early years. It sometimes seemed that an owner needed a new boat every year to remain competitive. Another source of displeasure was the mass obsolescence of virtually all preexisting offshore yachts—good boats that rated too high to compete effectively with the new crop of boats designed specifically to conform with the new rule.

Fortunately, just as the IOR seemed in danger of foundering in a sea of bad publicity, it became evident that the Mark III version was working quite well, and the cycle of obsolescence had slowed dramatically. The cooler heads in offshore racing recognized that to introduce yet another rating rule would very likely initiate a new wave of obsolescence as designers found ways to exploit a new set of weaknesses.

Since the mid-1970s, changes in the IOR Mark III have been relatively minor, and on the whole, it appears to be doing a fine job of rating those boats that are designed with the rule in mind. An amended version of the IOR Mark III, called Mark IIIA, gives a modest rating break to older boats to help them compete more effectively with the latest designs. This too appears to work fairly well, as long as the "old" hull is equipped with up-to-date deck gear, rigging, sails, fins, and electronics.

To summarize, the IOR rule in its mature form has become a conservative rating rule that encourages advanced development in certain restricted contexts such as hull construction, sails, and gear, but sharply curtails the overall range of permissible design configurations. The cream of the yachts conforming to IOR parameters currently enjoy extremely close, exciting racing in major offshore events—the so-called Grand Prix circuit of ocean racing.

International Measurement System (IMS)

In 1976, the United States Yacht Racing Union (USYRU) addressed itself to the plight of those sailors who wanted to race, but ". . . who prefer to own boats that differ from the optimal IOR concept." The boats in question are typically heavier, slimmer monohulls with more livable interiors than the IOR norm; the list of designs that are uncompetitive under IOR also includes exceptionally light displacement racing boats with undistorted hull lines. The USYRU decided to address this need by undertaking to develop a new handicapping system that would be sophisticated enough to allow boats of very different character to compete on a fair basis.

Fortuitously, a research group at the Massachusetts Institute of Technology had begun work three years earlier on the theory and practice of yacht handicapping. Using information from an extensive series of tank tests as well as some full scale experiments, the H. Irving Pratt Project, as it was called, developed a sophisticated **velocity prediction program** for sailing yachts. This program is, in essence, a high-powered computer model that determines the speed that a well-sailed yacht could be expected to attain in various sailing conditions. In general terms, the program works by computing the aerodynamic forward and side forces produced by the sails, then balancing these forces off against the righting forces and drag forces produced by the moving hull. Members of the newly formed Measurement Handicap Committee of the USYRU began working side by side with Pratt project researchers in order to develop a practical handicapping system based on the velocity prediction program.

The **Measurement Handicapping System** was first implemented in 1978. In 1985, after much testing and refinement in the United States, it was adapted by the ORC and renamed the **International Measurement System (IMS)**. The unique character of the IMS stems from its ability to accurately predict the speed of a sailboat on different points of sail and in different wind conditions. Rather than assign each boat a single time allowance that roughly reflects its average speed potential, an IMS certificate offers a series of time allowances that reflect predicted performance in different wind speeds and on several types of race courses (with varying proportions of upwind vs. offwind work). It is, of course, more difficult to implement handicaps that are linked to the wind conditions occurring during a race, and an amazing variety of objections have been raised. However, in the final reckoning, it is unreasonable to criticize the IMS for being complicated. Simpler systems are inherently unfair; and after all, the real goal of yacht handicapping is to produce time allowances that accurately reflect genuine differences in performance potential.

IMS hull measurement is performed using a computerized machine that establishes the X-Y-Z coordinates of a great many points on the hull surface. The process takes about eight hours and generates enough data to permit a full set of hull lines to be reconstructed electronically. After the hull form has been established, volume of the immersed portion is computed with the aid of freeboard measurements identical to those used by the IOR. An IOR-type inclining test is conducted to establish the stability and CG location of the yacht in measurement trim. Computations are then made to predict stability with sailing gear aboard and a full crew on the windward rail. A series of involved computations establishes the magnitude of skin friction, form drag, and wave-making drag at various speeds and heel angles.

A second subprogram analyses the aerodynamics of the rig and sails to derive the driving force and side force that can be expected under different sailing conditions. The program is set up to prescribe sail flattening and reefing options when the extra resistance associated with excessive heel begins to reduce predicted performance. Sail and rig measurements used are identical to those used by the IOR, except that mast diameters are also taken for spar windage computations.

The final portion of the IMS is an elaborate program that determines which combination of sail trim, heading, and crew-weight placement will provide the best possible performance for a particular boat under each particular sailing condition. In all, velocity predictions are made for twenty-six cases (including optimized upwind and downwind headings) in each of six true wind velocities from 8 to 20 knots. The net result is a performance profile that can be used to predict whether one boat will be faster than another in a given set of sailing conditions and by how much.

Although the IMS is clearly superior to any previous yacht handicapping system, it currently still has shortcomings. High-tech boats with very lightweight rigs, sails, hulls and deck hardware pitch less in rough seas, and hence enjoy a significant advantage that is currently unmeasured under both IOR and IMS (fig. 6–2). Furthermore, boats with lower-than-average displacement-to-length ratios may enjoy both an unmeasured downwind advantage in surfing/planing conditions and an unmeasured upwind advantage in rough seas. So far, all IMS performance predictions have been based upon a smooth water model, but research is under way to find ways of predicting rough water performance as well.

On the whole, the IMS is working quite well in the United States. A shortage of measurement machines delayed its debut elsewhere in the world, but at the time of writing the system was finally getting up and running in Great Britain. Already, however, there is real concern that too much pressure on the IMS from the most serious competitors in the sport may once again render a large fraction of the current racing/cruising fleet uncompetitive. For this reason, the ORC is promoting the IOR as the preferred handicapping rule for major international offshore events, hopefully leaving the IMS arena to recreational racers sailing the more conservative and cruisable designs. Since **level-class racing** is an important part of many of the top IOR venues, the IMS is probably a less suitable system for these events in any case, because under the IMS every boat has several different wind-specific handicaps rather than a single rating.

The performance predictions that are the heart of the IMS system have proven themselves to be of enormous value to serious IOR sailors as a tune-up and racing aid (see Chapter 17 on electronics). For

Fig. 6–2. Older Grand Prix IOR racers like this Ted Irwin design can be deadly under IMS, largely because their lightweight construction and empty ends currently give them an unpenalized advantage in rough water. *Photograph by Irwin Yachts.*

this reason, many serious IOR competitors today will have their boats measured for IMS even if they intend to race only IOR events. Conveniently enough, the measurements required for an IOR rating constitute a subclass of the measurements needed to generate an IMS certificate, so an IOR rating can be computed from IMS input data. At the time of this writing, machine measurement of hulls is finally being implemented on a worldwide basis, and before long it will no doubt be standard practice to measure for both IOR and IMS simultaneously.

The Midget Ocean Racing Club (MORC) Rule

North America's Midget Ocean Racing Club (MORC) caters specifically to cruisable keelboats of 30 feet overall length and less. Launched in 1954, following a much-publicized Atlantic crossing by the 18-foot *Sopranino,* this handicapping rule was intended to encourage racing in compact but seaworthy cruising boats. Prior to that time small yachts were effectively barred from competition in East Coast distance racing.

Over the years, the MORC rule has evolved considerably, but has remained remarkably successful at providing close competition for a mixed fleet of wholesome little cruisers. Like most rating systems less complex than the IMS, boats designed to the MORC rule can be optimized for either lighter or heavier air, and of course there is virtually no limit to the amount of money that a wealthy owner can spend on a custom design (even one less than 30 feet long). Nevertheless, many MORC championships continue to be won by production boats (fig. 6–3).

Under the MORC rule, displacement is measured by simply weighing the whole boat—a practical approach with smaller craft. Stability is estimated from ballast-to-displacement ratio; a rough-and-ready approach that in practice works quite well. The way that the MORC rule evaluates the effects of bow and stern overhang on effective sail-

Fig. 6–3. One of the most successful MORC designs of recent times, the S-2 7.9 is a 26-foot Graham and Schlageter design with a displacement of 4250 pounds and reasonable accommodations for a boat its size. A broad stern adds sail-carrying power while the steeply rising aft run confers a rating advantage.

ing length tends to encourage rather snub-ended boats, often with fairly convex buttock lines aft. Simple, sturdy rigs are significantly encouraged by the terms of the MORC rule, a feature that the IOR would do well to emulate. For the most part, sailors who want to race relatively inexpensive keelboats under an inexpensive rating rule seem well pleased with the MORC rule.

Channel Handicapping

A new handicapping system developed in the United Kingdom just a few years ago, Channel handicapping has gained a solid following in Western Europe. Like IOR it's a fairly simple measurement system, and like IOR it could, no doubt, be exploited by purpose-built designs except for one twist: the rating formula is kept secret by the administrators of the rule. High-tech sails and recent design dates incur rating penalties.

So far, Channel handicapping seems to be working very well and has attracted many older boats back into racing. While it seems quite likely that designers could eventually figure out how the hidden formula works by comparing the rating certificates of large numbers of boats, it is hoped that a healthy IOR and IMS can prevent these types of pressures from developing. Over the next few years, as the IMS makes inroads in Europe, it seems likely that the more dedicated cruising boat racers are apt to leave the Channel handicapping fold. Nevertheless, this cleverly administered rule is still likely to attract a substantial following, mostly among the cruising sailors who enjoy some racing on the side.

Portsmouth and PHRF

Even with IOR, IMS, MORC, and various other measurement systems to choose from, there are plenty of boats that fall through the cracks. In particular, unballasted sailboats, yachts with inefficient underwater fins, exceptionally heavy- or light-displacement boats, and multihulls either fare very poorly under all the measurement systems or are not eligible at all. Handicapping systems based upon the observation of race results help to fill the needs of these groups, as well as those of sporadic racers who are reluctant to incur the expense of a measurement-type rating.

One-design classes frequently sail around the same course at regattas starting at five- or ten-minute intervals. After comparing the elapsed times of the various class leaders in a number of races it becomes feasible to make valid comparisons of the relative speed potentials of these boats in a variety of wind conditions. This is the basis of the **Portsmouth yardstick**.

The USYRU version of the Portsmouth yardstick uses the Thistle, a popular class of centerboard dinghy, as its primary point of reference. The performance of the Thistle around a closed course in six different wind ranges (Beaufort 1–6) was in each case assigned a value of 83. Boats that sailed either faster or slower than the Thistle in given wind conditions were assigned higher or lower Portsmouth numbers as suitable data became available. For example, the Fireball dinghy has proven to be slower than the Thistle in light winds (Portsmouth 89 for Beaufort 1), but faster in a real blow (Portsmouth 80 for Beaufort 6). Its average handicap of 86.5 means that over a large number of races in a range of conditions, a Fireball can be expected to average 96 percent of a Thistle's speed.

Under the auspices of the USYRU, Portsmouth numbers have been assigned to some 1,500 classes of dinghies, day-racing keelboats, small multihulls, and offshore yachts. About seventy of these handicaps are regarded as reliable enough to serve as secondary yardsticks. Data gathering is an on-going process involving numerous yacht clubs.

The **Performance Handicap Racing Fleet** (PHRF) is another, more recently established system that assigns ratings on the basis of observed performance. It differs from the Portsmouth yardstick in that it deals exclusively with ballasted monohulls—for the most part cruising auxiliaries. PHRF handicaps are expressed in terms of seconds per mile and no attempt is made to assign individual handicaps for varying wind strengths.

Both Portsmouth and PHRF share a common failing: They are based on data that are inherently unreliable, or at any rate, very difficult to interpret. In many cases, race outcomes are decided primarily by the relative skills of the crews involved rather than by differences in the speed potential of the boats involved. Differences in sail quality or bottom preparation will also have a dramatic impact upon performance, often obscuring the real differences in performance potential. As a result, classes or designs that are favored by highly skilled racing sailors often are saddled with stiffer handicaps than the performance potential of these boats actually warrants, while other classes may get off too easily and be ripe for exploitation in the hands of a top crew.

Scientific Handicapping—A New Era Begins?

Rating and handicapping systems have been a part of sailboat racing for more than a century now, and, for better or worse, they have played a major role in shaping the sport. In the past, overly simplistic rating formulas that placed undue emphasis on certain speed-producing factors led to the creation of some strange and often rather unsatisfactory yachts. Only recently, thanks to the advances in computer technology, has it become feasible even to contemplate a fully balanced and universal handicapping system—one that gives all competitors an equally good chance to win on the basis of sailing skill alone. As the first attempt at this sort of system, it is not surprising that IMS falls short of perfection, but it nevertheless is a major step forward and a harbinger of things to come.

For the time being, the administrators of international offshore racing have chosen to use the IOR as a buffer to protect the fledgling IMS from an all-out assault by ''professionals'' of the big-boat racing game. This dual-system approach may well persist into the twenty-first century, but is unlikely to remain in effect indefinitely. Contemporary Grand Prix IOR boats have evolved to the point that they are of little value for anything except IOR racing, and as such have poor resale value. Over time, look to IMS or its successor to gradually supersede the IOR for all types of big-boat racing.

Even if a universal scientific rating system capable of handling everything from trailer sailors to big multihulls is eventually developed, there is still likely to be a place for less elaborate and costly handicapping. Simplified measurement systems like MORC, Channel handicapping, and even the venerable International Rule are likely to continue to thrive in some quarters. The same is true of the performance-based systems like Portsmouth and PHRF, which provide very inexpensive handicaps for recreational racers.

7

Multihulls: The New Frontier

For multihulled sailboats, legitimacy has come hard. However, exclusion from the mainstream of yachting for almost a century may well have ultimately improved the breed by encouraging multihull enthusiasts to take more daring and innovative departures from the conservative realm of conventional yacht design.

Notwithstanding this, multihull sailboats are fundamentally a lot more like monohulls than they are different, and this chapter is an extension of concepts introduced earlier in this book. The major differences between monohulls and multihulls relate to speed potential, sailing behavior, and onboard space distribution.

The Multihull Speed Edge

There are two main reasons why multihulls tend to be substantially faster than monohulls. The first is their superior transverse stability relative to weight. It's true that stability in both multihulls and monohulls stems from the same source—the lateral separation of the CG and CB that occurs when the boat heels. However, when two or three widely spaced hulls are involved, the CG and CB move apart much farther and more abruptly (fig. 7–1). This characteristic, sometimes called **straddle stability,** endows the typical multihull with enormously greater sail-carrying ability than a monohull of comparable displacement, which in turn allows a larger, more powerful rig to be used.

The second reason for superior multihull speed is that very slim, low-resistance hulls can be used because the form stability of each individual hull has virtually no effect upon the transverse stability of the complete boat. As for displacement itself—one of the most important determinants of hydrodynamic drag—multihulls again benefit because they are so stable at small heel angles that no ballast is required to provide ample sail-carrying ability.

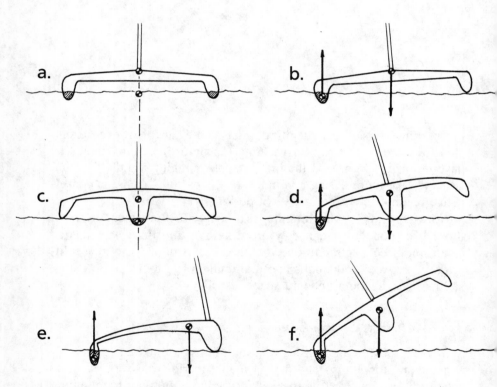

Fig. 7–1. The immense sail-carrying ability of multihulls results from a dramatic shift of the center of buoyancy to leeward that takes place at relatively small heel angles *(a–d)*. At the point of maximum stability, the righting couple for a cat and a tri will be the same provided both have the same displacement and beam *(b* vs. *d)*. On the other hand, a proa is potentially more stable than either when its CG is offset to windward *(e)*. Once the heel angle providing maximum stability is exceeded, the righting couple for any multihull decreases quite rapidly *(d* vs. *f)*.

As the length-to-beam ratio of a displacement hull climbs to 10:1 and more, the contribution of wave drag to total hull resistance rapidly falls away. Of course, several very slim hulls will have more wetted surface relative to displacement than a single wider one, but the added skin friction this causes is, on the whole, far less damaging than the substantially greater wave drag of the beamy hull at higher speeds. It is now common for multihulls to achieve speed-to-length ratios around 3.5 (compared to 1.4 for typical displacement monohulls) despite the fact that the dynamic lift provided by such narrow, knifelike hulls is, in most cases, quite limited.

Cats, Tris, and Proas

Catamarans (cats) have two identical or mirror-image hulls linked together by one or more transverse structural members called **cross beams. Trimarans** (tris), as the name implies, have three hulls: generally a larger central one and a pair of slimmer outboard hulls called **amas. Proas** are asymmetrical two-hulled multihulls comprised of one wider, larger hull and another slimmer one which may be positioned either to windward or leeward. For a variety of reasons, proas are specialized, problematical sailboats. They are far less popular than the other two types.

As compared to tris, cats are simpler to construct and potentially lighter because they have less hull surface area relative to length and displacement. For a similar size and displacement, cats also have less windage than tris, a major source of drag when the apparent wind is ahead of the beam at 25 or 30 knots. The chief weakness of the catamaran configuration is light-air sailing, because when both hulls are equally immersed, a cat's wetted surface is at its maximum (fig. 7–1a). Minimum hydrodynamic drag in a cat is achieved when heeling forces are just great enough to lift the windward hull barely clear of the surface (fig. 7–1b), and for this reason cats are usually at their best in a good breeze.

Trimarans are easier to rig than cats because the central hull furnishes a sturdy spine for stepping and staying the mast. If a tri is constructed so that only one ama contacts the water at a time, and provided the amas are properly shaped, its wetted surface in light air will be minimal (fig. 7–1c). For this reason, a good trimaran's light-air speed will usually be superior to that of a comparable cat.

Multihulls as a group are difficult to tack because they have little

momentum to overcome the aerodynamic drag of their big rigs. However, most tris come about more readily than cats because the amas
are largely clear of the water while the boat is passing head-to-wind.
All in all, trimarans tend to be more versatile sailboats than cats, but
the extra cost of building an additional hull that differs from the other
two cannot always be justified.

Transverse Stability and Safety

When a cat is "fully powered" and blasting along with the weather
hull just kissing the water (fig. 7-1b), the center of buoyancy is almost
all the way to leeward, while the center of gravity is situated to windward at a distance equal to half the beam (or a bit more if the crew
are perched on the weather hull). Exactly the same is true of a good
modern tri (fig. 7-1d), although many sailors don't realize it. The
key is to build enough volume (buoyancy) into each ama to support
the entire weight of the vessel with an adequate reserve. If this is
done, the tri, like the cat, can be sailed with its CB all the way to
leeward and the CG at the half-beam point. Virtually all modern tris
have buoyancy in each ama of at least 120 percent of the all-up displacement of the boat. Many designers now favor amas with around
200 percent buoyancy to minimize submarining.

Proas that are sailed with the larger, heavier hull to windward are
potentially the fastest multihulls of all because the center of gravity
of the entire boat is offset to windward even before the crew moves
to the rail (fig. 7-1e). However, proas also tend to be intractable and
potentially dangerous boats—inherently less stable whenever they are
sailing on the "wrong" tack. To maximize performance on both tacks,
some offshore racing proas have been double-enders with alternating
rudders at each end and a rig that can be switched bow for stern
during gybes!

The issue of lateral stability as it relates to safety is particularly
critical with multihulls because the peak righting forces in multihull
stability curves are usually reached at very low heel angles—usually
between 5 and 15 degrees. If heel increases any farther, the righting
tendency diminishes, because the CG and CB immediately begin to
converge again (fig. 7-1f).

Unlike most ballasted monohulls, an inverted multihull is extremely stable—generally even more stable than when upright because
the upside-down rig has a keel-like influence. It is no surprise that

both multihull designers and sailors treat the subject of capsize as a matter of grave concern. While innumerable schemes and systems for righting large capsized multihulls have been devised, built, and even tested, none so far have been proven reliable in the strong winds and rough sea conditions when a capsize is most apt to occur. The only viable solution to the multihull capsize problem currently appears to be prevention: the use of automatic sheet release gear (to let fly the sheets if loads become excessive), conservative sailing, and good seamanship. Masthead floats have been used on a few big cruising multihulls to prevent a serious 90 degree capsize from turning into a catastrophic 180 degree one, but at the cost of substantial added rig weight and windage.

Hull Shapes

Asymmetrical catamaran hulls and trimaran amas have been used extensively in the past in an effort to produce lateral resistance for upwind and crosswind sailing without the extra draft and complexity of centerboards or other underwater appendages. However, for the most part, this design approach is now out of vogue because it has been found that the asymmetrical hulls make rather inefficient lifting foils and create too much additional drag, particularly for efficient offwind sailing. Today the generally preferred cross section for cat and tri hulls is symmetrical and U-shaped (fig. 7–2a). This form ensures minimum wetted surface for low-speed, light-air sailing, while keeping the length-to-beam ratio high as all the weight shifts to the leeward hull in a breeze. Trimarans often gain an additional wetted-surface advantage in light air by having substantial bow and stern overhangs on the amas that only immerse as the leeward ama begins to load up (fig. 7–2b). To reduce added resistance while punching through waves, the forward topsides of both catamaran and trimaran hulls are frequently rounded and torpedo-shaped (fig. 7–2c).

Most monohulls have so much stability in the fore-and-aft direction that a forward capsize or pitchpoling is only possible under extraordinary wave conditions in ocean storms. Pitchpoling is more of a problem for multihulls because they weigh less, go faster, and usually have much bigger rigs relative to their overall lengths. Trouble typically arises when the leeward bow of a multihull digs in while hurling down a wave in a gust, causing the boat to "trip" and pitch violently forward. The solution chosen by most contemporary multihull de-

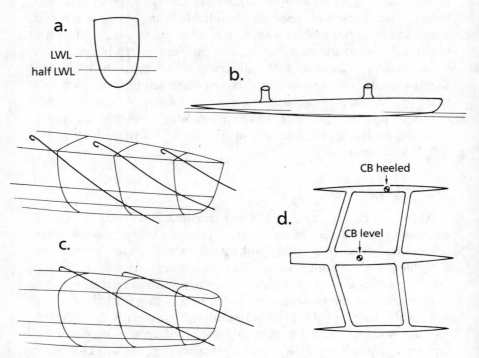

Fig. 7–2. Symmetrical hulls with U-shaped cross sections are typical of modern multihulls (a). The amas of trimarans may have considerable rocker to minimize wetted surface in light air and drawn out sterns to reduce turbulence when hard pressed and deeply submerged (b). Rounded sheerlines reduce both aerodynamic drag (c) and added resistance while piercing waves. Offsetting the amas of a trimaran forward provides a beneficial forward shift in the CB (d) thus helping to avert nose dives while driving hard.

signers is to design boats with ample reserve buoyancy in the bows so that the leeward hull becomes very difficult to immerse. In many cases it is also worthwhile to shape the hulls so that the center of buoyancy shifts forward as the boat heels—partly to improve resistance to pitching forward, but also to help maintain a balanced helm. In cats this effect can only be obtained by flaring the forward topsides more than the aft ones. In tris, it can also be achieved by locating the CB of the amas ahead of the CB in the main hull (fig. 7–2d).

Multihull Cruising Yachts

Although the Polynesians were crisscrossing the Pacific in multihulls hundreds of years ago, and as early as the 1950s a handful of pioneering yachtsmen were following suit, cruising multihulls are only now gaining widespread popularity. Debate continues to rage as to whether multihulls are more dangerous than monohulls (more likely to capsize), or safer (less likely to sink). Today it is widely believed that the risk of a wind-induced capsize in a good cruising multihull of moderate design is small provided prudent seamanship and routine vigilance are practiced. As for wave-induced capsizes in severe ocean storms, some of the latest evidence (wave-tank testing by Donald Jordan) suggests that a conventional ballasted monohull may be more at risk than a typical multihull when both are running before the seas trailing drogues. The reason? Because the weight of the monohull is concentrated much closer to its center of rotation, it has much less rotational inertia to counteract sudden heeling or rolling forces. Balanced against this, of course, is the fact that a multihull, once capsized, will ordinarily remain capsized, while a conservatively designed monohull should soon right itself, although often rather the worse for the wear.

For inshore cruising, there remains little question that multihulls offer an outstanding combination of virtues: superior sailing speed, superior powering speed, enormous deck area, outstanding shallow-draft capabilities, and almost no heeling while under sail. Probably the two greatest drawbacks of a cruising multihull are the shortage of mooring space for such beamy boats, and a substantially higher price as compared to monohulls with comparable accommodations. If a relatively small cruiser will suffice, a trailerable trimaran with retractable or demountable amas may solve the mooring problem. Higher cost is a much tougher nut to crack, because building any multihull entails making two or three hulls per boat along with a strong yet lightweight connecting structure. Furthermore, multihulls require much bigger, more expensive rigs than comparable monohulls if they are to perform to their potential. All this tends to offset the cost savings on a ballast keel many times over.

The most satisfactory cruising multihulls are probably catamarans of 40 feet or more, because in this size range a useful "main cabin" space can be provided in a rigid bridge structure that spans the gap between the hulls without compromising performance excessively.

Smaller cruising cats typically suffer either from too much bulk and windage or a desperate shortage of enclosed living space. A pair of tunnel-like cabins less than 4 feet wide may be OK for sleeping or navigation work, but they aren't much good for anything else. In contrast, tris as small as 25 feet can make reasonable cruising boats because the relatively deep central hull provides a corridor of adequate headroom while lateral extensions of the main hull above the waterline provide space for counters and berths. On the other hand, large, modern trimarans tend to offer only skimpy interiors for the price, because the amas are almost always too slender to use for living space.

Multihull Aerodynamics

Because multihulls are bulky but lightweight sailboats that travel at unusually high speeds with the apparent wind forward of the beam most of the time, aerodynamic drag comprises an unusually high proportion of the total resistance they must overcome. Successful attempts to reduce aerodynamic drag therefore pay significant dividends in multihull design.

Rounded, indistinct sheer lines are now common on high-performance multihulls, not only to reduce hydrodynamic resistance when penetrating waves but because wind-tunnel tests indicate that, given an identical topsides profile, a radiused sheer can reduce wind drag up to 20 percent (fig. 7–2c). Similarly, where upwind speed is a primary consideration, the cross-arm structures that interconnect the hulls should be as compact and aerodynamically "clean" as possible.

To minimize **parasitic drag**—the resistance associated with appendages—contemporary multihull designers strive to cluster or, better yet, to recess sail-handling gear, leaving their decks as sleek as possible. Above the deck, the rigging is subjected to similar attention. While all sailing rigs represent a trade-off between maximum aerodynamic efficiency and minimum weight, the optimum for performance multihulls tends to favor the aerodynamic side of the spectrum. The reason is that multihulls are so much more stable than other sailboats that they can tolerate more rig weight as long as it "buys" the "cleanest," most aerodynamically efficient rig available. This is why fully battened, rotating mast rigs and wing mast rigs are the rule rather than the exception in contemporary high-performance multihulls. These rigs, among others, will be discussed at some length in Chapter 13.

Strength vs. Weight in Multihull Construction

Stiff boats experience higher rig-induced stresses than tender ones, and big multihulls are by far the most stable of all sailboats. In addition, multihulls often experience large twisting or wracking forces as their widely separated hulls pass independently through waves. For these reasons, the structural engineering of multihulls is particularly critical and difficult. Only during the 1980s, with the rapid growth of big-budget sponsored racing and the concurrent development of sophisticated finite analysis computer programs, has the design of big multihulls advanced much beyond a "try and see" level. Fortunately, the horrific breakdown rates that plagued big-time multihull racing in the early to mid eighties are clearly tapering off. Enough has been learned about the loads on multihull structures that it is now feasible to build lightweight boats that are exceedingly unlikely to fail as a result of sailing stresses. On the other hand, high-speed collisions with large floating objects are a continuing problem. To protect against this hazard simply by beefing up construction is almost certain to incur an unacceptable weight penalty, so many large multihulls are now fitted with "sacrificial" bow sections and watertight bulkheads similar to those of ships.

Radical Trimaran Developments

Until recently, large racing cats were generally regarded as slightly faster than comparable tris, although the latter were acknowledged to have an edge in light air and while maneuvering. However, the 1987 championship of the intensely competitive and professional Formula 40 class was decisively won by a trimaran that showed a speed advantage over a field consisting mainly of high-tech cats, not only in light air, but in strong winds as well. During the 1988 Formula 40 season, the tris again prevailed despite rule changes aimed at "saving" the simpler and somewhat less costly cats.

Given that all competitive Formula 40s are built to the minimum displacement allowed by class rules, the design parameter that appears to be tipping the odds in favor of the tris is their ability to

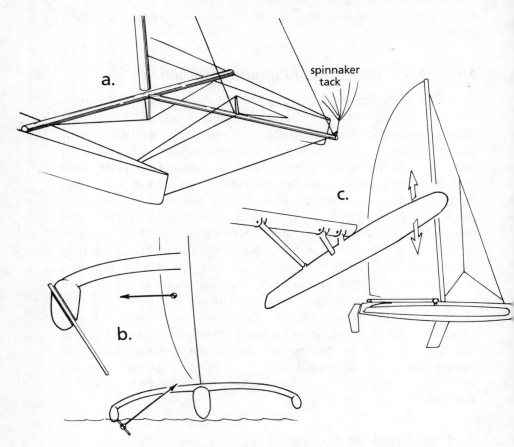

Fig. 7–3. Fixed bow poles are gaining popularity on modern high-performance cats because they provide a secure anchorage for the jibstay and a midline tack attachment point for big asymmetrical spinnakers *(a)*. Foil-stabilized trimarans utilize lift from the canted daggerboard in their leeward ama to reduce displacement without loss of stability *(b)*. The remarkable Formula 40 trimaran *Adrenalin*, designed by Mike Zuteck, Peter Steiner, and the Gougeon brothers, features amas that pitch independently of the main hull to reduce structural stresses and rough-water resistance *(c)*.

accommodate greater beam. The maximum workable beam of a racing cat is limited by three factors. First, it is necessary to step the rig of a cat between the hulls, generally on a trusslike structure consisting of tension and compression members (fig. 7–3a). If the distance between the hulls becomes too great, the loads on this ''tube-and-wire'' structure rapidly escalate to unmanageable proportions. Second, an overly beamy cat may be completely unable to tack in some conditions, while a tri with equal (or greater) beam can still successfully come about with comparative ease. Finally, it is essential to be able to reduce the wetted surface of a racing cat in light air by positioning crew weight to leeward to encourage the windward hull to lift out. However, if beam (and hence transverse stability) is too great, flying a hull to reduce light-air resistance will not be possible.

Currently the fastest big racing tris (Formula 40 and larger) have beams 30 to 40 percent greater than those of comparable racing cats. With sufficient buoyancy in each ama to comfortably "fly" both the main hull and the windward ama, these state-of-the-art trimarans have enough extra sail-carrying power to offset the weight and windage advantages of their catamaran competitors. One 1988 Formula 40 tri, the U.S. entry *Adrenalin,* tested **articulating amas** which were hinged so that they could pitch independently of the main hull (fig. 7–3b). This innovation was highly successful in reducing resistance in rough water by partially uncoupling the movements of the separate hulls. In addition, it greatly reduces stresses upon the hulls and cross beams.

Foil stabilization is another unusual avenue of trimaran development that may hold great future promise, although to date it has been problematical. The basic idea is to equip the amas with a pair of daggerboards that are inclined between 30 and 45 degrees from vertical (fig. 7–3c). When the boat is close reaching or hard on the wind, the inclined foil on the leeward side generates not only side force but an upward force that helps to counteract the heeling forces which are tending to submerge the leeward ama.

The key to improved performance with foil stabilization lies in reducing the size, weight, and resistance of the amas. In most cases, instead of each offering a comfortable 130 to 200 percent buoyancy, they must be pared down to less than 100 percent with the lift from the foil making up the difference. This means that foil-stabilized tris lose much of their stability whenever they slow down—a characteristic that is unlikely to endear them to the average sailor! A further drawback is that the lift produced by an inclined foil is associated with extra induced drag, so the gains achieved by savings in weight, windage, and wetted surface will not be entirely free. Worse yet, unless the foils are retractable, the added hydrodynamic drag they create in light air when no vertical lift is needed will more than offset the drag savings associated with smaller, lighter amas. These difficulties notwithstanding, the foil-stabilized trimaran holds considerable future promise, as does its logical extension: the hydrofoil sailboat. Experiments with foil-supported sailing craft have been attempted off and on since the 1930s and several inventors now appear to be on the verge of developing genuinely practical foil control systems.

Racing Multihulls: A Crucible for Development

Any doubts that racing is the dominant motivating force behind technological developments in sailing would be quickly dispelled by even a quick overview of multihull racing. Because they offer superior performance (and perhaps because they have for so long been the black sheep of the sailing world), multihulls have attracted some of the most innovative sailors and designers. Developmental classes in multihull racing tend to be among the least restrictive, often governing only overall length, beam, and sail area.

This is not to brush over the many flourishing multihull one-design classes that today are mileposts for what was state of the art five, ten, or even twenty years ago. Multihull one-designs are no different than other one-designs—the ultimate testing grounds for the small-scale refinements of sails, gear, and sailing techniques.

As far as large multihulls are concerned, the major driving force behind the developments of the past decade has been the emergence of sponsored professional ocean racing as a major spectator and media sport. Currently, the trend is away from the 85-foot "Super-Maxi" multihulls of the mid-1980s because these monsters have generally proven too dangerous for shorthanded events and too costly for all but the very richest of sponsors. On the other hand, participation and sponsorship for professional multihull racing is stronger than ever as more attention is focused on designs of 40- to 60-foot overall length. In this size range, the potential of rotating rigs can be more readily exploited and the boats are far faster to maneuver and trim. As a result, Formula 40s often nip at the heels of the 85-foot Super-Maxis in European inshore events.

Perhaps the ultimate arena for multihull development is the so-called Little America's Cup that is contested in C-class cats. C-class boats are 25 feet long and 15 feet wide, with a maximum sail area of 300 square feet including spars. Today, the C-class has become a battleground for remarkably sophisticated "solid" rigs that look more like aircraft wings than sails. C-class boats are so refined that boat

speeds in excess of twice the true wind speed are routinely obtained—
the most efficient performances so far achieved by water-borne sailing
craft. *Stars and Stripes,* the 65-foot catamaran that easily outran New
Zealand's big monohull in the peculiar and rather unfortunate 1988
America's Cup, was by and large just a scaled-up C-class cat. However, with its extra length and unrestricted sail area, it was also almost
certainly the fastest light-air sailing machine ever built.

8

Dinghies, Beach Cats, and Sailboards

Relative to size, modern small sailboats easily outperform their larger brethren, and a few types—notably sailboards—can even outsprint the fastest large yachts under the right conditions. This level of performance is achieved in somewhat the same way that an automobile manufacturer goes about creating a sporty model.

The basic recipe for a sports car calls for a small, low-slung chassis to minimize weight and wind drag coupled with a powerful engine, sophisticated suspension, and sticky tires for efficient power transfer and roadability. By analogy, a high-performance small boat is also compact and light, but has a high sail area-to-displacement ratio, very workable sail-handling gear, and the great stability needed to take advantage of its powerful rig. Ballast is unnecessary because the weight and strength of the crew are sufficient to muscle the boat back to its feet in the event of an accidental capsize. The specifics of how these features are brought together varies from one boat type to another, but in every small, quick sailboat, all these ingredients are invariably present.

Conventional Performance Dinghies

Sailing dinghies stabilized primarily by crew weight represented the leading edge of sailboat development from the early 1900s—the era when Uffa Fox pioneered the modern planing dinghy—until the 1960s, when they begin to share the limelight with the up-and-coming multihulls. During this time, planing hulls, bendable spars, genuinely lightweight construction, efficient underwater foils, and a multitude of gear innovations ranging from travelers to ball-bearing blocks all originated in the world of dinghy racing. Even today, big-boat development often lags behind the small-boat field, and draws heavily upon small-boat advances made years earlier.

Developmental dinghies, particularly the International 14 class established in 1928, played a major role in the evolution of efficient planing hulls that could also perform adequately in a displacement mode for upwind and light-air sailing. As a rule, such hulls are comprised of a slim, wedge-shaped bow that flairs into wide, fairly flat-bottomed after sections. The hull bottom typically has only a modest amount of **rocker** (fore-and-aft curvature as viewed from the side) to minimize downward suction forces developed as water flows over the back half of the boat at high speed.

The key to the versatility of this sort of hull is that it really represents three boats in one. With crew weight forward and to leeward, the immersed portion of the hull becomes quite short and deep-chested—a shape well suited to light-air sailing where wetted surface and form drag are of paramount importance (fig. 8–1a). In this light-air trim mode, much of the broad expanse of bottom in the aft third of the boat lifts completely clear of the water.

When sailing near the top end of the "displacement speed" range (as when beating to windward in a good breeze), the dinghy crew moves aft a little to approximately the middle of the hull's length and hikes out to windward to completely eliminate heel. In this second trim mode, the quarter wave rises to immerse the broad stern sections, increasing form stability and providing an effective sailing length that is more or less equal to the length of the hull (fig. 8–1b).

At planing speeds, dynamic lift causes the hull to gradually rise higher in the water, yielding a net reduction in wetted surface and wave drag (fig. 8–1c). While planing, the water flows smoothly across the nearly flat aft sections and breaks cleanly away at the lip of the transom. However, since most traditional dinghy hulls have a rounded or V-shaped bottom instead of a completely flat one, the water flow across the underbody is also displaced laterally, causing the flow to "climb" the curved topsides of the hull to some extent and causing

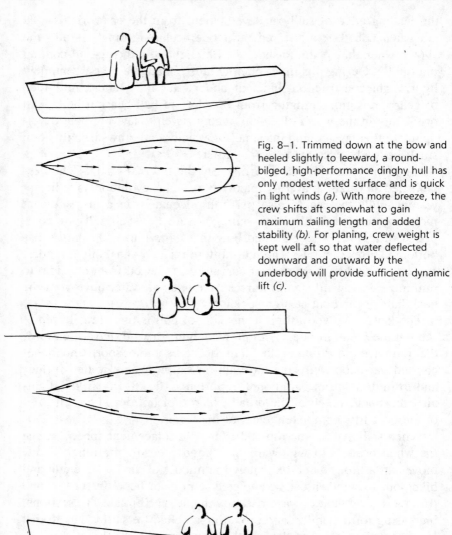

Fig. 8–1. Trimmed down at the bow and heeled slightly to leeward, a round-bilged, high-performance dinghy hull has only modest wetted surface and is quick in light winds *(a)*. With more breeze, the crew shifts aft somewhat to gain maximum sailing length and added stability *(b)*. For planing, crew weight is kept well aft so that water deflected downward and outward by the underbody will provide sufficient dynamic lift *(c)*.

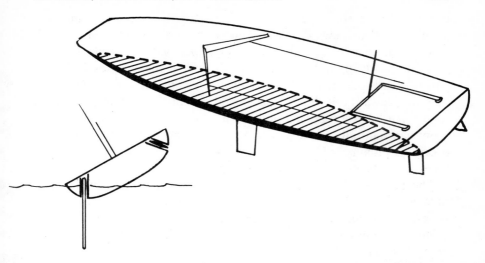

Fig. 8–2. The traditional scow hull achieves an efficient hull shape for upwind work by being sailed with substantial heel. Canted twin centerboards and rudders are often fitted to improve the efficiency of these foils.

a little extra resistance. Although improved planing performance can be achieved by incorporating certain features borrowed from power-boat design, the resulting losses in light- and medium-air performance may be unacceptably high.

As an indication of the all-around excellence of the basic round-bilged dinghy configuration, consider that some of the quickest small monohulls currently racing are relatively ancient designs (Thistle '46, Flying Dutchman '52, and 5-0-5 '54). Of course, although the hull shapes of these one-designs have been more or less ''frozen'' by class rules, the actual racing speeds of the boats have increased markedly over the years thanks to improvements in sails, spars, gear, and perhaps most importantly, sailing techniques.

On sheltered waters, another venerable small-boat configuration—the **inland lake scow**—can still provide outstanding all-around performance. Scows have flat-bottomed hulls that maintain substantial beam all the way forward to a squared-off bow (fig. 8–2). The overall effect is not unlike a plank with rounded edges. Sailing to windward or in light air, a scow is encouraged to heel about 30 degrees. With only the leeward edge of the hull immersed, it acquires a slender, low-resistance hull shape not dissimilar to that of a multihull. Of course, the rig surrenders some effectiveness because it is inclined substantially to leeward. Nevertheless, the underwater foils remain efficient because a typical scow is equipped with not one, but two asymmetrically mounted **bilge boards** and in many cases a similar pair of small rudders that angle outward from the midline. Ordinarily, only the leeward bilgeboard is extended. On breezy offwind legs, with both bilge boards retracted and the flat-bottomed hull hiked level, a scow can naturally plane like crazy. Their greatest weakness is the excessive pitching and added resistance caused by the blunt, buoyant bows when beating to windward in strong winds and big waves.

The scow concept was more or less fully developed by the late nineteenth century, and until surprisingly recently, it produced the fastest of all sailboats. The largest of the traditional scow classes—38-foot A-scows—might hardly appear to qualify as small boats, but being unballasted vessels of only 1850-pound displacement, they actually behave a lot more like dinghies than offshore yachts. Parallels between a traditional twin-rudder, twin-board scow and a modern catamaran are quite striking, if you stop to think about it, and interestingly enough, the Melges-20—one of the more recent scow designs (1962)—even features a concave or tunnel bow!

Recent Advances in Dinghy Technology

As mentioned earlier, it is possible to significantly enhance the planing performance of a conventional sailing dinghy hull by borrowing design features from fast powerboats. These include eliminating all rocker and deadrise variations in the aft half of the bottom and perhaps even introducing some steps or discontinuities to help reduce wetted surface while up on a plane. In practice, such powerboat-like hulls seem to suffer much more in light to moderate winds than they improve in heavier weather. One feature that does seem to promote planing without hurting light-wind performance too much is a single chine along the turn of the bilge in the aft half of the hull (fig. 8–3). Like the sharp lip of the transom, the chine causes high-speed flow to break away sharply rather than climb up the hull sides.

The most extreme planing dinghies ever developed are the famous 18-foot skiffs that are raced primarily in Sydney, Australia. Contemporary "Eyedeens" are handled by three highly athletic sailors who trapeze from the tips of wide aluminum hiking racks to counterbalance the heeling forces generated by rigs that tower as much as 40

Fig. 8–3. High-performance dinghies of recent vintage like this custom Australian 14 footer commonly feature a hard chine that disappears around the middle of the hull.

feet above deck (fig. 8–4). Sail areas for light air are about 500 square feet for upwind work and as much as three times that off the wind. One invention from 18-foot skiff racing—the fixed centerline spinnaker pole—has recently been adopted by a variety of other high-performance classes including the evergreen International 14. With an asymmetrical spinnaker tacked to the end of the pole and equipped with twin sheets like a jib, gybing is greatly simplified and a considerably larger spinnaker becomes manageable. Unfortunately, the idea only works really well in boats that are fast enough to go downwind efficiently with the apparent wind forward of the beam.

As testbeds for hull and rig configurations, advanced control systems, and high-speed sailing techniques the "Eyedeens" are in a class all their own. On the other hand, the costs of campaigning a top-flight 18-foot skiff for a season have mushroomed to about $100,000 per year at the time of this writing, making it a game that only well-heeled corporate sponsors can afford to play. Of course, there are potentially plenty of these, but with other forms of professional racing gaining strong footholds in Europe and North America, the 18-foot-skiff class is having trouble attracting a following outside of Australia and New Zealand.

A Beach Cat Revolution

While Aussie 18s win top marks for being outrageous, hair-raising and spectacular, a host of modern beach cats, in most cases mass-

Fig. 8–4. Aussie 18s are the most radical (and expensive) dinghies in existence. Planing is routine even in light air (inset).

produced in low-tech fiberglass, offer similar performance at a fraction the cost while falling within the skill range of the average sailor. The reasons why multihulls have a speed advantage over monohulls were discussed at length in the previous chapter. In practice, scaling catamarans down to 20 feet in overall length or less often tends to make them faster rather than slower because it eliminates one of the chief limitations on the performance of big multihulls: fear of capsizing. Thanks to their small size and weight, beach cats can be readily righted, so speed-hungry crews routinely push them to their limits.

A second important reason that small multihulls are often as fast or faster than their larger sisters is again the old story of proportionally greater stability relative to weight. Beam in a multihull is a major stability-inducing factor, but one that is ultimately limited by handling problems and structural headaches. On the other hand, the crew of a small multihull can obtain a dramatic boost in lateral stability by moving their body weight to windward of the weather hull with the aid of trapezes, hiking platforms or both. Similarly, shifting crew weight as far aft as possible on hairy reaches can considerably improve longitudinal stability and resistance to pitchpoling. In light air, the crew can hike out to leeward to lift the weather hull out of the water for a big reduction in wetted surface and associated drag. Of course, the evolutionary refinement of gear and techniques that results from intense one-design racing has, over time, also had a dramatic effect upon the speed of small multihulls just as it has in the monohull dinghy classes. In classes where this evolutionary process has been pursued most intensely, the net speed improvements are, of course, greatest. Hence, the Olympic Tornado, a 20-foot cat designed in 1966, is still at least as fast around a triangular course as any more recent beach cat excepting some radical developmental boats like the C-class designs.

Sailboards: Something New under the Sun

The idea of attaching a universal joint at the base of a small unstayed rig and using one's body to hold up sail has been credited to two different inventors: Hoyle Schweitzer and James Drake. Since its inception less than fifteen years ago, sailboarding has become a major new watersport that combines some of the best features of both sailing and skiing.

For a novice boardsailor practicing in light winds, the first challenge is learning to become a major working part of the boat itself— using muscles, balance, and body weight to counter the forces from the rig while steering by subtle adjustments in rig position. However, once a basic level of competence has been achieved and the new boardsailor begins to venture out in strong winds, the unique elegance of the sailboard concept really begins to shine forth.

In creating a new kind of rig that is free to pivot or tilt in any

direction, Drake and Schweitzer happened upon a nifty way to eliminate much of the resistance that stems from the displacement of more
conventional sailboats. In anything more than a light breeze, a boardsailor leans backward and inclines the sail into the wind (fig. 8–5).
As a result, the net aerodynamic force from the sail acts upward as
well as forward and sideways. In strong winds, the upward component of the sail force is enough to support almost all the weight of
the boardsailor's body, which in turn reduces the downward load on
the board (hull) to a small fraction of what it would otherwise be.

Because the loads they must support are so small—generally not
more than 40 to 50 pounds—high-speed boards are generally small
to minimize weight and wetted surface. At speed, they obtain almost
all their support from dynamic lift, making them the only sailboats
that plane in the same sense that high-speed motor boats do. Sailboards designed for strong winds are often so small that they lack
enough buoyancy to support their riders, a feature which turns the
task of getting under way into an acrobatic feat in its own right!

For several years now, sailboards have held the absolute sailing
speed record for boats of any size or type. Traversing a half-mile
speed trial course at an optimal reach, expert boardsailors routinely
exceed 30 knots, and the current record holder recently cracked the
40-knot "barrier"! Of course, to attain these speeds requires specialized conditions: beam-reaching winds in the 40- to 50-knot range
combined with fairly smooth water. On an upwind-downwind course
in more moderate conditions, multihulls are faster and likely to remain so. The main reason is the size of the human body relative to
the size of the sailboard's rig. When closehauled with the apparent
wind well forward, the parasitic drag and flow disturbance caused by
the boardsailor's body retard his board a great deal more than when
sailing on a reach. Upwind, the superior aerodynamics of advanced
multihulls put these larger boats at a distinct advantage, while downwind, the extra sail area they can set while under way again gives
them the edge.

Sailboards for general recreational use and course racing must be
competent in light air as well as a good breeze. To achieve this end,
they have more volume and buoyancy than high-speed boards. Course-
racing boards, because they must go upwind well at displacement
speeds, tend to be shaped quite a bit like slim, small racing dinghies
with rounded or V-shaped forward sections that blend into a nearly
flat bottom at the stern.

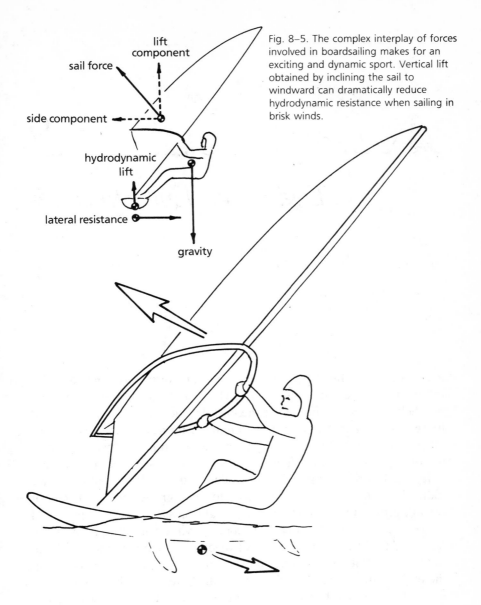

lift
component

sail force

side component

hydrodynamic
lift

lateral resistance

gravity

Fig. 8–5. The complex interplay of forces involved in boardsailing makes for an exciting and dynamic sport. Vertical lift obtained by inclining the sail to windward can dramatically reduce hydrodynamic resistance when sailing in brisk winds.

The first, explosive growth phase of boardsailing is tapering off now, and the equipment is becoming more standardized. On the other hand, because boardsailing gear is relatively inexpensive, and because the sport is inherently dynamic and exciting, there continues to be a great deal of experimental work under way in this field—quite possibly more than in any other branch of sailing.

9

Engineered Hull Structures

Although most sailors probably equate "state of the art" in boatbuilding with advanced materials like Kevlar™ and carbon fiber, the progress achieved in this field over the past decade is actually a great deal more sweeping in scope. Serious engineering has finally assumed its proper place in yacht design. Rather than cautiously "overbuilding" to conservative rules of thumb, today's designers are performing detailed studies of sailing loads and specifying scantlings that may vary radically from one part of the boat to another. At the top levels of racing, efforts to eliminate excess weight have become ruthless, and in some cases even fanatical. Of course, while trimming away every ounce of fat, there is a real risk of inadvertently nicking a vital bone or two, as a spate of structural failures in offshore racing yachts during the early to mid 1980s has graphically illustrated. On the whole, however, the new emphasis on "scientific" design and construction is yielding improvements in sailboats that are probably greater than those resulting from developments in any other area.

The Stresses of Sailing

Although upon occasion sailing can be mentally stressful (as when caught in stormy weather aboard a boat whose structural integrity is suspect) the word **stress** as used here is an engineering term which refers to a force acting within a material. In most sailboats, stresses within the hull and rig are maximal during a tough beat, so imagine an offshore-type keelboat sailing hard on the wind in a force-8 gale and slamming into ugly head seas. Normal water pressure on the immersed portions of the hull is intermittently boosted by wave impact pressures near the bow. Lift forces generated by the keel, and the very substantial weight of the keel itself, create large, fluctuating stresses that are concentrated in the region where this fin joins the hull. Other highly localized loads are encountered within the rudder shaft and its supports. The downward thrust of the mast, the corresponding upward pull of the weather shrouds, and the upward pull of the force and backstays together subject the hull-deck structure to a variety of wracking and bending stresses. Winches, lock offs, sheet leads, and weight of crew members impose high, although localized, stresses upon the deck structure.

At first glance, this cacophony of internal forces might appear to defy analysis, but with modern analytical techniques it is possible to break the whole mess down into comprehensible parts. Calculating the combined peak stress in each and every part of the structure is another, vastly more difficult undertaking, but one that professional designers are beginning to subdue with the help of sophisticated computer techniques such as **finite element analysis**. For our purposes it is sufficient to look briefly at the main external forces acting upon a hull and to describe the stresses or internal forces that result from each.

Pressure Forces on the Hull

To begin with, the water surrounding any boat presses inward on all submerged portions of the hull. This **hydrostatic pressure** is proportional to the depth of immersion—32 pounds per square foot acting on portions of the hull that are 6 feet below the surface, 64 pounds per square foot on areas 1 foot down, and so forth.

Slamming into waves causes momentarily higher pressures on fairly small regions, although possibly not as much higher as the noise and excitement might suggest. In compiling the data base used to develop the American Bureau of Shipping scantling rule (see Chapter 12), designer Gary Mull mounted accelerometers in the bows of yachts beating into rough seas. Peak decelerations observed were only about one-fourth gravity, which corresponds to a **head** or pressure of about 200 pounds per square foot above and beyond hydrostatic pressure.

Of course it is only prudent to assume that ocean-going yachts in extreme storm conditions might sustain wave-impact decelerations more severe than those Mull measured. Indeed, data collected by Nautor Swan from a fully instrumented competitor in the 1986 Whitbread Round-the-World Race (as well as a number of structural hull failures aboard other boats in that race) suggest that localized wave-impact loads during unusually rough conditions can be considerably higher than previously anticipated. More dangerous still are the highly concentrated local pressures induced by collisions with floating debris—something that can happen in almost any sailing waters.

Localized Hull Loads

Distinct from the stresses imposed by external pressure on the hull are the stresses associated with rig, keel, and rudder loads. The mast of an ordinary stayed rig operates under compression and tends to push the bottom of the hull downward in the area where it is stepped. Simultaneously the windward shrouds pull upward on the hull-deck structure at the chainplates with an equal, but opposite force. The net result is a tendency for the hull to become narrower and deeper amidships while sailing (fig. 9–1).

An end-to-end bending stress on the hull is caused by the upward pull of the headstay in the bow, backstay(s) (and mainsheet) near the stern, and the mast pushing downward in between. These longitudinal bending forces translate into tensile stress on the bottom surfaces of the hull and compressive stress in the deck and cabin structure (fig. 9–1, bottom). If the hull is momentarily supported by separate wave crests at the bow and stern, the weight of the boat itself will be added to this longitudinal bending load. Conversely, support by a single wave crest amidships will momentarily reduce it.

The common practice of attaching a deep, thin fin keel using cast-in-place keelbolts creates a situation where the tensile stresses within the keelbolts skyrocket as the boat heels. It is easy to envision how, at large heel angles, the keel is, in effect, trying to lever itself off the hull. With a keel of modern IOR proportions attached using port-starboard paired bolts, the tension on the windward bolts increases fifteen-fold over what it is at level trim during a severe knockdown (fig. 9–2, top). If the same keel is attached by a single row of bolts,

Fig. 9–1. Conventional rigs impose severe tensile (T) and compressive (C) stresses upon hulls that are additional to the stresses caused by hydrostatic pressure. Longitudinal bending loads on a hull typically peak when the hull is supported by a wave at each end. When this happens, stresses from rigging loads are added to the bending loads created by the weight of the boat.

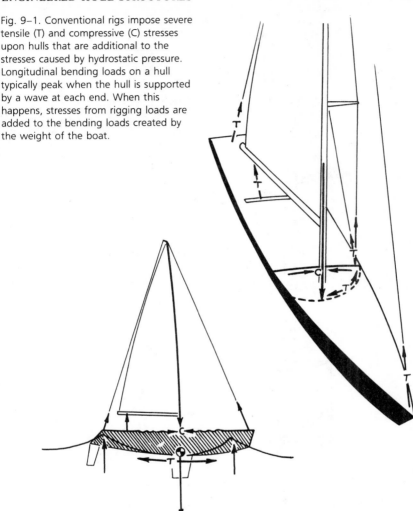

maximum tension on the bolts is even greater—a total of about twenty-five times the keel's weight. Although the lift generated by the keel counteracts gravitational forces very slightly, stresses within the keel-bolts and the nearby root area are nevertheless formidable.

Stresses within the shaft of a conventional spade rudder take two forms: torsional (twisting) stress and bending stress. The first is uniform throughout the exposed upper portion of the shaft, while the latter peaks very sharply where the shaft passes through the hull (fig.

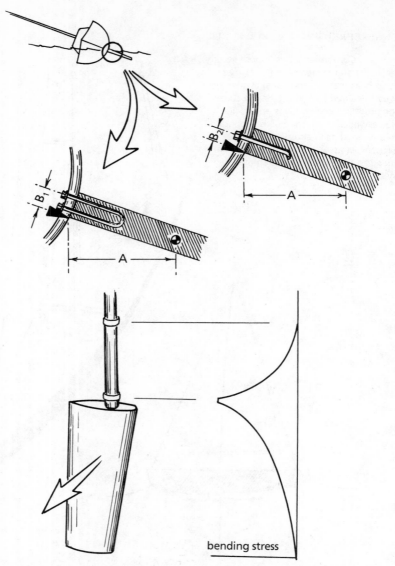

Fig. 9–2. During a knockdown, stress on keelbolts (and the adjacent hull structure) can reach very high levels. In this situation, the keel acts as a lever with its fulcrum at the lower edge of the root. Mechanical disadvantage (from the viewpoint of the keelbolts) is the ratio B/A (when A is the distance from the ballast CG to the fulcrum). The bending stresses on a spade rudder peak sharply where the shaft is supported by the lower rudder bearing.

9–2, bottom). These stresses are rarely extreme, but can be awkward to handle when a designer is striving to minimize rudder thickness and hence shaft diameter; while at the same time keeping weight at the ends of the boat to a bare minimum.

Stiffness vs. Strength

Each of the stresses acting within the hull and deck of any sailboat causes these structures to distort to some extent. For some, this may be an unnerving thought because we like to think of our boats as rigid and solid. In reality, however, no structure can ever be absolutely unyielding because the only way that a solid material can sustain a load is through a springlike action. In other words, for a structure to resist a force it must be temporarily bent or deformed.

Of course, the materials we regard as stiff distort a great deal less under a given load than the ones we describe as flexible. Even a thick concrete slab flexes slightly beneath the footsteps of a kitten, but the temporary dimples created by the tiny paws are almost immeasurably small.

A little excess weight is not a matter of grave concern in the case of a concrete floor. However, in a performance-oriented sailboat it's quite a different matter, because unnecessary weight increases displacement and hence hydrodynamic drag. On the other hand, inadequate hull stiffness can also reduce performance, partly because rig tension and sail shape will vary too much, and partly because drag increases and propulsive energy is dissipated as the hull flexes.

Excessive water pressure can sometimes cause a flat or nearly flat portion of the hull surface to invert—a problem graphically described as **oil-canning**. This is highly undesirable for several reasons. First, the fairness of the hull is degraded, causing an increase in turbulence and drag. Second, some buoyancy is lost without any compensatory decrease in wetted surface, so the hull sinks a little deeper and produces more drag. To appreciate how much extra resistance can be produced by an overly flexible hull, try rowing an underinflated rubber dinghy. Then pump it up firmly and notice the dramatic improvement.

The challenge confronting designers and builders is to create sailboat structures that combine adequate stiffness and minimal weight, with the added criterion that every part be strong enough not to break. Although strength and stiffness are often mentioned in the same breath, these properties are just as frequently found separately. A soda cracker is fairly stiff, but very weak; while an automobile tire is strong, but flexible.

In the days of planked wooden boats and single-skin fiberglass, a hull that was built robustly enough to feel rigid and solid under way was pretty much guaranteed to be strong enough for even the worst weather. A similar building philosophy is used in ordinary frame house construction. Domestic building codes specify large, closely spaced joists (floor timbers) in order to ensure that the floor feels solid and unyielding underfoot. The size and number of joists required to obtain this stiffness would greatly exceed the requirement for strength if expensive prime lumber was used, so rather inferior construction-grade lumber with numerous knots, checks, and other flaws can safely be substituted.

In the case of modern sailboats it is no longer safe to assume that acceptable structural stiffness will automatically be accompanied by adequate strength. The widespread use of **sandwich construction** using skins made of advanced composite materials on either side of a low-density **core** has made it relatively easy to build featherweight parts which deform only minimally up to the moment they break.

Overall stiffness in the case of a complex, hollow structure like a boat hull is determined less by the material(s) from which the parts are made than by the shape and orientation of components such as frames, bulkheads, webs, and the skin itself. Major structural components are usually structures in their own right—the boxes-within-boxes concept.

Building Stiff, Light Panels

Panels—sheets of material spanning the distance between one supporting member and the next—are the real building blocks of most modern sailing hulls. Often, of course, a continuous skin will be used to envelope many skeletal supports. Nevertheless, for purposes of calculation, the designer or engineer normally treats each unsupported sector as a separate panel (fig. 9-3).

Crew weight on a flat deck or hydraulic loads on a flat bottom apply pressure perpendicularly to the panels. This applied load induces tensile stress toward the inner (opposite) face of the panel and compressive stress near the face to which the external load is applied (fig. 9-4a). Halfway between is the **neutral plane** where longitudinal stresses are nil. The stiffness of a flat panel is determined primarily by its thickness, increasing approximately as the thickness is raised to the third power.

On the other hand, if significant curvature is present in a panel, the picture changes considerably. Cambered decks and hulls function either like the tension cables of a suspension bridge (fig. 9-4b) or,

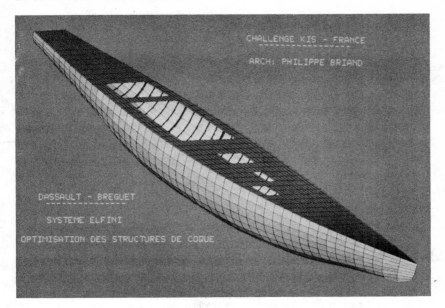

Fig. 9–3. The elemental building blocks of any modern hull-deck structure are the panels which span the spaces between frames. This panel diagram was prepared as part of a sophisticated structural study for a French 1977 America's Cup challenge using software developed by Avions Marcel Dassault.

more commonly, like the compression arches and domes often found in terrestrial architecture (fig. 9–4c). In either case, cambering the panel substantially increases its ability to withstand external pressure and allows thinner, lighter scantlings or larger unsupported spans to be used.

Advantages of Stressed Skin Construction

Cruisable sailing hulls must be largely open on the inside to accommodate people, gear, and so forth. Practical hulls must also be tough enough to take minor impacts in stride. For these reasons, most designers favor a modification of the **monocoque**, or unit-body, style of construction. By starting with a shell that is strong and stiff in its own right, only a modest number of stringers, bulkheads, webs, girders and ring frames need be added. In many cases, these widely separated supporting elements can double as essential furnishings like berth fronts, cabinets, and partitions.

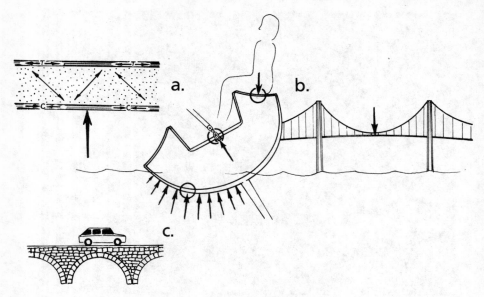

Fig. 9–4. A flat sandwich panel such as the cockpit sole of the boat diagrammed here sustains tensile stress in one skin, compressive stress in the other, and shear loading on the core in between *(a)*. Concave panels function like the cables of a suspension bridge with both skins working as tension members *(b)*. The rounded bottoms of most hulls resist hydrostatic pressure by operating as compression structures like the arches of a stone bridge *(c)*. Satisfactory core materials must therefore be capable of sustaining moderate crushing loads and transverse tension stresses as well as shear.

The alternative extreme to a monocoque boat is one in which the hull skin sustains only hydraulic loads while an internal **space frame** rigidly holds keel, rudder supports, mast step, and rigging terminals in their correct positions with respect to one another. This style of construction was made famous by Ron Holland in 1981 with an IOR racer named *Imp*. The one real advantage of this approach is that it becomes comparatively easy to engineer the space frame structure that must sustain the largest sailing forces. Unfortunately, the hull skin must, in practice, be overbuilt to withstand bumps and knocks, while the space frame intrudes horribly on the interior layout. Nevertheless, many all-out racing boats today continue to use elements derived from this approach such as full height longitudinal bulkheads (with cutouts) that extend much of the boat's length, or compression struts to hold the chainplates apart (fig. 9–5).

Most lightly constructed keel boats require a system of floors—transverse girders—to distribute keel-induced stresses over a substantial portion of the boat's bottom. In production fiberglass yachts, these floors often take the form of a corrugated fiberglass **hull pan**, or "force grid," that is lowered into the hull and bonded into place.

The Importance of Engineering

The hull and deck of a custom 42-foot offshore racer can easily weigh as little as 1500 pounds these days. To put this figure in perspective, consider that 1500 pounds represents just 10.5 cubic feet of fiber-resin composite plus about 70 cubic feet of plastic foam or honeycomb core material. If constructed from aluminum, the same 1500 pounds "buys" only 9 cubic feet of material with which to work. Obviously, the way that this skimpy supply of building materials is arranged and distributed is of overriding importance in creating a sound, reasonably durable hull structure.

The properties of modern boatbuilding materials have been deliberately downplayed in this chapter to draw attention to the importance of structural design considerations. In reality, of course, the characteristics of the building materials themselves are also very important and will be the subject of the next two chapters.

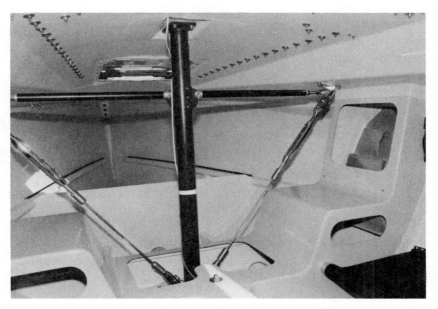

Fig. 9–5. Lightweight racing boats often utilize a metallic substructure to handle transverse rigging loads so that the hull itself can be designed and fabricated more easily.

10

Fundamentals of Fiber Composite Construction

Fiberglass and other fiber composites are the most popular materials in boatbuilding today. In all probability, they will become even more dominant in the future. However, before getting into a discussion of these materials in particular, it's well worth taking a little time to become acquainted with the properties of good structural materials in general. A satisfactory boatbuilding material must be "strong" for its weight, "tough" or fracture resistant, and impervious to environmental degradation. Some inherent stiffness is also essential, despite the fact that whole-boat stiffness is largely determined by the distribution of material within the hull structure, as was discussed in the preceding chapter. Let's look a bit more closely at what these desirable characteristics mean.

Tensile strength is a straightforward measure of the "pull" required to break something. It is ordinarily expressed in pounds per square inch of cross-sectional area (abbreviated psi). **Sheer strength—** the ability of something to resist forces tending to make one part slide past another—is also expressed as stress in psi at failure. **Compressive strength** is a little harder to pin down because compression failure can occur in three different ways: buckling, diagonal shearing, or crushing. For this reason, compression strength measurements obtained in lab tests often vary dramatically depending upon the sizes and shapes of the samples used.

Toughness is the ability of a material to resist fracture under sudden loading. A tough material like fiberglass will absorb a great deal of energy before it breaks, while a brittle one like plate glass obviously cannot. Fracture mechanics—the way things break—will be discussed further in Chapter 12, which deals with structural failures in yachts. For now, it's enough to remember that strength and toughness are often found separately, but should both be present in a good boatbuilding material.

Durability in the marine environment demands not only toughness but resistance to the degradative effects of salt and moisture. Metals must either resist corrosion themselves or be totally covered with an impervious barrier coating. Typical fiber composites do not corrode and are largely, although not always completely, waterproof. However, some of the core materials used in composite boatbuilding can absorb water and may degrade if the outer skins leak.

To evaluate the **stiffness** of a material requires that stress be related to the strain or deformation caused by that stress. Stress divided by strain gives a number known as Young's modulus of elasticity.*

Strain itself is ordinarily expressed as a fraction or percentage: unstressed length divided by stressed length. Therefore when stress in psi is divided by strain, which is nondimensional, the resulting modulus is still expressed in psi. In effect, the Young's modulus of a material is the stress that would extend a sample of the material to twice its original length if it didn't break first.

Few satisfactory building materials can survive strains of even 5 percent, let alone the 100 percent strain that would be involved in an actual doubling of sample length. This is only reasonable, since if they weren't fairly rigid, inelastic substances they wouldn't be suitable for building things. The Young's moduli of conventional boatbuilding materials in their raw form generally range from about 1.5 million psi for wood to about 30 million psi for steel. This might seem like a huge range, but if differences in density are taken into account, both materials behave very much on a par (see Table 1). Ordinary fiberglass composites are less stiff for their weights than wood, steel, or

---

*Thomas Young was a British mathematician who, in 1790, successfully pinned down the concept of elasticity. Modulus simply means "little measure" in Latin.

aluminum, because they contain a considerable volume of relatively flexible resin. On the other hand, some "exotic" fibers—notably carbon—have more than enough inherent stiffness to offset this dilution effect.

Table I

The relative stiffness of boatbuilding materials.
Young's modulus is shown on the left, and Young's
modulus divided by specific gravity on the right

Material	Young's Modulus (psi × 10)	Specific Young's Modulus (psi × 10)
Wood (Sitka spruce)	1.9	3.8
Steel	30.0	3.8
Aluminum	10.5	3.9
Glass fiber	10.0	4.0
Kevlar™ fiber	19.0	13.1
Carbon fiber	60.0	27.3

Why Composites?

Fiberglass is a tough material because the relatively weak matrix of plastic resin that separates the strong glass fibers serves to interrupt the spread of cracks laterally from one fiber to the next. The resin matrix also helps to distribute and equalize tension loads among the fibers, so that flaws in individual fibers end up having no measurable effect upon the strength of the laminate as a whole.

Today, fiber composites dominate the pleasure boat industry. "Brush and bucket" fiberglass construction is popular, not so much because it ensures a genuinely superior product, but because a good-looking boat can be built quickly using relatively unskilled labor and with only a modest investment in tooling and equipment. The structural strength and durability of female-molded fiberglass boats often vary enormously, but almost all of them look fantastic on a showroom floor or dealer's yard.

On the other had, thanks to recent advances in the structural analysis of sailboats and major improvements in fibers and resins, composites are now almost always selected as the primary building materials for sophisticated high-performance boats. Because a composite hull or deck is created right in the mold, it is very easy to

build extra strength and rigidity into highly stressed areas (or to minimize weight in lightly loaded ones). The more advanced composites
can be breathtakingly expensive, but they offer mechanical properties
that currently cannot be matched using a similar weight of any other
materials. Considering that even the most painstakingly constructed
hull represents just a fraction of the cost of a finished yacht, it usually
makes sense to choose the best possible materials for the job.

Boatbuilders have traditionally used fiberglass in three forms:
chopped mat, cloth, and woven roving. **Mat** consists of short lengths
of randomly oriented glass fiber, lightly glued together to form a felt.
Cloth is relatively fine textured and woven using yarns that are, to
some extent, twisted together (fig. 10-1a). A **woven roving** is made
from bundles of parallel fibers (fig. 10-1b). Because friction between

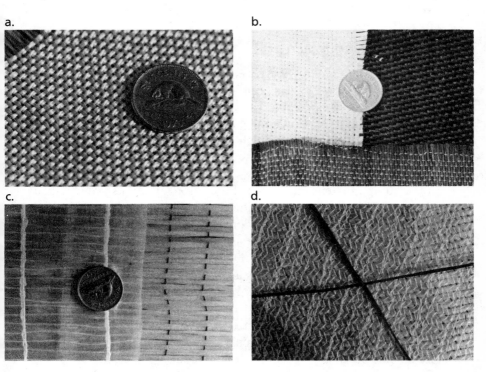

Fig. 10-1. An assortment of contemporary reinforcing materials: *(a)* Kevlar/E-glass cloth
with slight twist in the glass strands only; *(b)* three rovings: a twill woven carbon fiber *(left)*,
a square woven S-glass *(right)*, and a harness woven Kevlar *(bottom)*; *(c)* unidirectional fibers
held in place prior to lamination by adhesive strips *(left)* and a harness weave *(right)*; *(d)*
sixty-degree biaxial material made up of two layers of unidirectional roving stitched together. (A balanced triaxial material would incorporate a third layer in the stack.)

fibers during manufacture and subsequent handling is the principle cause of the superficial flaws that initiate breakage in stressed fibers, cloth is typically weaker than comparable woven roving.

These days, glass and other fibers are also available in the form of **unidirectional rovings** which consist of large numbers of straight parallel fibers held loosely together by a few transverse fibers that are glued or stitched into place (fig. 10-1c). Unidirectional materials are, of course, superior in situations where a high load is anticipated in one particular direction. The latest in fiber reinforcements are bi-directional and tri-directional materials—two or three layers of unidirectional material in a stack, each with a different orientation (fig. 10-1d). These are stronger than woven rovings because the fibers follow straight instead of crimped (zigzag) paths, and because the fibers rub against each other less during manufacture.

Fibers for Reinforcement

Ordinary boatbuilding fiberglass is a type known as **E-glass**, or electrical glass. Good E-glass can have excellent mechanical properties, but there is considerable variation. A higher quality glass fiber known as **S-glass**, or structural glass, is chemically a bit different from E-glass and extruded as much finer strands. It's about 30 percent stronger than typical E-glass, but costs twice as much.

Kevlar is the DuPont company's trade name for synthetics of the aramid group. In tension, it is a little stronger for its weight than S-glass and it loses less of its initial strength during preparation and handling. On the other hand, it's compressive strength is considerably lower than even E-glass, most resins don't adhere to it well, and it costs about four times more than E-glass.

Allied Chemical's **Spectra**™ is a refined, highly cross-linked form of fibrous polyethelene. Its chief virtues are a tensile-strength-to-weight ratio that is even higher than Kevlar and excellent resistance to physical abuse. However, resins tend to adhere to it poorly and it floats in most resins, which can make layup difficult. At this stage, it must be classed as an experimental boatbuilding material.

Carbon fiber is made from acrylic strands that are carbonized at high temperatures in vacuum ovens. It is a little stronger for its weight than S-glass and a great deal stiffer. In fact, carbon-fiber composites are the only materials popular in modern boatbuilding that are appreciably stiffer for their weights than wood, aluminum, or steel. Carbon fiber currently costs about eight times more than E-glass. Aside from cost, its greatest shortcoming is its inability to withstand localized impacts and other physical punishment. To a large extent, this is an inherent problem that goes hand-in-hand with its exceptional stiffness. However, the toughness of carbon-fiber laminates can be markedly improved by using hybrid lay-ups that contain a proportion of other fibers such as Kevlar or glass. Some newly developed resins also appear to help in this regard.

Resins and Resin/Fiber Ratio

Conventional hand-laid fiberglass boatbuilding yields a composite with only mediocre mechanical properties, partly because cured polyester resins are too brittle to allow the full strength of the glass to be utilized, and partly because the ratio of weak resin to much stronger glass is usually far too high (70 percent resin by weight is the norm). To illustrate the first point, typical E-glass fails at a strain (elongation) of about 4.5 percent, while cured polyester resin fails at a strain of around 2.5 percent. To take advantage of the full strength of the glass fibers, progressive boat builders are turning to vinylester and epoxy resins which can be formulated to fail at strains of around 5.5 percent (the approximate breaking strain of S-glass).

Kevlar, being stiffer than glass, has a tensile stress at failure of only about 2.5 percent. Carbon fiber, being stiffer still, fails at a strain of around 1.5 percent. Thus both are potentially compatible with ordinary polyester resins. Nevertheless, to avoid adhesion and possible water-permeability problems most builders working with these expensive fibers elect to go with premium resins.

Building weight-effective composites requires that the ratio of strong fibers to weak resin be as high as is feasible. The amount of resin needed to "wet out" a reinforcing material will depend upon its small-scale architecture—how densely packed the fibers are. Cloth and roving absorb less resin than mat, and unidirectional materials absorb the least of all. Skilled hand-laminators can attain resin-to-fiber ratios of 50 percent by using rubber squeegees to remove excess resin. When a vaccuum bag is subsequently used to provide uniform clamping pressure on the laminate during cure (fig. 10–2), additional resin can be soaked up by a disposable absorbant layer to attain ratios as low as 40 percent.

To do better yet, sophisticated equipment must be substituted for

Fig. 10–2. In a common use of vacuum-bagging techniques, precut core material is set onto the wet outer skin lay-up before a plastic sheet is positioned over the laminate and sealed around the edges. When air is subsequently evacuated from the bag, external air pressure squeezes the laminate together while it cures. Photographs by Moore Sailboats.

shop workers to perform the task of resin application. **Pre-pregs** (pre-impregnated reinforcing materials) come from the factory with a very thin, uniform resin coating already covering every strand of fiber. Of course, the resins used to manufacture pre-pregs must be fully mixed prior to the impregnation process. For this reason, resin-catalyst combinations that cure at room temperature cannot be used—they would quickly gum up the continuous application machinery and make the shelf life of the finished pre-preg material unreasonably short. Instead, hot-curing epoxy formulations are used, and pre-preg laminates must be cured at elevated temperatures. The first generation of pre-pregs needed several hours at 120 degrees Celsius to cure properly, which meant that an oven large enough to contain an entire boat had to be found (or built) for each project. The latest ''low temperature'' pre-pregs cure at about 75 degrees C, a big improvement because electric blankets or heat lamps can supply enough heat to achieve a good cure in most cases.

Pre-pregs are a shop worker's delight, at least as compared to the messy wet lay-up techniques. At room temperature they are only slightly tacky and can be readily repositioned if accidently misoriented. In addition, the **open-mold time** using pre-pregs is exceptionally long, an important advantage when large hulls are being laid up in one go. Unfortunately, even the hot-curing resins used in pre-pregs will gradually gel at room temperature, so pre-pregs must be transported and stored frozen. Pre-pregs are expensive to begin with, and these handling problems further increase the cost of using them. Nevertheless, there is every chance that their popularity will continue to grow because no other composite materials can match their high fiber-to-resin ratios and challenge their weight efficiency.

Core Materials

The crucial properties in a good core material are low density and sufficient sheer and compressive strength to withstand the relatively modest stresses it will encounter in use. Three main groups are commonly used in conjunction with composite skins: plastic foam, woods, and plastic or aluminum honeycombs. Polyvinyl chloride (PVC) is the most common plastic used for foam cores. Acrylic foam, although mechanically superior to PVC, is not yet widely available.

The most popular wood for core material is balsa, oriented so that the grain is perpendicular to the plane of the panel. On a microscopic

Fig. 10–3. End-grain balsa *(left)* consists of tiny, elongated hex cells (scale bar: 0.1 mm). Honeycomb cores like the aluminum version shown on the lower right are strikingly similar to balsa, but on a much larger scale. Most versions of Nomex also feature hexagonal cells, but some utilize a rectangular format *(upper right)* so that the core material can be wrapped around tight bends.

level, balsa looks a lot like a fine-scale version of a synthetic honeycomb (fig. 10–3, left). Evaluated without skins, it offers better sheer strength and compressive strength than PVC foams of similar density. Unfortunately, the strength-to-weight advantage of balsa may be diminished by the tendency of the open, elongated cells at the ends of the grain to fill with resin. To some extent, this problem can be minimized by precoating the balsa with a quick-setting resin before laying up skins. On the whole, balsa has proven to be an economical yet highly efficient core material for both production and custom boatbuilding.

Strictly on the basis of mechanical performance, the most impressive core materials currently available are the so-called **honeycombs**—synthetic imitations of the vertical-celled matrices built by bees (fig. 10–3, lower right). Surprisingly strong honeycomb cores can be made out of ordinary paper, but any contact with water is likely to reduce these cores to mush. For marine use, most honeycomb cores are made out of either aluminum foil or a papery aramid film that is usually sold under the brand name of Nomex™. Both aluminum and Nomex honeycombs have at least twice the sheer strength of PVC or balsa of equal density, and are noticeably superior in tension and compression as well. In theory, at least, very little resin needs to be added in assembling a Nomex-cored panel because the area of contact between the edges of the honeycomb and the skins is small. In practice, however, it's often very tricky to bond composite skins reliably to honeycomb cores without either flooding the cells with excess resin or producing weak, resin-starved joins in some areas. In many cases, good results can only be obtained using pre-pregs and vacuum-bagging techniques.

Composites and the Future of Boatbuilding Materials

Wood, steel, and aluminum are all excellent boatbuilding materials and will undoubtedly continue to be used for many years to come in certain applications. Laminated wood in various versions continues to be an excellent choice for smaller custom and semicustom hulls, because it lends itself to building without molds, while providing an excellent combination of strength, stiffness, durability, and light weight, plus an undeniable aesthetic appeal. Specific applications for these materials will be discussed in the next chapter.

Nevertheless, it's safe to say that the future of pleasure boatbuilding by and large belongs to composites. The much-publicized problem of gel-coat blistering (and associated internal delamination) is a specific failing of certain materials and building techniques more than a blanket condemnation of fiber composite construction as a whole. As the technology of resins, coatings, reinforcing fibers, and cores continues to evolve, there is every reason to believe that composite construction will continue to increase its current lead over other materials, both for series-built yachts and custom performance boats.

11

Roles for Woods and Metals in Contemporary Boatbuilding

Alongside the rapidly evolving field of fiber-composite boatbuilding, woods and metals may appear to be staid and old-fashioned materials. However, both continue to provide excellent alternatives to composites for some types of projects, and, of course, are used to at least a limited extent in virtually all boats. This chapter will examine woods and metals, both in general terms as structural materials and specifically as they are used in leading-edge yacht construction.

Why Wood?

Particularly for smaller one-off or semicustom sailboats, wood is quite often the building material of choice because it is the simplest and least expensive way to achieve adequately light weight together with good stiffness, strength, and impact resistance. To appreciate how wood can compete with the modern "miracle materials," it is necessary to understand something about the way it is put together.

The structural substance in all woods is cellulose, an organic polymer (long chainlike molecule) based on a simple sugar. However, unlike table sugar, cellulose is an exceedingly strong material. On an equal weight basis, many woods match the tensile strength of high-tension steel, or in other words are about four times as strong as the mild steels in everyday use.

Cellulose fibers form spiral arrays within the walls of long, tubular cells. In the trunks of trees, these tubular cells form massive parallel clusters, a feature which gives wood its characteristic "grain." Across the grain, the cellulose-containing cells are for the most part held together with relatively weak natural adhesives, although a few woods like the oaks have small clusters of cellulose-containing cells oriented radially, giving them better than average cross-grain strength.

Woods are typically tough materials with excellent fatigue resistance and impact resistance. As in fiber-reinforced plastic composites, cracks tend to be stopped by the weak interfaces between the strong cellulose-containing cells. In addition, wood goes one step further than fiberglass. To break wood across the grain, the built-in spiral pattern of the cellulose fibers within the cell walls must first be straightened in the path of the break—a process that absorbs additional energy.

On the debit side, the "bundle-of-tubes" structure of woods makes them relatively weak in compression—typically less than one-third their tensile strength. When walls of one tubular cell buckle, those of adjoining cells are pulled out of shape as well, often leading to a chain reaction failure.

Before wood can be used in boatbuilding or other construction, it must be seasoned or dried to reduce its water content from 50 percent by weight to 12 percent or less. In the latter stages of this drying process, wood not only gets lighter but, as a result of minor chemical changes in the cellulose, becomes stronger and stiffer as well. It also shrinks dramatically in cross-grain dimensions—a characteristic that may cause it to split.

Unfortunately, the seasoning of wood is fully reversible. If exposed to moisture, it will promptly absorb water again; in the process losing strength, stiffness, and of course, swelling out of shape. Since boats get wet all the time, this characteristic of wood has caused endless difficulties over the years.

Finally, wood suffers from the drawback of being edible, at least to a small but prolific group of organisms that can break cellulose down into its component sugars. Dry-rot fungi and "shipworms" (wood-boring clams) have probably destroyed more wooden vessels than warfare and shipwreck combined.

Plying and Laminating

Techniques for slicing wood veneers date back to the Egyptians, but the ability to bond these veneers together into a waterproof plywood suitable for boatbuilding had to await the invention of heat-setting phenolic resin glues in the 1920s. Plywood offers better dimensional stability and resistance to splitting than lumber. In addition, the quality and uniformity of a laminated wooden structure can be greatly improved because most of the hidden defects within a log will be exposed and eliminated during fabrication.

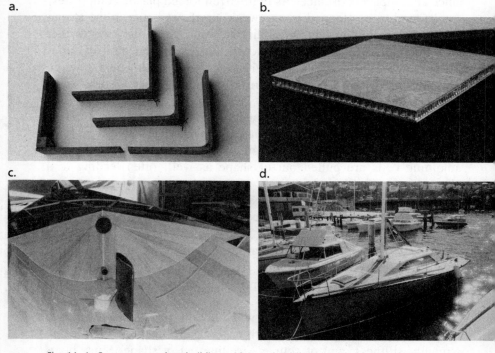

Fig. 11–1. Contemporary boatbuilding with wood: *(a)* "Stitch and glue" plywood construction employs epoxy adhesives and fillers *(sequence on right)* instead of conventional timber chine logs *(left)* to construct strong joints between hull panels. Wire ties temporarily fasten the precut panels together until an epoxy fillet on the inside of the hull has cured. *(b)* Thin plywood skins can be readily bonded to a honeycomb core to fabricate light, stiff panels. *(c)* Half-inch balsa planking with thin fiberglass skins inside and out will result in a panel weight of only 4 ounces per square foot for this (admittedly fragile) Aussie 18-foot skiff. *(c)* Custom 31-foot "beer-can racer" designed by New Zealand's Jim Young has 14-foot beam and only 5000 pounds displacement. Construction in 1983 was glass over longitudinal balsa planking, but today Durakore™ planking could provide greater impact resistance for the same weight.

Plywood is widely used in the construction of all kinds of yachts including those with fiberglass or metal hulls. For small, homebuilt boats it has been the material of choice for forty years, largely because it it easier and more pleasant to work with than any of the alternatives. The development of epoxy adhesives capable of filling wide gaps and forming sturdy fillet joints has made plywood boatbuilding easier than ever (fig. 11–1a). Plywood skins can even be used over lightweight cores like Nomex honeycomb to fabricate very light, strong panels (fig. 11–1b). Unfortunately, prefabricated plywood, like other flat panel materials, is highly resistant to bending in two directions at once and is therefore ill-suited to building the compound curves characteristic of most modern sailing hulls. To create these shapes using wood, other approaches must be used.

Wooden vessels constructed from three or more layers of crossed diagonal planking were in use even before the turn of the century. However, because waterproof glues did not exist at the time, mechanical fastenings had to be used and extensive caulking was necessary to prevent leaking. The comparatively recent development of waterproof glues that cure at room temperature makes it feasible to laminate wooden hulls over simple male molds. These **cold-molded** hulls are, in essence, sheets of plywood fabricated in the shape of a boat.

Low-density woods are generally preferred for cold molding because they permit a thicker and hence stiffer hull to be constructed for a given weight. The actual wood substance is much the same in all species, but dense woods like ash and oak contain less air than light woods like balsa and red cedar. For cold molding, the ability to ''hold'' fastening, at one time a top priority in the selection of boatbuilding lumber, is of much reduced importance.

Epoxy Sealing

When it comes to blocking the passage of moisture into (or out of) a wooden structure, epoxy coatings are admirable performers. The moisture content of boats finished with several layers of epoxy inside and out can reasonably be expected to remain almost constant for many years. Without much water and with very little oxygen, fungi cannot grow, so epoxy-encapsulated wood becomes essentially rotproof. However, no epoxy coating should be expected to block all moisture passage, although it can reduce it to a very low rate. For this reason, most builders do not recommend coating bulky timbers with epoxy; if these swell even a little, the epoxy film is likely to split. Large laminations containing many small pieces of wood are preferred because the mass of wood is then divided into subunits that are isolated and physically restrained by the surrounding plastic.

Wood-Fiberglass Boats

A modern variant of traditional carvel-planked construction has evolved in Australia, New Zealand, and, more recently, the United States (fig. 11-1c, d). The basic technique involves bending, fitting, and edge gluing longitudinal planks of balsa or other lightweight wood over a set of mold frames. After sanding and fairing, one or more layers of fiber reinforcement material and epoxy resin are applied to the outside of the hull. It is then lifted off the mold frames and additional layers of reinforcement applied to the inside. The wood planking, besides acting as a low-density core, furnishes longitudinal strength, so the fiber-composite skins can be oriented primarily to provide diagonal and transverse reinforcement. Unlike conventional cold molding, which requires a substantial male mold, wood planks will bend smoothly over a mold that consists of nothing more than a series of station frames. As a result the technique lends itself to the construction of custom racing boats.

A recent variation on this approach utilizes prefabricated strips and panels made of longitudinal hardwood veneers bonded to an end-grain balsa core. Developed by the Baltek Corporation, a major international supplier of balsa products, these materials are sold under the brand name Durakore™. They are most commonly used to strip-plank a custom hull over a rudimentary male mold. Assembly goes very quickly, and the finished interior can have an attractive wood finish provided the inner skin is made of transparent fiberglass.

Of course, it can be argued that strip-planked boats with composite skins are actually just fiberglass boats that happen to have wooden cores, but this is nit-picking. If the shape of the hull is initially defined by its wooden components and wood comprises from 60 to 80 percent of the finished product, it seems only fair to call the result a wooden boat.

Modern Metal Construction

Structural metals are strong, very stiff, relatively dense materials. However, the truly wonderful thing about many metals is that under excessive loads they will deform a great deal before reluctantly breaking—a property known as **ductility**. Of course, once the metal has begun to yield, it will not thereafter spring back to its original shape, but the deformation is a useful advance warning of incipient failure. When metals are flexed repeatedly, most tend to lose ductility and become work-hardened—a change that is also known as **fatigue**. Cyclic loading caused by wave impacts is a potential source of fatigue in metal boat hulls. Fortunately, this problem rarely arises, because practical limitations dictated by the construction techniques available usually lead to significant overbuilding and generous safety factors (fig. 11–2). On the other hand, fatigue has been known to cause failures in sailboat standing rigging, and certainly it should be considered wherever metals are used aboard boats in a structural capacity.

In practice, the most telling drawbacks of metals for boatbuilding are corrosion, weight, and cost. Oxidation—the most familiar type of corrosion—presents no problem in the case of stainless steels, bronzes, aluminum alloys, and titanium, because these rapidly become coated with rugged oxide films which subsequently serve to protect the underlying metal from further attack. In contrast, the soft, flaky coating of iron oxide that forms on unprotected iron or common steel provides no such protection for the underlying metal, so effective barrier coatings are essential.

All marine metals in common use are prone to galvanic or electrochemical corrosion, although some are vastly more susceptible than others. In addition, some metals, particularly stainless steels, are prone to accelerated corrosion while sustaining a load. This makes good sense if you remember that stress on a material means stress on its chemical bonds which renders them more susceptible to chemical attack. Stress corrosion is a particularly nasty problem in sailboat standing rigging (see Chapter 13).

When cost, availability, strength, toughness, ease of fabrication, and ability to resist corrosion are all taken into account, the only metals that are serious candidates as hull-building materials are mild steels and "marine grade" aluminum alloys. Steel, although strong, cheap, and readily available, is not a practical material for lightweight racing hulls because of its high density. If a steel panel is made thin

Fig. 11–2. Modern metal boatbuilding: *(a)* Steel cruising hulls with radiused chines are easier to construct than true round-bilged designs, yet are more esthetically attractive than chined ones. *(b)* Once completed, a good steel-hulled boat is indistinguishable from a wood or composite one. *(c)* Obtaining a fair hull shell with the exceptionally thin-gauge aluminum plates used for this 43-foot IOR racer required that the welds be made skillfully and in proper sequence. *(d)* Note the much heavier framing needed to meet scantling requirements for the 12-meter class.

enough to match the weight of lighter building materials, it will lack either adequate stiffness or will require an excessively complex rib-and-stringer framework to back it up. Worse yet, a very thin steel hull would be extremely vulnerable to rusting through, like an auto body, should its protective coating fail.

On the other hand, for yacht designs that can tolerate the additional structural weight, steel is an excellent way to go. The impressive reserve strength that comes automatically with the selection of plating thick enough to provide a cushion against corrosion is a reassuring thing in a cruising yacht. An additional benefit of relatively thick plating is an increase in usable interior volume (stemming from a reduction in the amount of framing required).

The stronger aluminum alloys have yield strengths similar to mild steels, but weigh only about a third as much. They are less stiff than steels (Young's modulus 11 million vs. 30 million). However, because the stiffness of a beam or panel is so dependent upon its thickness, an aluminum panel need only be 20 percent thicker to equal the rigidity of a steel counterpart. In practice, welded aluminum alloy hulls typically weigh about half as much as similar steel ones. Unfortunately aluminum alloys cost around five times as much as steel.

A few Grand Prix racing yachts, beginning with *Intuition* in 1980, were built using flush rivets and epoxy adhesives to fasten cold-formed, full-length plates to one another. In this way, the strength losses and heat distortion associated with welding were avoided, and very thin metal could be used in low-stress areas. An aluminum honeycomb core between much thinner skins was used for the deck. The technology for these projects was borrowed directly from the aircraft industry, which for years has been refining methods for gluing, riveting, forming, and relieving internal stresses in light-alloy structures.

Unfortunately, the exceptionally thin sheet metal and high-strength alloys used in these ultrasophisticated aluminum boats did not stand up well in the corrosive marine environment. Furthermore, during the past five years, new advances in composite construction have continued to tip the balance away from aluminum for raceboat construction. However, conventional welded aluminum may well be the best available choice for custom cruising yachts.

When it comes to corrosion problems, aluminum is somewhat paradoxical. On the one hand, its surfaces are well protected by an oxide film that is tough enough to make painting largely unnecessary, save for cosmetic reasons. On the other hand, it is even more susceptible than steel to electrolysis and galvanic corrosion. Fortunately, these destructive processes are well understood and preventable. The keys to corrosion control in an aluminum boat are a properly installed electrical system, the avoidance of incompatible metal fittings and fastenings, and good sacrificial anodes.

The Future of Metals in Boatbuilding

For any boat that may be beached or ground against rocks, there is no substitute for metal construction. Among sailboats, trailerable pocket cruisers are probably the most likely to fall into this category, followed perhaps by offshore yachts making hazardous voyages. Currently, there is a growing trend among serious offshore sailors to build yachts out of heavy-gauge aluminum which is left unfinished. By saving the considerable expense of a quality paint job, building costs can come in quite close to those of a steel boat (which must be painted), while maintenance is significantly reduced.

Of course, metals will always have a place in sailboat fittings, fasteners, rigs, and deck gear. The variety of metals used in these applications today goes well beyond a simple choice between mild steels and aluminum alloys. Bronzes are a classic standby that offers good looks, a low melting point for easy casting, and tensile strength that rivals many steels. The stainless steels as a group offer exceptional corrosion resistance and good strength, although they are not particularly easy to work. Titanium alloys are unmatched for a combination of strength, corrosion resistance, and low density—the weight of aluminum with the strength of steel. All these metals are too costly to seriously consider for hull construction, but bronze and stainless steel are extensively used for fittings. Titanium is still considered an exotic material, and to date has been used almost exclusively on custom racing boats. However, as the techniques needed to cut, shape, and weld this somewhat intractable metal continue to improve, there is a reasonable chance that it will eventually find widespread application on all sorts of sailboats.

12

Structural Failures
and How to Avert Them

Boats have been leaking, splitting, and sinking since mankind first took to sea. However, during the much shorter history of recreational sailing, structural failures have fortunately been quite rare. The good overall safety record of sailing yachts reflects both a generally high regard for seamanship on the part of amateur sailors, and the fact that until recently, most recreational sailboats were relatively expensive craft, carefully built to time-tested standards.

Few will dispute that today's sailboats still tend to be expensive. On the other hand, there is a growing trend among performance-oriented sailors to spend their money on weight-saving composites rather than beefy, conservative construction. In recent years, structural failures in offshore racing boats, monohull and multihull alike, have become prevalent enough to evoke serious concern. The reasons why boats sometimes break (and may be breaking with increasing frequency) are the focus of this chapter.

Cracks and Stress Concentrations

When any solid material fractures, the chemical bonds holding the molecules of that material together are physically pulled apart. The energy required to do this—the energy of fracture—varies enormously from one material to another. Brittle materials such as ordinary window glass, in addition to containing numerous tiny flaws that act as "crack starters," also possess little in the way of molecular impediments to the spread of cracks. Other materials, like most metals and fiber composites, are "tough" primarily because they possess fine-scale mechanisms to circumvent the weakening effects of small defects. To break a good structural material requires very extensive disruption of the molecular architecture, not just at the plane of fracture, but down into the material as well. Because many extra molecular bonds must be deformed or broken in this process, the energy of fracture is greatly increased.

Whether a particular object breaks under a given stress is determined by the shape of the object as well as upon the material from which it is made. Corners, notches, grooves, and steps all generate sharp localized increases in stress—**stress concentrations**—that are far higher than the average stress in the material at large.

The existence of stress concentrations was first deduced by C. E. Inglis in 1913 when he sought to discover why steel ships sometimes broke up in rough weather despite the fact that calculations and even

Fig. 12–1. Radiused corners, smooth joint fillets, and a complete absence of rough edges are critical in modern lightweight composite construction if potentially dangerous stress concentrations are to be avoided.

direct measurements of strain within ships' plating seemed to indicate safety margins of better than six to one. Prior to Inglis' work, naval architects had overlooked the effects of hatchways and other abrupt discontinuities upon the local distribution of stress, although plenty of mariners had noticed that cracks usually started at sharp corners. When actual measurements were eventually taken at the corners of square hatchways, stresses ten to fifty times higher than those in the hull at large were uncovered. In general, the sharper a notch or discontinuity, the more intense the local stress concentration. For this reason, bulkhead and hatch openings should be well rounded, while right-angle joints should ideally incorporate a generously radiused fillet (fig. 12–1).

Extreme stress concentrations on a very small scale occur at the tips of cracks (fig. 12–2). As the flanking areas just behind an advancing crack tip relax, all the stress they had previously sustained is

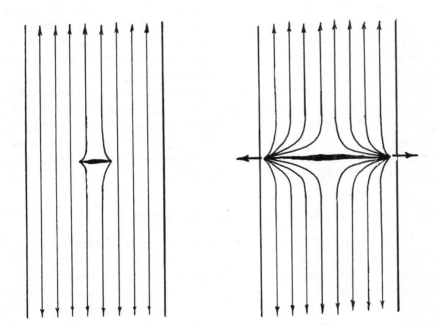

Fig. 12–2. For a particular material and level of internal stress (represented by parallel stress trajectory lines), a sufficiently small crack is "stable" *(left)* and will extend only slowly if at all. However, once a crack or flaw reaches critical length, the concentration of stress at its tips becomes too great and rapid failure ensues *(right)*.

thrown forward to bear upon a relatively small number of molecular bonds just ahead of the crack tip. It's the ancient principle of divide and conquer in a microscopic context. The longer the crack, the greater the stress at its end (or ends). Once a crack extends beyond a particular **critical length** (which depends upon the particular material and the level of internal stress), it will become unstable and may spread with almost explosive rapidity.

Fatigue and Resonance

Besides breaking from direct or localized overload, many materials weaken gradually when repeatedly strained. As mentioned in the previous chapter, tough metals can become "work-hardened" and brittle when bent repetitively—the reason why a paper clip or wire coat hanger eventually breaks when flexed forth and back. Fiber composites fatigue as a consequence of occasional but cumulative fiber fractures. Even woods, although superior to many other structural materials in this respect, eventually weaken with repeated bending. Since a yacht hull going through waves is inevitably going to experience cyclical stresses, the fatigue of hull materials is an important design factor that should be taken into account—particularly when every effort is being made to minimize weight.

It is also possible that violent impact with waves or floating obstructions may, in some circumstances, trigger shock waves within the hull structure that focus and cause damage somewhere other than at the impact site. The damping effects of the surrounding water and low-density core materials reduce the chances of this sort of failure, but the possibility cannot be entirely discounted.

Trouble in Paradise—Composite Failures

On the face of it, fiber composites seem perfect for boatbuilding. They are tough, very strong for their weights,* waterproof, noncorrodible, and can be formed into complex shapes with a minimum of waste. By varying core characteristics and the orientation and types of reinforcing fibers in the skins, different portions of a one-piece hull

---

*Very fine fibers of glass and most other materials are proportionally much stronger than large pieces of the same materials because the fibers contain fewer defects that can serve as crack initiators.

or deck can be tailored to sustain the stresses they will actually encounter in use. Unfortunately, advanced composites are new and relatively unfamiliar to many boatbuilders. Used correctly, they perform spectacularly, but to date, there seems to be an increased likelihood of engineering and building errors when these sophisticated materials are used.

Creating the actual boatbuilding material (the fiber-resin composite) on site is both an asset and a major drawback of composite construction. Offsetting the advantages listed at the beginning of this section is the potential for three serious drawbacks: First, modern resin systems must be mixed precisely and fiber reinforcement materials handled carefully for optimal results. Both can readily deteriorate if stored improperly. Second, application is critical, particularly with unidirectional-type materials where fiber orientation can easily be disturbed. Sharp bends and abrupt angles must be avoided (fig. 12-2). Even small air bubbles "frozen" within a highly loaded composite part can create dangerous stress concentrations!

When it comes to composite problems, carbon fiber tends to be particularly troublesome because of its great stiffness and associated low energy of fracture. Carbon-fiber laminates often fracture under impacts that would not harm more flexible materials because they deform only minimally and thus dissipate comparatively little energy. For similar reasons, carbon fiber must be used with great care as a supplementary reinforcement and stiffening material for lightweight rudders, spars, and hulls. If too little carbon fiber is applied, the rigid carbon fiber may break before the more flexible underlying material begins to shoulder any appreciable share of the load. In general, it's safest to use enough oriented carbon fiber to sustain 100 percent of the load along the axis of highest stress (while allowing the foundation material to handle the secondary loads). But paradoxically, hybrid laminates, containing approximately 40 percent aramid (Kevlar) and 60 percent carbon, are proving to be substantially tougher than laminates containing only carbon fiber.

Core failures in modern composite boats seem to be cropping up with increasing frequency, perhaps simply because cored construction is becoming more commonplace. Nevertheless, it is becoming evident that a core must do more than just hold two load-bearing skins apart. In the case of a rounded hull loaded in from the outside by water pressure both skins are typically loaded in compression with transverse tensile forces tending to pull the skins away from the core.

The cores of nearly flat panels such as decks experience shear stresses. In either case, core failures typically occur immediately adjacent to the inner surface of the skin because, as you no doubt anticipated, the abrupt change in mechanical rigidity at this juncture creates a stress concentration.

Chapter 9 described how top racing boats are designed for maximum structural stiffness with just enough strength thrown in to keep everything in one piece. Advanced composite sandwich panels are superb for fulfilling these design criteria because they tend to be considerably stiffer for their strength and weight than metal or laminated wood. On the other hand, using these very stiff panels results in a smaller safety margin in terms of strength, making accurate structural analysis a virtual necessity. Unfortunately, although it is not particularly difficult to resolve the gross stresses at work within a boat, it is considerably harder to ascertain all the fine-scale stress concentration effects. Predicting the degradation in material performance that may result from builder's error adds further uncertainties. For these reasons, even the most up-to-date scantling guidelines have been formulated largely on an experiential basis and continue to advocate substantial safety factors (or margins for error).

Policing Construction Standards

Lloyd's Registry of Shipping, with headquarters in London and offices in over 100 countries, is the world's oldest and largest surveying organization. To obtain Lloyd's classification or a Lloyd's building certificate, a yacht must not only be built from approved plans and in accordance with prescribed specifications, but either the individual yacht itself or the builder's operations must be subject to regular surveys. Naturally, many owners and would-be owners are reluctant to absorb this added expense. An additional drawback from the viewpoint of many contemporary racing sailors is that Lloyd's standards are highly conservative and slow to evolve. As a result, some of the more exotic and fashionable varieties of composite construction will probably not be approved for some time. The only contemporary racing boats required to carry Lloyd's certification are the 12-meters, and now this class has been supplanted for future America's Cup competitions, and it seems unlikely that others will be added to the list.

Since 1981, another set of construction standards, those of the

American Bureau of Shipping (ABS), has rapidly gained favor in yachting circles. This development is scarcely a surprise, in that the ABS guidelines for Offshore Yachts were developed through a collaborative effort involving the New York–based Bureau and the International Technical Committee of the Ocean Racing Council—administrators of the IOR. The ABS guidelines provide a system for determining minimal **scantlings**—specifications for every part of hull-deck structure as well as the rudder and keel root. The thickness and composition of each panel is calculated on the basis of its size, curvature, and the **design head** or inward pressure that is anticipated during service. The formula used for these calculations were developed with the help of scantling data from a variety of yachts, some of which had failed in heavy weather and others which remained intact. Provided good information is available regarding the actual mechanical properties of the materials as used, the ABS guidelines appear to provide an adequate safety margin with almost any sort of hull construction. While some designers criticize the ABS system as being overly conservative in certain areas, it has been well received by many yacht owners who like to see the value of their investments, as well as the safety of their craft, protected. Like Lloyd's, ABS offers several classification services ranging from plan checking and approval to ongoing surveys of individual yachts during and following construction. At the time of writing, there are no specific scantling standards for the great majority of offshore racing events. However, the ORC has recommended that ABS compliance be made a requirement for newly constructed yachts competing in the particularly strenuous Category I offshore events such as the Whitbread Round-the-World Race.

Can legislated scantling standards genuinely advance the cause of safety at sea, or are they simply another intrusion on individual freedom that will mainly benefit marine surveying companies? There are plenty of arguments, both pro and con, but on the whole, the current movement toward establishing the ABS system as a universal standard for offshore monohulls appears worthwhile, if only because a surprisingly large proportion of yachts are still being designed and built by people who have little or no background in engineering.

With the current shift in emphasis from "strong enough to take anything" to "as light as possible yet strong enough to hold together," it is perhaps inevitable that the frequency and severity of structural failures in yachts has increased. An extra willingness on the part of professional and semiprofessional racing crews to take risks and push their boats to the limit has, no doubt, exacerbated the problem, and may well be causing failures in yachts that could have survived unscathed in an earlier era.

On the positive side, new materials and computer-assisted design techniques are making it feasible to build boats that are both lighter and stronger than ever before (as the advertisements often claim). The major difficulties seem to arise either when construction is substandard due to a poor batch of materials or bad workmanship, or when computer stress modelling is used to design boats "right to the edge." When the latter is attempted, any minor underestimation of shock loads, local stress concentrations, or seemingly trivial errors in workmanship can have grave consequences. Because neither the forces exerted by the sea, nor the interplay of stresses within a yacht's hull are fully understood at present, a substantial margin of safety seems only prudent.

13

Recent Developments in Stayed Rigs

Although the wind makes no distinction between the sails and the spars and rigging that support them, the useful air flow alterations that propel most sailboats are produced by the sails alone. With just a few exceptions, the spars and rigging are necessary evils—essential for holding the sails in position and transferring forces to the hull(s), but undesirable due to their weight and the flow disruption they produce. To minimize these adverse effects, enormous effort has been devoted to reducing the sizes and weights of rig components while retaining adequate strength.

Distilled to its basics, a stayed sailing rig consists of two kinds of structural elements: a mast and perhaps some spreaders, both of which function as struts or compression members, plus the standing rigging which operates under tension to hold the mast upright against the lateral forces produced by the sails. This simple model accurately represents a masthead sloop sailing with only its genoa set (fig. 13–1). Halyard tension adds extra compressive stress on the mast—enough to justify using **halyard locks** in some racing spars to halve this portion of the load.

With contemporary rigs, deliberate fore-and-aft mast bend is frequently induced by the pull of the mainsail leach, the forward thrust of the boom at the gooseneck (produced by vang action), and the

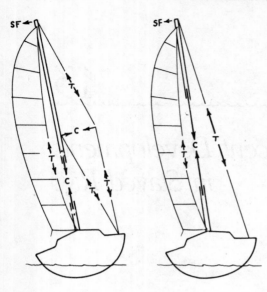

Fig. 13–1. The geometry of most stayed rigs ensures that even modest forward and side forces (SF) from the sails will translate into much larger compression stresses (C) within the mast. Most spreaders serve as secondary compression elements to increase the effective shroud angles *(left)*. Without them, the tension on the shrouds and compression on the mast would be unacceptably high in many cases *(right)*.

Fig. 13–2. Mast bend in most modern rigs is induced by a combination of mainsail leech tension, boom thrust (from the vang), and masthead backstay action. Note how a masthead rig with a backstay crane responds to backstay tension just as a fractional rig would.

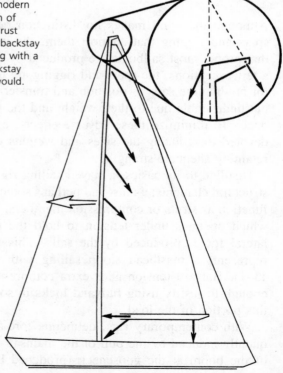

action of a masthead backstays (fig. 13–2). Although the overall stress level within the mast is not changed much by this bending, the pattern of stress distribution can be affected in ways that must be understood by the spar maker (fig. 13–3a–b).

When a stayed mast fails, it is usually the result of a rigging failure that allows the spar to bow until its walls buckle and rupture. Engineers call this mode of failure Euler buckling (pronounced "Oiler"). Of course, the same thing can happen if one or more of the **panels**— the lengths of unsupported spar between shroud insertions—is made too long, or if the mast is simply too limber for the compression loads it encounters.

A second type of failure, known as Brazier buckling, occurs when an adequately stayed mast becomes so heavily loaded in compression that a crease abruptly develops in its walls, usually at the site of a minor side load or other stress concentration. Spectacular failure then follows almost instantaneously. For a simple but dramatic demonstration of this, balance yourself on one foot atop an empty aluminum drink can, then ask someone to gently poke the side of the can with the blunt end of a pencil.

At one time it was widely believed that fore-and-aft mast bend in an offshore yacht was only safe if the total amount of bend was limited to about half the mast's longitudinal dimension. The idea was that the load axis—a straight line from masthead to butt—should never stray outside the mast itself.

Today, of course, it is routine practice to deliberately bend all sorts of sailboat masts a good deal more than this in order to accommodate extra mainsail girth and to permit a wider range of draft control. The reason failures are still comparatively rare has to do with the distribution of stress within a typical bent spar. When fore-and-aft bend is induced in a mast at dockside (while it is not being subjected to much compression), tensile stress occurs near the front of the section and compressive stress toward the back (fig. 13–3a). However, when the large compression loads generated by sailing are superimposed upon these much smaller bend-induced stresses, the whole mast goes into compression, with the peak compression loads being shifted a little toward the back of the spar (fig. 13–3b). Many modern mast sections are designed to handle this uneven distribution of stress, with more metal toward the back of the section and a boltrope groove that effectively stiffens the aft face of the mast against localized buckling (fig. 13–3c).

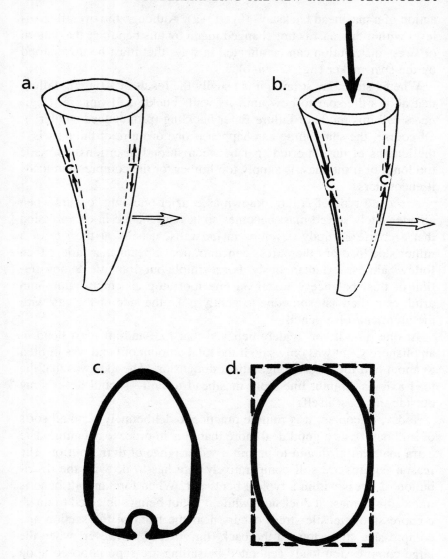

Fig. 13–3. When a mast is bent without being subjected to compression loading (a), the forward (convex) wall undergoes tensile strain while the aft wall sustains mild compression. However, when heavy compression loads from sailing are superimposed on this stress pattern, the entire mast goes into compression, although a greater share of the compressive stress is borne by the aft wall (b). Sophisticated "bullet-shaped" racing masts (c) typically have the most metal toward the rear of the section, and use variations in wall thickness to obtain greater stiffness for a given weight. The oval mast section (d) has the same X and Y dimensions and weight per foot as the box section shown as a broken outline, but is significantly more limber.

Mast Section Design

In selecting a cross-sectional shape for a mast, the designer must steer a middle road between the conflicting requirements of aerodynamic and structural efficiency. Turbulence caused by a nonrotating mast does considerable mischief to the orderly flow of air over the leeward side of the mainsail, and surprisingly slight reductions in mast size have measureably improved racing speeds. On the other hand a larger diameter mast with thinner walls is dramatically stiffer relative to its weight (although more vulnerable to Brazier buckling).

Spar builders compare masts with different cross sections and wall thicknesses not only by weight per linear foot (or meter) but with the aid of a mathematical expression from engineering called the **fourth moment of inertia**, which evaluates stiffness. This expression interrelates the amount of material in a mast's walls and the distance of that material from the central axis. Because the "moments" of a mast section increase as the square of this distance, overall sectional size has a much more dramatic effect upon mast stiffness than adding material to the mast walls. For example, an oval section of uniform wall thickness that is 60 percent as wide as it is long will have a transverse moment of inertia that is only 42 percent of its longitudinal moment.

Spar designers use a number of tricks to improve the "moments" of their masts without increasing either their dimensions or their weights per foot. Consider an oval mast section and a rectangular one, both possessing identical X and Y dimensions and containing identical amounts of alloy (fig. 13–3d). Clearly the box section will be the stiffer of the two, not only because the metal near its four corners is situated considerably farther from the central axis. Unfortunately the poor aerodynamics of the rectangular mast section would preclude its usefulness on a performance-oriented sailboat. However, some of the same advantage can be gained by varying the wall thickness of a low windage, bullet-shaped section, to increase the proportion of the material that is situated farthest from the central axis (fig. 13–3c).

In selecting a modern racing mast, the spar designer strives for the optimal balance between weight and cross-sectional size. Whenever two masts of slightly different sectional size are both built to minimum weight and minimum acceptable stiffness, the smaller spar with thicker walls will inevitably be substantially heavier. Although the windage saving from reduced sectional size has a significant positive effect upon mainsail efficiency and performance, the price of these gains is the loss of some rough-water speed due to increased pitching. Extensive pragmatic testing in the crucible of top-level racing has zeroed in on optimal sections for each size of racing yacht, with marginally smaller, heavier masts being given the edge for inshore races in smoother waters.

The heart of a modern spar is an **extrusion** made by forcing heat-softened aluminum alloy through a steel die, like toothpaste from a tube. The shape of the die selected determines the mast section, as discussed above, but the choice of the alloy used is also important. Most performance masts are made from 6000 series aluminum that is alloyed with silicon and magnesium. Its virtues are adequate strength, fairly good weldability, and satisfactory corrosion resistance. The 7000 series aircraft alloys, which contain zinc, are stronger but more prone to corrosion problems and very difficult to weld without a substantial loss of strength. To date they have been used for only a handful of racing spars. Series 2000 alloys are stronger still, but very troublesome because they are difficult to extrude and impossible to weld. Epoxy adhesives, flush rivets, and backing strips must be used to assemble the multi-part masts built from this alloy. At the time of this writing, only high-budget programs such as Admiral's Cup and America's Cup campaigns have experimented with Series 2000 masts.

Engineering Masts for Localized Loads

Aluminum mast blanks as supplied by the mill are uniform from one end to the other, but the actual stresses on a mast vary considerably at different locations. Compression is incremental in masts rigged with spreaders, so the lowest panels sustain the greatest loads (fig. 13–4). Modern rigid spreaders impose very high localized stresses in the vicinity of the spreader roots, which must be carefully designed and reinforced. In addition, the main boom and spinnaker pole apply substantial inward forces to the walls of the mast in specific places. Finally, where holes or slots are cut to allow internal halyards to exit a mast, it may be important to add local reinforcement. For these reasons, it is always desirable to alter a basic mast blank so that the mechanical characteristics in each part of the finished mast will better match the stresses in that area.

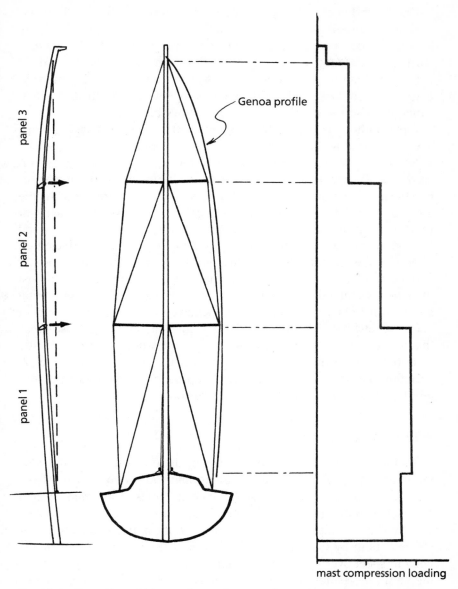

panel 3

panel 2

panel 1

Genoa profile

mast compression loading

Fig. 13–4. Rigs with multiple panels are the norm for performance-oriented offshore monohulls today, partly because they permit slimmer, more aerodynamic sections to be used, and partly because they allow overlapping headsails to be sheeted more effectively. Sophisticated racing masts may be "tailored" to efficiently handle the steplike pattern of compression loading found in a spar of this type.

The most basic and popular step toward this end is masthead tapering, because the top few feet of any mast are comparatively lightly loaded, while unnecessary weight and windage here do the greatest harm. Masts made from weldable alloys are ordinarily tapered by cutting out one or more long, wedge-shaped sectors, forcing the new edges into contact, and welding them together. Heat-treated extrusions or those made from unweldable alloys are much more difficult to taper, although epoxy-bonded seams with aluminum backing strips and cold-forming techniques have both been used.

Beyond a masthead taper, relatively few spars are tailored for localized stress variations because of the costs involved, but many sophisticated techniques are available. Basically, there are two possible approaches: add more material to beef up highly stressed areas or remove material from low-load zones. The former can be achieved by adding **doublers**—extra thicknesses of alloy that are riveted or bonded either to the inside or the outside of the spar. A smoother surface results if the doublers are attached inside, but the spar must then be assembled from left/right or front/back halves. Removing alloy from lightly stressed areas is achieved either by machining or chemical etching. The latter technique involves masking those areas that are to remain thick before suspending the whole mast in a caustic soda bath which dissolves exposed alloy at a slow, uniform rate. A variation on the ''chemical milling'' approach can be used to gradually taper the wall thickness of an extrusion.

The Spreaders' Roles

As in other areas of stayed-rig design, there is a trade-off between the complexity of the standing rigging and the sectional size of the mast itself. If the shrouds meet the mast at angles of less than around 10 degrees, compression loads are likely to soar unacceptably (fig. 13-1 right). Because the shroud base of most larger yachts is restricted, both by the relative narrowness of the hull itself and by the need to sheet overlapping genoas far inboard for efficient upwind sailing, multiple panel rigs are popular (fig. 13-4). Even without any reduction in compression loading, short panels are less susceptible to Euler buckling than long ones. Better yet, with multiple panels, larger shroud angles and a net reduction in mast compression are obtained with no increase in spreader length.

Naturally, designers of multi-panel rigs are quick to take advantage of this reduction in compression loading to use slimmer, more limber spar sections. The extra flow disturbance over the mainsail luff that results from a thicker mast appears to harm performance more than the extra windage produced by additional spreaders and standing rigging.

The spreaders of modern rigs not only push the shrouds outward, but are often used to deflect them in the fore-and-aft plane as well. Indeed, in some high-performance dinghies, this is the spreaders' sole function. As the pull of the mainsail leech and the forward thrust of the boom bow the mast forward, the shrouds impose a backward, restraining pressure on the spreader tips (fig. 13–4 left). Provided the spreaders and their root attachments are sufficiently rigid, this bend-limiting effect will be applied to the mast itself. In essence, even in-line shrouds often serve a secondary function as intermediate stays. Of course, when the chainplates are situated aft of the mast plane, as in many smaller fractional rigged boats like the J-24, this staying effect is greatly increased.

Even with rigid spreaders, slender racing rig masts often have too little support in the fore-and-aft plane to prevent the mast from over-bending under normal sailing loads. One or two pairs of **checkstays** are commonly used to further restrain the tendency of the mast to bow forward, and to fine-tune its bending characteristics for optimal mainsail shape. Note that the purpose of checkstays is not the same as that of the **running backstays** on a fractional rig which lead to the hounds where the forestay intersects the mast, and are used exclusively to control forestay tension. When multiple checkstays, or runners plus checkstays, are fitted, they are usually lead to a common tail to avoid having to release and retension each pair of stays separately during tacks and gybes.

The Standing Rigging

Thanks to the advent of hydraulic controls, it is now easier than ever to adjust backstays, checkstays, babystays, jumper shrouds and in some cases the length and sweep angle of spreaders while under way. As a result, the distinction between standing and running rigging is becoming blurred. Nevertheless, it is still conventional to classify the forestay, masthead backstay, and the shrouds (which are still rarely adjusted while under way) as standing rigging.

Recently, more and more designers and riggers have been specifying **rod rigging** for shrouds and stays in place of twisted wire rope. Compared to conventional 1 × 19 wire of the same diameter, rod rigging is about 30 percent stronger because there are no air spaces in its cross section. On racing boats, it is common practice to take advantage of this difference by substituting a smaller rod in order to reduce windage. An additional benefit is that the twist-free rod stretches substantially less than a wire rope as it loads up, making complex rigs a great deal easier to tune. On the other hand, it is likely that this same lack of "give" in rod rigging increases the chance of shock damage and dismasting in exceptionally rough going.

The chief bugaboo in the design of any tensile structure is devising satisfactory end fittings, and sailboat rigging elements are no exception. Swaged ends work well with wire rope, but are unreliable with all but the smallest rods because the surface of the latter is too smooth. Threading the rod ends to accept screw-on fittings obviously involves removing metal and therefore reduces strength. This problem was neatly solved when Navtec introduced the **cold-formed head,** or "mushroom head," for anchoring rod terminals. The technique employs a powerful hydraulic press to flare the end of the rod so that it cannot slip out of a variety of special receptacles (fig. 13-5a, b).

However, even with this major headache resolved, rod rigging can cause difficulties. A number of rig failures, including some famous ones like the dismasting of *Ceramco New Zealand* in the 1981 Whitbread Race, have been traced to rod rigging being incorrectly installed where a shroud extending up from deck level was bent over spreader tips. It turns out that whenever **continuous rod rigging** of this type is fitted, it is critical not only that the rod be preformed to bend over the spreader tip with an accuracy of better than 1 degree but that the bent area be protected by a special sleeve that is also accurately prebent (fig. 13-5c).

Continuous rod rigging is convenient when all the rods extend down to turnbuckles at deck level where they are readily accessible for tuning. On the other hand, so much care and precision is needed to install these systems correctly that trouble is bound to arise at least occasionally. For this reason, **discontinuous rod rigging**, with separate rods between every spreader, has become increasingly popular. With discontinuous rigging it is necessary to go aloft in order to adjust the tension of the intermediate shrouds, and the increased number of end fittings drives up costs. However, the extra weight of these fittings is largely balanced by weight savings in the rods themselves, because

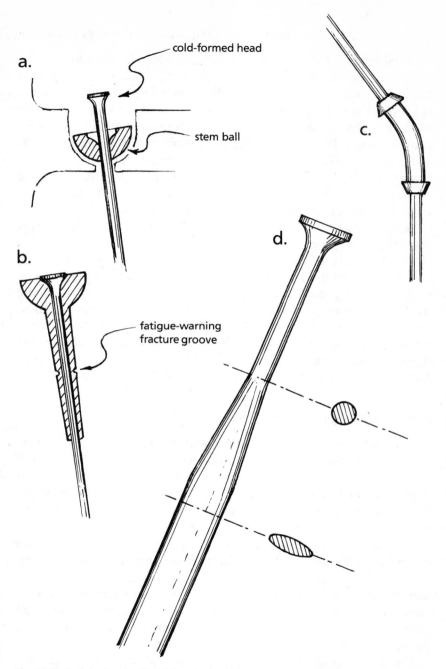

a. cold-formed head

stem ball

c.

b.

d.

fatigue-warning
fracture groove

Fig. 13–5. Rod rigging details: *(a)* Standard cold-formed head backed up by a stainless steel stem ball will easily exceed the tensile strength of the rod. However, fatigue can occur where the rod emerges from the stem ball if the latter fails to move freely enough in its socket. *(b)* A more recent stem ball design not only gives better lateral support to the rod end but warns of gradual fatigue by fracturing long before the rod itself fails. *(c)* Rod protectors for spreader tips and the rod they contain must be prebent with great precision to obtain satisfactory longevity from continuous rod rigging. *(d)* Lenticular rigging made by re-forming ordinary rod is aerodynamically efficient, but very expensive.

the total length of rod in the system is considerably reduced.

Originally rod rigging was made from type 302 or 304 stainless steel—the materials most commonly chosen for 1 × 19 wire rope. However, the rod rigging proved more prone to stress corrosion, so today the more resistant (and expensive) Nitronic 50 stainless is generally selected. Premium rod rigging is made of NP-35 nickel-cobalt, a still more costly material. For top-flight racing applications, a lenticular or teardrop cross section is occasionally specified to reduce windage (fig. 13–5d). However, besides the breathtaking costs involved, **lenticular rod rigging** seems quite susceptible to wind-induced vibration, which may lead to fatigue failure within a surprisingly short time.

The reliability of the more down-to-earth varieties of rod rigging has improved to the point that it has become a fairly popular option on pure cruising boats. Advocates of this new technology often cite the well-documented problem of stress corrosion inside swaged ends, particularly in tropical climates. On the other hand, a serious blue-water cruiser must consider the difficulties of finding replacement rod rigging in out-of-the-way places and should probably carry some spare 1 × 19 wire with appropriate end fittings (Norseman or Sta-Lok).

Booms and Spinnaker Poles

Engineering a satisfactory main boom or spinnaker pole is generally easier than designing a good mast because with these spars it is unnecessary to minimize cross-sectional size or to seek closely controlled bending characteristics. In most cases, comparatively large, thin-walled sections can be chosen for a net gain in stiffness relative to weight.

Spinnaker poles are pure compression structures, but most main booms must be designed to resist high-bending loads imparted by vangs, and in some cases, mid-boom sheeting arrangements. To sustain bending loads as efficiently as possible, contemporary racing booms frequently take the form of deep boxes—sometimes fabricated with relatively heavy extrusions on the top and bottom, and very thin gauge sheet aluminum for the sides (fig. 13–6a).

The use of advanced composites such as carbon fiber in masts has been effectively banned in most forms of racing—a curiously reactionary stance considering how widespread the use of these materials in hull structures has become. However, the ban on exotic composites

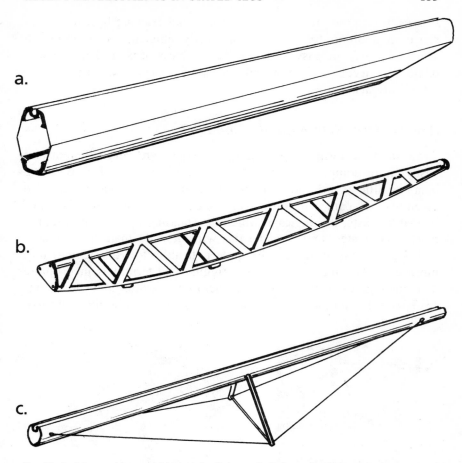

Fig. 13–6. Advanced booms: *(a)* Maxi-depth boom built from aluminum extrusions top and bottom with lightweight side plates formed from thin alloy sheet. *(b)* Triangular truss-type boom—stiff and light, but difficult to fabricate. *(c)* A stayed boom.

has been considerably less comprehensive when it comes to booms and spinnaker poles, so a good many have been made using carbon fiber and epoxy. On the whole these tend to be delightfully light and very strong, but poor at withstanding knocks and scrapes.

Exceptionally efficient booms, at least from an engineering viewpoint, can be built as truss structures (fig. 13–6b) or stiffened against bending with struts and rigging wires much as a mast is stayed (fig. 13–6c). However, the former are formidably difficult to fabricate, while the latter could conceivably decapitate an unwary crew! Open trusses hold some promise as unconventional cruising boat masts because in addition to being mechanically efficient as compression structures, they are easy to climb. Nevertheless, it is unlikely that any of these concepts will soon find widespread acceptance in the mainstream of yachting.

Are Modern Rigs Reliable Enough?

The high-performance stayed rigs of today are very different and vastly more complicated than the rigs used aboard offshore racing boats as little as a decade ago. Single- and double-spreader rigs have given way to spars with four, five, and even six panels. In this era of bendable masts, the angles at which the standing rigging intersect the mast, chainplates, and spreader tips will often fluctuate through several degrees. Since this can be quite unhealthy for rod rigging, it is more important than ever that the rigging and terminals incorporate efficient **toggles** so they can align themselves while under load (fig. 13–7 left). Despite numerous innovations, there can be no doubt that

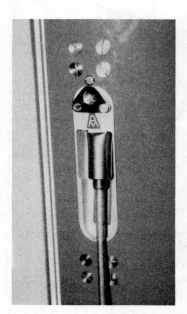 

Fig. 13–7. A stayed rig is only as reliable as its weakest link. Sophisticated components like the recessed, free-toggling shroud tang shown on the left would not have prevented the obvious failure of the improperly tapered mast on the right.

a modern full-race rig is a temperamental beast that demands frequent inspections and ongoing maintenance.

Considering how often masts are lost in contemporary offshore racing, it is surprising that, to date, there has been little call for rig scantling guidelines. Perhaps some sailors have rationalized that rig integrity is less of a safety concern than hull integrity because, after all, "you can always power home." If so, this represents a dangerously cavalier attitude, and it could be argued that rig scantling regulations are needed simply to protect people from themselves. Currently, the IMS makes some allowance for the extra aerodynamic drag of a larger mast section, but this alone is unlikely to entice the more serious competitors.

A state-of-the-art racing rig is a creation of spare elegance with every component just strong enough to perform its appointed role. Unfortunately it takes only one failure out of a hundred or more highly stressed components to bring the whole thing tumbling down. Likewise, any oversights on the part of the spar builder are likely to become painfully obvious (fig. 13–7 right), and there's precious little margin for errors on the part of the crew.

On a more positive note, the combination of advanced engineering and a whole lot of build-and-break experimentation has greatly increased our understanding of stayed-rig design. By taking the lessons learned in racing and applying them to cruising spars, it is now feasible to equip cruising boats with lighter, stronger, yet more reliable rigs than ever before.

14

Freestanding Rigs, Rotating Masts, and Rigid Sails

Stayed, nonrotating rigs are used on a majority of sailboats, but a variety of alternatives are currently gaining in popularity. Freestanding rigs, the oldest type of all, are staging a revival thanks to recent technological advances. Some sophisticated rotating rigs function as sails in their own right, not just as unavoidable aerodynamic handicaps. Although conventional rigs offer real advantages for many types of boats and are unlikely to ever vanish from the scene, odds are that more radical rig types will find increasingly widespread application in the future.

Design of Unstayed Rigs

From an engineering viewpoint, an unstayed mast works in an entirely different way from a stayed one. Rather than being a compression strut that thrusts upward against the tension of the rigging, a freestanding mast operates as a **cantilevered beam** and sustains mostly bending loads. Whenever any beam is subjected to a lateral load, the material comprising one face of the beam is subjected to tensile stress, while the opposite side goes into compression. The portion of the beam in between undergoes shear, or diagonal, stress (fig. 14–1 left). The only compression stress in an unstayed masts comes from halyard

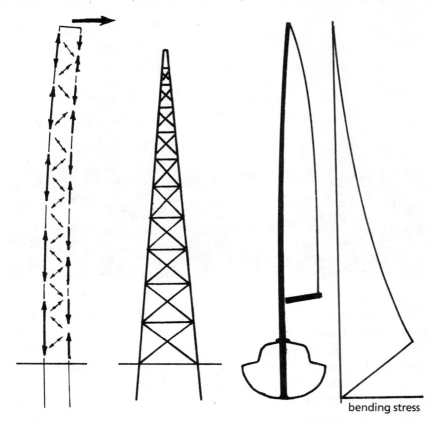

bending stress

Fig. 14–1. A lateral force applied to a beam imparts compressive stress toward one side of the beam, tensile stress on the opposite side, and shear stress in between. The arrangement of elements in a truss-type structure like a tower mirrors this stress pattern. Like the tower, an unstayed mast should be tapered because it sustains peak bending stresses where it passes through the deck.

tension (together with the associated downward pull of the sheets, cunningham, etc.). Wind loads induce bending stresses.

A nonrotating, unstayed mast will bend in a different direction with every change in wind angle. For this reason, each part of the mast wall must be capable of sustaining tensile, sheer, and compressive stresses with equal competence. On the other hand, all these stresses range from zero at the masthead to a maximum where the spar passes through the deck (fig. 14–1 right). For these reasons, the most efficient shape for a nonrotating, unstayed mast is a symmetrically tapered tube.

Until recently, the most logical choice for building a freestanding mast was the trunk of a tree, which has, after all, evolved to perform a very similar function. Today it is possible to build a more weight-efficient, hollow spar from either spun-tapered aluminum or fiber composites. One particularly elegant technique involves using specialized equipment to spiral resin-coated reinforcing fibers onto a rotating form or madril, which is later removed. Fibers are usually wound on in both directions and deliberately applied at varying angles. The majority of the fibers are applied at low fiber angles (close to the long axis of the mast) to provide the necessary tensile and compressive strength. Others, wound on at larger angles, furnish sheer strength and resistance to longitudinal splitting. Due to its enormous stiffness and high strength relative to weight, carbon fiber has found favor in unstayed-mast construction. Its chief drawbacks—low resistance to impact and vulnerability to highly localized stresses—are not serious shortcomings in this application.

Unstayed masts, being substantially thicker than stayed ones, create more turbulence and degrade mainsail performance to a much greater extent. Bending characteristics are largely built in, and due to the absence of adjustable rigging elements, the options for fine-tuning sail shape by altering mast bend are limited. For these reasons, few freestanding rigs are used in big-boat racing, although they are popular

Fig. 14-2. The unstayed masts used on an increasing number of contemporary cruisers are almost always circular in cross section and nonrotating *(left)*. The Garry Hoyt–designed Freedom 25 *(right)* is one of the few examples of a freestanding, rotating rig to date. Upwind efficiency is comparable to a conventional sloop, while tacking is simplified.

on singlehanded dinghies and board boats. On the other hand, they are appreciated by cruising sailors because they have very few parts that could fail, and therefore require virtually no maintenance (fig. 14-2).

In the future it may become feasible to fabricate more compact unstayed masts by incorporating either longitudinal webs or internal ring frames to stiffen a thin walled tube against buckling (fig. 14-3). The latter design strategy is represented by bamboo stalks, which are remarkably stiff and tough considering their slenderness and light weight.

Rotating the Mast

Most sailboat mast sections are oval, not so much for streamlining, but because it is more difficult to provide fore-and-aft support using stays than lateral support via shrouds. Consequently, the mast itself must have greater strength and stiffness in the fore-and-aft plane. Even when closehauled, the airflow impinges upon a conventional mast at quite a large angle which creates substantial turbulence, especially on the leeward side of the sail near its luff (fig. 14-4 left). Since this is the portion of the mainsail that potentially could generate the largest propulsive forces, mast-induced turbulence is quite costly

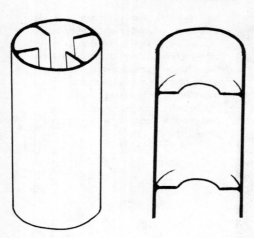

Fig. 14–3. Internal webs or bulkheads may be used in future freestanding masts to pare down sectional size without too much loss of stiffness.

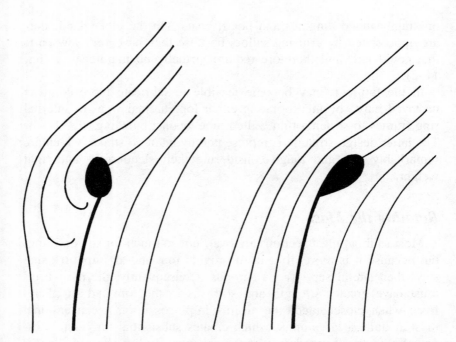

Fig. 14–4. Because air flow in the immediate vicinity of a rig is quite "lifted" due to the upwash from the mainsail (left), an extensive turbulent zone forms on the leeward side of most nonrotating masts. A rotating mast will largely eliminate this turbulence (right).

to performance. On the other hand, if the mast can be pivoted so that the longer dimension of the section faces more or less directly into the local airflow, the propulsive force from the mainsail increases considerably—often in the neighborhood of 15 percent (fig. 14–4 right).

On the debit side, rotating masts are more difficult to stay than fixed ones because diamond shrouds must be used to stiffen the section laterally and only a single pair of upper shrouds can be used to actually hold the rig erect (fig. 14–5a). Worse yet, the upper shrouds must lead directly to the deck without the help of spreaders to increase shroud angles, requiring that the rig be short or that the chainplates be positioned exceptionally far outboard. The usual impact of these staying limitations is to increase panel lengths and mast compression, necessitating, in most cases, a stronger, heavier mast section. Monohull designers, wrestling with limited transverse stability and a narrow shroud base, are likely to find that the aerodynamic gains from a rotating mast are insufficient to offset the losses associated with greater weight aloft. On the other hand, multihulls, with their very high initial stability, wide shroud base, and greater need for high-speed aerodynamic efficiency, lend themselves beautifully to rotating masts and often benefit considerably. The few monohulls that use rotating masts are comparatively small boats with the high beam-to-length ratios needed to furnish an adequate shroud base.

Of course, an unstayed rotating mast could be used on even the narrowest monohull. However, there are formidable problems associated with engineering a mast that is thin enough transversely to make rotation aerodynamically worthwhile, strong enough to stand alone, and light enough not to compromise stability too much. The Garry Hoyt–designed Freedom 25 shown on the right of figure 14–2 features a sophisticated carbon-fiber wing mast, and is one of the first experiments along these lines to date.

From Rotating Mast to Wing Mast

Wing masts differ from rotating masts not so much in concept as in proportions. While the objective with a rotating mast is still merely to minimize the adverse aerodynamic effect of a having a mast at all, a wing mast is intended to furnish useful propulsive forces in its own right. This is accomplished by chosing a section that is much larger, particularly in the fore-and-aft dimension, than the corresponding ro-

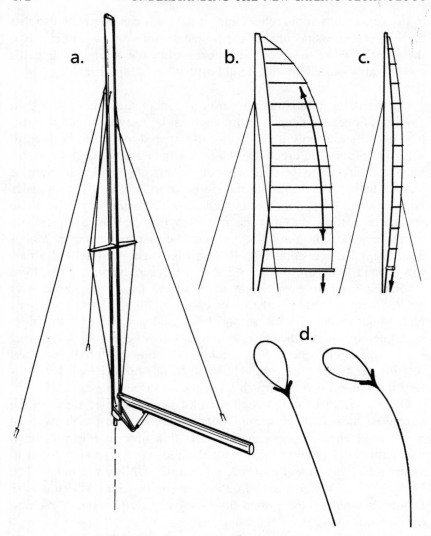

Fig. 14–5. Details of rotating rigs: *(a)* Conventional arrangement permits only one pair of shrouds with no spreaders, although panel(s) below the hounds can be stiffened with diamonds. Rotation is controlled by a lever linked to the boom. *(b)* Wing masts are ordinarily stayed like other rotating masts, although greater sectional stiffness may allow a reduction in the standing rigging. *(c)* A radiused trailing edge on a wing mast will cause the luff to sag to leeward when the mast is rotated, allowing twist to be controlled using less leech tension. *(d)* Limited-swing hinge fittings on the inboard batten ends enable mast rotation to control mainsail draft.

tating mast would be—a section that provides considerable sail area in its own right.

Because stiffness increases so dramatically with even a small increase in sectional size, any wing mast worthy of the name is vastly more rigid than the corresponding fixed or rotating mast would be. This makes it feasible to partially offset the extra weight that would otherwise result from its extra size by opting for low-density construction materials like wood and cored composites instead of aluminum alloy. Even so, most wing masts are considerably heavier than their smaller counterparts, and are again best suited to multihull use.

A number of wing masts for recent ocean-racing multihulls have incorporated radiused trailing edges (fig. 14–5b). This invention, credited to British designer Austin Farrar, serves to reduce the leach tension needed to control mainsail twist by introducing a complementary leeward curve in the sail's luff whenever the mast is rotated (fig. 14–5c). The fully battened mainsails used by these powerful boats have huge roaches, which makes leach sag extremely difficult to control through the application of mainsheet tension alone.

Solid Rigs

If the wing mast represents the transitional point in the quest for aerodynamic efficiency, where the mast itself ceases to be a handicap and becomes an asset, the next logical step is a rig consisting solely of a giant wing mast. Strictly from an aerodynamic viewpoint, solid rigs make excellent sense because they can provide significantly higher lift per unit area and superior lift-to-drag ratios than conventional thin sails. On the other hand, the drawbacks of additional weight aloft, breathtaking cost, and potentially daunting handling difficulties have limited the use of solid rigs to a few esoteric developmental sailboats such as 18-square-meter and C-class catamarans (fig. 14–6), and the defending yacht in the bizzare 1988 America's Cup.

Unlike aircraft wings, which can be permanently asymmetrical in cross section, a solid rig must work equally well on either tack. Therefore any asymmetry in its sectional shape must be temporary, produced by adjusting movable nose sections, flaps, and the like.

Of course modern aircraft use similar adjustments to enable the wings to support the weight of the plane either at fast cruise (with minimal drag) or at much lower takeoff and landing speeds. Sophisticated solid rigs are set up to work much like the wings of a modern

Fig. 14–6. Modern solid rigs are masterpieces of aerodynamic design and painstaking craftsmanship. This one originally propelled *Wild Turkey*, an 18-square-meter catamaran, but more recently has been used to power a successful hydrofoil sailboat.

jetliner. For upwind sailing and windy reaching where a favorable lift-to-drag ratio is often more important than maximum aerodynamic force, solid rigs are set up with modest camber (curvature) and "sheeted" at low angles of attack (fig. 14–7a). Sailing offwind, when both lift and drag are useful propulsive forces, the rig is set up with a great deal of camber, and slots may be opened to ward off stalling at large angles of attack (fig. 14–7b).

The similarity between solid rigs and airplane wings extends to construction, which in both cases is usually a thin skin stretched over a framework of transverse ribs and longitudinal spars or stringers. Achieving adequate strength without excess weight using this approach demands some very sophisticated and expensive engineering—the approach used in the development of new aircraft. Because boatbuilders rarely have the resources available to aircraft designers, the alternative is patient (and often depressing) build-and-break experimentation.

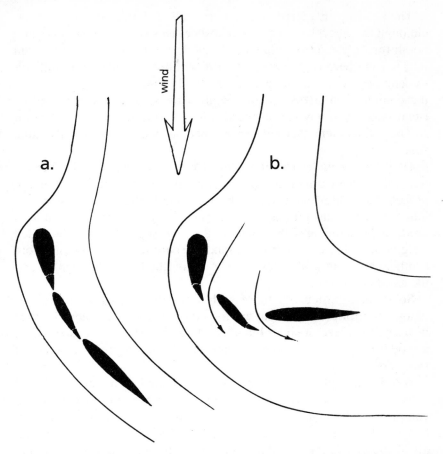

Fig. 14–7. An advanced solid rig set for upwind sailing *(a)* has modest camber to ensure a high lift-to-drag ratio. Off the wind *(b)* camber is dramatically increased by rotating major elements and angling trailing edge flaps on the forward two elements. Air passing through the resulting slot "revitalizes" flow along the leeward side of the rig, thus preventing stalling despite the large angle of attack.

Controlling Advanced Rigs

When an 8-knot wind gusts to 12 knots, the propulsive and heeling forces produced by a rig will more than double unless sail camber is adjusted. Most stayed, bendy rigs offer an excellent set of familiar controls which make it comparatively easy to keep sail forces manageable. Harnessing the sail power of unusual rigs can be more difficult.

The bending characteristics of freestanding rigs are largely built in, although the interplay between mainsheet tension and vang-generated boom thrust has some influence. Rotating masts and wing masts run into trouble because these large, stiff sections are inherently difficult to bend appreciably. One popular method of draft control is to adjust the compression stress on full-length battens, a common presailing ritual familiar to any cat or board sailor. Unfortunately, the range of camber adjustment that can be attained in this way is usually quite small.

Deliberately under-rotating a mast is aerodynamically inefficient, but can reduce camber and depower a sail. A refinement of this approach that is used with some advanced rotating rigs employs special inboard batten and fittings that prevent the battens from exceeding a predetermined angle with respect to the mast (fig. 14–5d). When such a rig is over-rotated, the battens (and sail) are forced to assume more camber, but with a little less mast rotation the battens straighten and the sail flattens out.

Solid rigs, particularly those with adjustable flaps and slots, have unique control problems that are too complex to discuss here. Suffice it to say, the maze of small lines, blocks and push rods housed within a modern wing mast would frighten off all but the most fanatical of tinkerers.

A different type of control problem associated with wing masts and solid rigs is an inability to reef beyond a certain point or to douse sail completely while moored or in a squall. While most of these rigs will behave like weathervanes as long as the wind does not swing too far aft of the beam, the possibility of getting trapped on a wild offwind ride with no way of reducing sail or even rounding up is a frightening one. Practical considerations like this are likely to limit the use of wing masts and solid rigs for some time to come. Nevertheless, they represent a fascinating aspect of sailboat design and one where rapid development is taking place.

15

Sails and Sailmaking in the High-Tech Era

The 1980s have brought a striking number of worthwhile technological developments to the sailmaker's trade. These fall primarily into two areas: new materials, and new techniques for designing and assembling sails. At the moment, the techniques seem to be having a more widespread impact upon the sport of sailing generally, but advanced sailmaking materials are of great importance in some types of racing and will almost certainly come into more general use in the not-too-distant future.

A sail, as described in Chapter 1, is a thin airfoil made of flexible material whose sole purpose is to redirect air flow, and in this way to produce a useful propulsive force. The only practical way yet discovered to build one is to piece it together out of relatively small, flat pieces of fabric called **panels.** Until quite recently, it was standard practice simply to sew together enough straight-sided strips of sailcloth to create a single expanse of material that was large enough to contain the overall outline of the desired sail. Sails made this way had no built-in three-dimensional shape and would therefore lie flat on the sail loft floor. In use, they naturally did not remain flat, but acquired a cambered **flying shape.** This three-dimensional curvature or **draft** was often deliberately induced by making the sail's luff (and sometimes its foot) more convex (or less concave) than the spar or wire to which it was fastened (fig. 15–1a). In addition, because early natural-fiber sailcloths were all highly elastic, fabric stretch played a major role in generating draft, particularly when the wind piped up.

When synthetic sailcloths were introduced following World War II, they proved to be a great deal more stretch-resistant than their natural fiber predecessors. Working with these new, more dimensionally stable materials, sailmakers soon discovered that it was desirable to make sails with a considerable amount of built-in three-dimensional shaping. Built-in camber is often induced by curving the edges of the individual panels so that each panel is a little wider in the middle than at each end (fig. 15–1b). At one time, this effect was achieved by varying the width of the seam overlaps (fig. 15–1c) and the process is still usually known by traditional names like **broadseaming** or **seam dilation.**

By the early 1970s, skilled racing sailors had developed a very good idea of optimum sail shapes for all conditions. Also, by this time, the rigs of racing sailboats had been refined to the point that sail draft, fore-and-aft draft location, and sail twist could all be readily adjusted while under way. Although much fine-scale experimentation with entry angles and camber distribution continues to take place, it is generally conceded today that optimum sail shapes are pretty much the same shapes that had proven optimal during the 1970s. The single most dramatic improvement in today's sails is that they will retain a near-optimum shape across a much wider wind range and with far less attention on the part of the crew.

What makes today's sails more stable than those of the 1970s? In the case of racing boats with "exotic" sail wardrobes, the materials used in constructing these sails obviously play an important part—one that will be discussed later in this chapter. On the other hand, a majority of today's sails are still being built with sailcloths that are very similar to those available in the 1970s, yet are nevertheless more stable, mannerly, and durable. Much of the credit here goes to computerized sailmaking techniques that make it feasible to take better advantage of the strong points in all sorts of sailcloths without driving production costs through the stratosphere.

Computer-Assisted Sail Designing

Try, for a moment, to visualize a sail as a shallow, triangular bag. Wind pressure—the load being carried in the bag—induces tensile

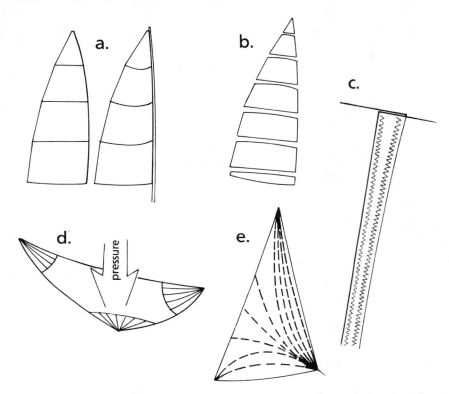

Fig. 15–1. Mechanics of sail shape: *(a)* A convex luff translates into extra sail camber when set on a straighter mast (or concave headstay). *(b)* Additional "built-in" camber is provided by shaping the panels, as in this simple example. *(c)* Traditional broadseaming or seam dilation—not as common as in the past, but the principle still applies with computer-designed sails. *(d)* The wind-induced pressure differential across the sail membrane is like a load being carried in a shallow, tightly stretched bag. *(e)* The tension stresses within the sail membrane follow trajectories determined by the shape of the sail and the way it's supported.

stresses within the plane of the sail material (fig. 15–1d). The pattern of the **stress trajectories** (stress pathways) produced by the wind pressure depends in part upon how this load is distributed, and in part by the way that the sides and corners of the sail are supported. However, in all cases, the stress trajectories follow curved paths that arc across the sail membrane, converging and concentrating in the corners (fig. 15–1e). Ideally, the strongest axis of the sail material will be aligned with these stress trajectories—a goal that has only recently been achieved.

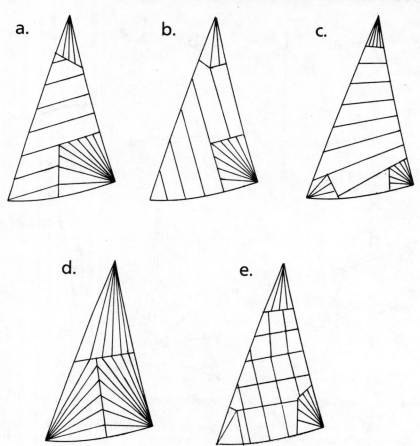

Fig. 15–2. Popular panel layout alternatives: *(a)* Cross cut with radial head and clew inserts. *(b)* Vertical cut with radial inserts. *(c)* Fan cut with inserts. *(d)* Full tri-radial. *(e)* Spider cut (modified vertical with horizontal shaping seams).

As mentioned earlier, the all-important flying shape of a sail—the three-dimensional shape it assumes when set and in use—is determined by a complex combination of edge shaping, broadseaming, sheeting parameters, mast bend/headstay sag, and fabric stretch. The effect of fabric stretch is particularly difficult to control due to major differences in stress levels from one part of the sail to another. Until quite recently, sail panel layouts were rather crude compromises between the desire to align the threadlines of the fabric in the sail with the stresses sustained by the sail, and the need to build the sail sufficiently quickly and economically to show a profit.

Today, thanks largely to the "computer revolution," it is feasible to take a much better approach to managing differential stretch throughout a sail. The key is to use more complex panel layouts that align the strongest axis of each individual panel with the stress trajectories within that part of the sail. Heads, clews, and tacks are now often constructed radially, using a fairly large number of narrow, wedge-shaped panels arranged in fanlike arrays.

Aside from some radial corners, the body of many contemporary sails consists of either conventional horizontal or vertical panels lying parallel to one another (fig. 15–2a, b). In more advanced designs of the horizontal type, panels in the body of the sail may be "rocked" to better align their threadlines with the stress trajectories (fig. 15–2c). Alternatively, the radial "corners" may be extended inward until they meet one another to form the entire sail (fig. 15–2d). Because stresses vary tremendously from one part of a sail to another, it is frequently desirable to change the weight and/or the type of material used for different groups of panels.

Radial sails, particularly tri-radial and starcut spinnakers, have been around a lot longer than computer assisted sailmaking, but in days gone by, the radial portions of the sail were either constructed "flat" (with three-dimensional shaping added in the joining seams) or with the edge shaping in the radial panels determined through experimentation. A particularly complicated approach, still occasionally used today, is to assemble the entire sail using flat radial and/or vertical panels; then slice it up horizontally to introduce the necessary broadseaming (fig. 15–2e).

One of the first successful efforts at computer-assisted sail design was a spinnaker panel pattern developed by Californian John Palmer during the mid-1970s. Palmer has continued working in this field to become a major supplier of software for the sailmaking industry worldwide. At about the same time, Tom Schnackenburg of North Sails successfully adapted a software program from the automotive industry that was used to determine the exact outlines of a set of flat panels needed to smoothly envelope any compound curved surface. With this tool (known as the "tin sail program" because it made no allowances for fabric stretch) it was feasible to break away from conventional cross-cut layouts and begin building radial and vertically paneled sails with reasonably predictable results.

The rationale behind radically constructed sails is self-evident once one appreciates the pattern of stresses sustained by a sail in use, but the reason why vertical panels are sometimes preferred over a horizontal layout is less obvious. In the early 1980s, when vertical-paneled sails were the "latest thing" for racing boats, this layout took better advantage of a peculiarity of the sailcloth manufacturing process. With some of the lighter weight woven sailcloths and early laminates, it was easier to make a material in which the strongest, straightest yarns extended along the length of the roll rather than across it. With more recent material, this difference is no longer significant, but vertical construction is still sometimes preferred because it eliminates highly stressed horizontal seams. Vertical seams run more or less parallel to the stress trajectories in the highly loaded leech of a sail and therefore need not sustain high loads. Even if one does start to fail, there's a better chance that a vertical-cut sail will hold together long enough to lower and repair.

In the current decade, computer-aided sail design has progressed from the outer fringes of the sailmaking world to a normal, everyday tool found in numerous sail lofts. Several popular packages are available to sailmakers from independent software developers, while a few of the larger sailmaking firms have created their own proprietary systems. The more elaborate programs can model a sail on the computer screen in the form of a multicolored, 3-D–perspective presentation, permitting the designer to view it from any angle. More importantly, by changing input data, the designer can rapidly assess the effects of trim adjustments or fine-tune the vertical profile of an overlapping genoa so that it will just clear all the spreader tips when closehauled.

It should be stressed that while sail design programs can help a sailmaker make good sails, they cannot ensure a superior result. The human sail designer must still ultimately determine sail shape and panel layout. Furthermore, there are quirks and gray areas in virtually all existing programs that the designer must learn to manipulate or circumvent. For example, even the most stable sail materials inevitably stretch at least a little while under load, and it is generally left up to the sailmaker to judge how this strain will affect the flying shape of the sail and to consider possible compensatory changes in the design. Some sailmakers are working on stress/strain analyses of sails comparable to the finite element analyses of hull structures that were discussed briefly in Chapter 9. However, at the time of writing, this work is still largely experimental. Eventually, however, it is likely to be of great value in learning how to construct sails that are as light as possible, yet stretch only imperceptibly under sailing loads.

The Cloth's the Thing

In the late 1940s, the ancient art of sailmaking took a great step forward with the introduction of synthetic sailcloths made from polyester and nylon fibers. During the decades that followed, further development was steady and evolutionary, as manufacturers learned to make increasingly stable sailcloths and as sailmakers gradually worked out improved methods for cutting and assembling sails using these materials. For mainsails and headsails, tightly woven polyester sailcloths, heat shrunk after weaving and sometimes further stabilized with plastic resin finishes, were state of the art into the late 1970s. For spinnakers and drifters, lightweight rip-stop nylon materials, stronger but more elastic than polyester cloths on a weight-for-weight basis, became the industry standard.

Interestingly enough, the vast majority of sails today are still being made from woven sailcloths that are, at best, only marginally improved over the materials in use during the 1970s. On the other hand, a highly visible and growing number of racing sails are made of **laminated materials** featuring fibrous reinforcements that are either bonded to a thin plastic film or sandwiched between two such films. Laminated sail materials were developed primarily to minimize elongation under load, and, in this way, to maintain more constant sail shape across the broadest possible wind range. Good ones typically stretch* only a few tenths of a percent under normal working loads as opposed to the 1 or 2 percent that can be expected from high-quality woven sailcloths.

As compared to most conventional woven sailcloths, the chief drawbacks of the laminated materials are reduced toughness and higher cost. Toughness as expressed in terms of resistance to tearing and ability to withstand high shock loads tends, unfortunately, to be

---

*In talking about cloth stretch, a clear distinction should be drawn between elastic and nonelastic deformation. Good sail materials generally behave elastically under normal working loads, but if stressed excessively they will yield and never again return to their original dimensions. Some woven sailcloths have the property of stretching quite noticeably and permanently when first flown, but subsequently stabilizing to a considerable extent. Naturally, anticipating the sail shape implications of this ''one-time'' stretch is a difficult task.

incompatible with good dimensional stability. The reason for this apparent paradox is that resilient materials will "give" to disperse localized loads over a large area, while inextensible materials tend to fail in the most highly stressed spot because stress in adjoining areas remains low. A laminate incorporating a "rip-stop" style of construction—relatively large, strong yarns spaced out over a fragile film—generally offers better tear resistance than an equal-weight laminate comprised of a uniform woven scrim bonded to the film. However, neither will stand up to punishment like a soft-finished woven sailcloth of similar weight.

While the lower tear resistance of laminates may never be entirely overcome, their higher costs are largely artificial and unlikely to hold up over the long term. Weaving and finishing good sailcloth is fundamentally a more complex and demanding task than manufacturing laminates, and, indeed, the day may come when laminated materials become less expensive than woven ones.

Shorter working life is frequently cited as another major drawback for laminated sailcloths, but this is not necessarily a valid criticism, particularly when working life is defined as the time period that a sail retains a truly satisfactory flying shape. While a woven sail might well survive for a few more seasons before it literally disintegrates, most performance-oriented sails are bagged for the last time long before they deteriorate to this extent.

The first laminated sail materials were tested in the 1977 America's Cup defense and, while not outstandingly successful, were almost immediately recognized as having great potential. Before laminated sail materials made their debut, sailcloth manufacturers had only two avenues open in their ongoing quest for greater cloth stability. Tighter weaving and heat shrinking improved bias stability, but generally at the expense of stretch resistance along the threadlines because these processes increased the amount of **crimp** or zig-zag in the yarns. Alternatively, the manufacturer could lock up the weave with a plastic resin treatment. Unfortunately, these firm finishes made the sailcloth stiff to handle, and in most cases the plastic resins broke down after a fairly short time. On the other hand, it should be noted that new one-design sails made from firm-finished woven sailcloths have, to date, usually proven to be faster than laminate sails. This, along with the naturally conservative bent of many one-design sailors, is probably the reason why many small-boat racing classes have been slow to adopt laminate sails.

Mylar™ is the trade name for polyester in film form as manufactured in the United States by DuPont. Evaluated on the basis of equal cross-sectional areas, it is significantly weaker and more elastic than the fine polyester filaments used to make woven sailcloth, because the long chain molecules of the film are entangled in a felt-like mat rather than being aligned with one another in parallel arrays. On the other hand, Mylar film has uniform mechanical properties in all directions (no bias) and, of course, there is no secondary stretch due to crimp.

The first Mylar sail materials consisted of film bonded to a light nylon backing similar to an unfinished spinnaker cloth. The nylon backing was too elastic to improve the stability of the laminate and its sole contribution was to upgrade the dismal tear resistance of the film. However, in the early days of the "Mylar revolution," manufacturers were too busy striving to overcome problems with laminating adhesives that were too brittle or too weak to worry much about maximizing the mechanical efficiency of their products.

However, once the early delamination problems had been licked, manufacturers soon abandoned nylon backings in favor of low-crimp polyester substrates. This second generation of Mylar materials still relied upon the Mylar film to sustain virtually all bias loads, but longitudinal and transverse stresses were shared by film and substrate. Where the dominant loads in a sail ran parallel to one of the threadlines, the substrate could often carry more than its share of the load due to the superior mechanical properties of polyester in its extruded form.

Ironically, the lack of a "bias" in Mylar films is of reduced importance today, as more and more sails are being constructed with numerous small panels oriented to conform closely to the stress trajectories. The third and latest generation of laminated sail materials uses Mylar film as an assembly substrate whose main role is to make the sailcloth airtight and to hold the load-bearing fibers in position. These fibers may take the form of threadlike yarns, but are more often made into flat, narrow bands or tapes so that they can be bonded more securely to the film. Polyester is still often used for reinforcement, but proprietary high-strength fibers like Kevlar 49 and Spectra 1000 are increasingly favored, particularly for large racing sails.

Kevlar was introduced in Chapter 10 as a fiber useful in high-tech composite boatbuilding. It is several times stronger than steel for its weight and lends itself to making very stable, lightweight sails. Its chief shortcoming is durability. Kevlar fibers do not take kindly to being bent sharply or repeatedly. For this reason, luffing a Kevlar sail or handling it roughly on deck can dramatically reduce its lifespan. Some of the latest Kevlar sail materials are reinforced with bands of unidirectional Kevlar fibers sandwiched between two layers of Mylar (or between a Mylar film and a woven polyester scrim). These seem to be more rugged than alternative constructions consisting of woven Kevlar fabric laminated to a single Mylar film because the Kevlar is better protected against both internal chafe with neighboring fibers and external abuse.

Spectra is a highly oriented, extensively cross-linked variety of polyethelene developed by Allied Chemicals. At the time of writing, its use is being championed by one major sailmaking firm, Hood Sails, while other sailmakers have tried it on an experimental basis. Spectra is even stronger than Kevlar for its weight and is substantially more resistant to bending, chafe, and fatigue. If it has an Achilles' heel, it's a tendency to "creep" or gradually elongate under long-term loading. Allied Chemicals and Hood Sails both indicate that this is not a problem with the higher denier (finer filament) versions of Spectra now being produced, but there are many who remain unconvinced. If the optimists are proven correct, expect to see a lot more Spectra sails in future years, not only on racing boats but on performance-oriented cruisers as well.

New Technology in Sail Manufacture

After a computer-aided sail designer has fine-tuned the 3-D shape of a sail and selected the material(s) to be used, it's time to actually build the thing. At this point, the design computer goes to work, quickly determining the precise shapes of the individual panels. In most cases, a subprogram known as a **nesting program** is then used to help position the various panels on the width of yard goods selected in order to minimize waste (fig. 15–3).

It is perfectly feasible to manually outline the panels of even the most complex computer-designed sails by locating the X and Y co-ordinates of a large number of control points on a gridlike plotting table and subsequently connecting these points with a fair line. Obviously, however, this is a laborious process, so an increasing number of sailmakers these days are buying automatic, computer-controlled plotters. Those who continue to manually plot computer-generated

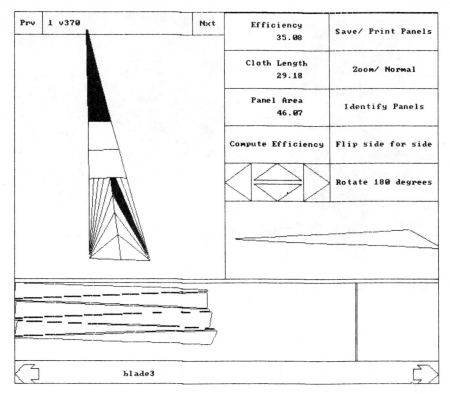

Fig. 15–3. A nesting program allows the panels of a particular sail design to be maneuvered individually on the computer screen until they are fitted together as closely as possible. Output from this program goes directly to a full-scale plotter in many cases.

sail designs generally do so for economic reasons, because while the cost of a design computer and adequate software is only a few thousand dollars, a plotter installation comes to at least $30,000.

Plotters suitable for sailmaking are expensive primarily because they are big machines that must perform reliably with great accuracy (fig. 15–4). Most consist of a rigid table 60 feet or so in length with toothed rails along its edges. These rails guide a carriage that spans the width of the table. The carriage contains a sophisticated servomotor and drive system which engages the toothed rails to propel the car to and fro along the table. A second servomotor and drive mechanism moves the pen carrier back and forth across the width of the car. Both motors run simultaneously and independently at the varying speeds required to control the movements of the pen with accuracy

Fig. 15–4. A typical plotter used in sailmaking. The large computer visible in the center of the background is the "brain" of the machine.

to a fraction of a millimeter. A fairly high-powered computer is, of course, essential to coordinate the operation of the servomotors. Furthermore, the drive mechanisms must be skillfully engineered to prevent the inertia of the carriage from causing inaccuracies as it alternately gathers speed and slows down.

Next step up from a plotter that simply draws the outlines of the panels (together with the seam overlaps) on a length of sailcloth is a similar machine that automatically cuts the panels. Several types of cutters have been tried, but lasers have so far proven most satisfactory. Unfortunately, gaining cutting capability involves more than just buying a suitable laser and attaching it to the plotter carriage in place of a pen. For one thing, the laser cutter (and in many cases its power supply) must be mounted on the carriage, which greatly increases the weight and inertia of the moving parts. Secondly, the laser optics must be precisely focused on the cutting plane, which means that the tabletop and guide rails must be very flat and smooth. Finally, the tabletop itself must be impervious to the laser beam, which usually means heavy metallic construction.

Despite these drawbacks, automated plotter-cutters are already finding their way from the high-volume garment industry into sailmaking. Some of the large sailmaking chains are now installing a high-capacity plotter-cutter in one central location and taking advantage of computer links to feed in design data from their individual sail lofts.

New Emphasis on Battens

The late 1980s will no doubt be remembered as the time when the fully battened mainsail made its way from the multihull/boardsailing fringe to the mainstream of recreational sailing. Using a few stiff rods to support and shape a flexible foil is hardly a new idea—the necessary inspiration can be gleaned from a superficial inspection of any flying insect, bat, or fish. The principal reason why the majority of sailboats today still lack luff-to-leech battens in their mainsails is once again historically rooted in racing regulations. At one time, mainsail roach area was limited by restricting the length and number of battens. Even after girth measurements for racing mainsails became commonplace, relatively short battens remained the norm until recently.

Full-length (more accurately, full-girth) battens offer several important advantages. Most importantly, they stretch the sailcloth uniformly without creating a hard spot or stress concentration where each individual batten ends. The result is a smoother, more aerodynamically efficient sail that tends to retain a desirable flying shape over a longer lifespan. Indeed, many ''blown out'' mainsails can be given a new lease on life with the addition of one or more full-length battens.

A second advantage is the ability to support more roach area where this is not restricted by racing rules or the proximity of a fixed backstay. A third is the ability of the long battens to quiet the sail while it is luffing.

Of course, there are also drawbacks. Longer battens and batten pockets add weight and cost to the sail. Furthermore, the substantial forward thrust of the battens can cause a great deal of wear and tear at the batten-luff intersection—a problem that sailmakers have not yet managed to fully resolve without resorting to elaborate batten end fittings. Even the task of finding batten stock that is sufficiently light and stiff, yet rugged, is a significant challenge. Battens for multihull mainsails with huge roach areas are often custom-made using exotic materials and may cost as much as the sail itself! On the balance, however, full-length battens are a real asset and will probably be the norm aboard most sailboats by the turn of the century.

The Frontiers of Sailmaking Today

The main thrust of leading-edge sailmaking over the past ten years has been toward sails that either change shape as little as possible during gusts and lulls or, better yet, change shape automatically to optimally suit the conditions of the moment. It has proven quite possible—and often worthwhile—to build fractional and unstayed rigs that bend aft and to leeward during puffs, causing the mainsails set on these rigs to twist off and flatten near the head. On the other hand, it is exceedingly difficult to devise jibs, genoas, and spinnakers that will flatten automatically in gusts rather than get fuller under the influence of increased luff sag and fabric stretch. The line of development that has shown greatest promise to date involves the use of a band of strong, inelastic material to resist stretch in the "belly" of the genoa while intentionally building the leach area so it will "give" and fall off slightly during gusts (fig. 15–5). Much work remains to be done in this area.

Laminated sail materials are currently associated almost exclusively with serious racing, but there is reason to believe that they will eventually find more widespread application. Efforts are under way to develop softer, more manageable laminates. Currently, there are hybrid materials available for cruising sails that feature a Mylar film sandwiched between two layers of woven polyester, but this approach would not appear to be a very economical one. Of course, with the increasing popularity of roller furling systems (see Chapter 16), soft, limp sailcloth is no longer the priority it once was aboard many cruising boats.

It is becoming evident that there is a limit to the shape stability that can be achieved by building sails with all the load-bearing fibers arranged to conform exactly to a computer-generated stress map. The problem is that the stress trajectories shift significantly depending upon how the sail is set, sheeted, and so forth. To help handle these variations, one major North American sailcloth manufacturer—Dimension Sailcloth—has developed laminates in which the reinforcing yarns are laid down at three different angles that span a 12-degree range.

Another approach to this problem, as well as a method of reducing the material wastage that occurs when radial panels are cut from conventional roll goods, involves bonding Kevlar tapes to either an assembled sail (see dustcover photograph) or to the panels prior to

Fig. 15–5. A Kevlar-reinforced panel radiating up from the tack helps to restrain the central portion of this genoa from bulging during gusts. Developments along these lines may eventually lead to headsails that effectively flatten as the wind builds.

assembly. If desired, some of the reinforcing tapes can be arranged at varying angles to accommodate changes in stress trajectories caused by sheeting variations, reefing, and so forth. One of the leaders in this field, Sobstad Sailmakers, is working up a patented process in which each panel of a sail is custom made. This system utilizes horizontal construction with 60-inch-wide panels, but the reinforcing fibers in every part of each panel are laid out in orientations and densities appropriate for that section of the finished sail.

As in the past, the majority of future developments in the field of sails and sailmaking will no doubt be small and incremental. Thanks to accurate computer plotting and cutting, the intricate bi-radial and tri-radial jibs and genoas being produced today are, on the average, considerably smoother and more wrinkle-free than those being made just a few years ago. No doubt the actual construction of sails will continue to be done by hand for some time to come, but with adhesive technology advancing rapidly, it is probably only a matter of time before they are routinely being glued rather than sewn together!

16

A Revolution
in Sail-Handling Equipment

There is no hard-and-fast dividing line between rigging and deck gear. Taken together, they form the sail-handling system—probably the single most elaborate (and often costly) system aboard a sailboat. My choice of equipment to discuss in this chapter is somewhat subjective, in that much of the gear discussed here could easily have been included in the preceeding sections on rigs and rigging. In general, the focus in this chapter will be on newly developed equipment that facilitates sail management and reduces the physical demands of crewing. Without question, there has been spectacular progress in this area over the past few years.

Big Boats, Big Loads

While it may be true that the real work of sailing is done by the wind, sails must be hoisted and trimmed to get the boat moving and keep everything working efficiently. Pitted against the forces generated by any fair-sized yacht, the muscle power of even the strongest crew is puny indeed. For this reason, deck gear is ordinarily rigged to provide a **mechanical advantage** (abbreviated MA), so a small force acting over a large distance will be converted into a large force acting over a small distance. Otherwise it would be absolutely impossible to handle any sailboat larger than a rather small dinghy in any kind of breeze.

There are really only four ways to achieve a mechanical advantage: levers, pulley systems (tackles), interconnected hydraulic cylinders, and wedges (inclined planes). All four are commonly used aboard sailboats with levers and tackles being the most common.

Winches are devices which look a little like tackles, but actually operate as levers. In recent years the trend has been to use winches more and more to replace other mechanical-advantage systems. Why? Because, first, a winch, unlike a tackle, allows line to be recovered freehand and very quickly when loads are light, yet can be promptly brought into play when needed. Second, a geared winch can provide an extremely high mechanical advantage that could only be duplicated by a cumbersome tackle incorporating enormous lengths of line. Third, the development of refined self-tailing mechanisms has greatly improved operator convenience. And finally, a separate invention, the modern **lock-off**, or **rope clutch**, has made it feasible to use a single expensive winch to handle up to half a dozen separate functions (fig. 16–1). Since winches play such a basic role in the gearing of modern sailboats, it is worth explaining them in some detail.

Fig. 16–1. Modern rope clutches on this yacht allow two winches to handle six controls.

The Basics of Winch Design

As mentioned a bit earlier, a winch is a lever-action mechanism. To visualize this, imagine a simple winch consisting of a cylindrical drum mounted on a central shaft (fig. 16-2 left). The line being tensioned comes off one side of the drum as a tangent to a circle. This means that, in effect, the load is attached to the end of a short lever whose length is equal to the radius of the winch drum (or to be strictly accurate, the radius of the drum plus the radius of the tensioned line). To turn the winch drum, a longer lever—the winch handle—is attached to the drum and a force applied to its end. Disregarding frictional losses, the mechanical advantage of this simple winch is the ratio of length of the handle (measured from the center of the central shaft) to the radius of the winch drum.

Geared winches, although more complicated, are also based en-

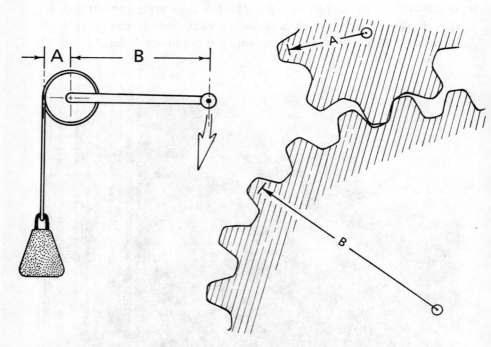

Fig. 16-2. All winches, geared or otherwise, work on the lever principle. Total mechanical advantage is the multiplicative product of all the leverage ratios B:A that occur in that particular winch.

tirely upon the lever principle, because once again, the ratio between the radii of each driving gear and the corresponding driven gear is the mechanical advantage for that stage in a gear train (fig. 16–2 right). These intermediate MAs are multiplied to obtain the MA of the winch as a whole.

With most sailing winches, the loaded line is generally attached to the winch solely by friction that comes from taking two to four wraps of line around the winch drum. This makes friction a two-edged sword. Without it, winching would be impossible; but on the other hand, friction associated with moving parts inside the winch, as well as the line deforming and rubbing against itself on the outside of the drum, result in efficiency losses that are rarely less than 20 percent. In the case of inferior or poorly maintained winches, frictional losses can reach 50 percent.

Obviously, the reduction of internal friction is a matter of great importance in winch design. Because the line leading onto the winch pulls the drum sideways against the central shaft with a force approximately equal to the load on the line itself, the bearing between the main shaft and the inside of the drum is the single most important potential source of friction within a winch. Most contemporary winch manufacturers use roller bearings here (rather than sleeve-type bearings) in the majority of their models.

Geared winches contain two or more secondary shafts to support the elements of their gear trains. Although the side loads on these secondary bearing surfaces are generally lower than upon the main shaft, the friction adds up, particularly in the more complicated multi-speed winches. Consequently, an increasing number of manufacturers are providing roller bearings or ball bearings for these secondary shafts as well. Even the basic winch handle can be improved in this regard. Ball-bearing grips now fitted on some premium winch handles can noticeably reduce the overall friction in a winch system.

As mentioned earlier, not all frictional losses take place internally. Both braided synthetic lines and wire ropes absorb a significant amount of energy as they bend, flatten, and spiral their way up the winch drum. For this reason, large winch drums are generally preferable to small ones despite the fact that a larger radius drum will require higher gearing to achieve a given mechanical advantage. In addition, a larger drum requires fewer turns to provide adequate grip making it quicker to load and unload.

Virtually every contemporary winch incorporates a ratchet mechanism to prevent the drum from unwinding when pressure on the handle is eased. Single-speed winches generally also have a secondary ratchet mechanism to permit the handle to be repositioned by rotating it in the "reverse" direction, while the primary ratchet holds the drum from slipping. Both ratchets consist of one or more spring-loaded pawls that bear against an array of saw tooth indentations on the inside of the drum. The characteristic clicking sound made by a winch as it spins is made by the pawls dropping into the valleys between the sawtooth ridges. Increasing the number of pawls in a winch enables it to sustain a larger load safely because the stress of each pawl is reduced (although on the debit side, friction is slightly increased).

In order to coax a line to spiral smoothly up a winch drum without binding or riding over itself, both the lead angle of the line and the shape of the drum itself must be carefully planned. Most modern winches accept a line that slopes up to the drum at an angle of 4 to 8 degrees. To help ensure that the line approaches at an acceptable angle, the bottom of most winch drums is sharply flared. An additional refinement seen in many winches is a slight top-to-bottom increase in the diameter of the working portion of the drum. This helps to ensure that the line climbs the drum instead of bunching up and possibly riding over itself.

Multi-speed winches can be shifted from higher or lower gear ratios as the load warrants. Two-speed models are far and away the most popular multi-speed designs because a very simple mechanism works well. In most cases, the handle is linked directly to the drum via the upper pawls for high gear. When the direction of handle rotation is reversed, the direct drive is bypassed and an idler gear near the base of the winch swings to engage a slower, more powerful geared drive.

Three-speed winches require much more elaborate gear shift mechanisms activated either by repeatedly reversing the direction of handle rotation and/or via a shift control in the base. Their use is primarily restricted to larger racing yachts where a few seconds saved in sheeting the genoa can justify the considerable complexity and extra expense.

These days, **self-tailing** is an increasingly popular winch option because it enables a single crew member to grind in a long stretch of line without interruption and eliminates the need for remote cleats. In addition, it permits both hands to be used to apply extra force to the winch handle (although the amount of added pressure obtained in

Fig. 16–3. The modern self-tailing winch has proven itself, not only for shorthanded cruising but for racing as well. One advantage is that a line wound on the drum can be tensioned instantly without first having to uncleat it.

this way is often surprisingly small). Atop the main drum of any self-tailing winch is a secondary drum with a single ribbed groove to grip the line (fig. 16–3). This secondary drum is attached to the main drum so both rotate together. The other element in the self-tailing mechanism is a motionless arm that projects over one side of the upper drum. This arm guides the line from the main drum into the self-tailer and strips it out of the self-tailer just before it has completed a full circle. Ideally, the groove in the secondary drum is shaped so that the line in the tailer is in vertical alignment with the line on the primary drum.

The **power ratio** or **velocity ratio** of a winch is really just its theoretical mechanical advantage—the mechanical advantage that would be achieved if the winch was totally friction-free. At one time, this was the only figure available from winch manufacturers, but some are now providing actual or measured mechanical-advantage data. This information is valuable in comparing the different winches within a model line, and in certain cases can also be used for limited comparisons between makes. However, don't assume either that all manufacturers will conduct their tests in the same way or that the winch mounted on your boat will do as well as the one the manufacturer tested in his lab. Lab measurements are typically performed using relatively few turns of small-diameter wire rope and a large tailing weight (later subtracted from the load). Like the EPA's fuel economy estimates for new cars, a winch manufacturer's performance data can probably be regarded as optimal rather than average. Therefore, when in doubt, it's generally safest to go up to the next size of winch.

Lines and Cleats

As anyone who has ever rigged one knows, the typical sailboat seems to be made of cordage. Sheets, halyards, and control lines together will commonly add up to hundreds of feet, and thousands in the largest, most complex racing boats. Not surprisingly, there is an enormous diversity in cordage available, with varying combinations or properties to suit different purposes. An ideal line for most rigging applications would be strong, durable, flexible yet virtually stretch-free, comfortable to handle, light in weight, and not prone to absorbing water. Preferably, it would also be inexpensive, but unfortunately this is rarely the case with cordage that meets the other criteria listed. On the other hand, in applications where one or another of the physical properties can be sacrificed somewhat, it is often possible to economize considerably.

Braided construction has largely supplanted **twisted construction** because it allows a stronger, less stretchy and more supple line to be made from the same amount of fibrous material. Most modern cordage for sailing applications is known as **double braid** because it consists of two braided components, a tubular cover that surrounds an inner core. However, when maximum strength and stretch resistance are essential the core may consist of a bundle of longitudinal fibers. As always, there is a trade-off involved: using parallel fibers for the core tends to make the line more vulnerable to being damaged as a result of twisting and kinking.

Polyester is far and away the most popular material for running rigging because it is modestly priced, resistant to environmental degradation, and has good mechanical properties. By subjecting their line to tension and elevated temperatures during manufacture—a procedure know as **prestretching**—the elasticity of a polyester line can be reduced to just a few percent under normal working loads. Unfortunately, suppleness tends to suffer, but low stretch is of greatest importance for halyards, which tend to be handled less than other lines.

For demanding applications where minimum line stretch and weight may represent important advantages, a variety of "high tech" lines are now available. Kevlar or Spectra fibers are usually used in the cores of these lines surrounded with a conventional polyester cover. Kevlar, in particular, is susceptible both to sun damage and chafe, so a protective outer sheath is very important to ensure reasonable longevity. Because Kevlar fibers are prone to fail as a consequence of rubbing against each other, it is also desirable to use blocks with special "Kevlar-scored" sheaves (fig. 16–4a). Likewise, sheave diameter should be at least forty times line diameter, a standard that is often difficult to meet. These drawbacks notwithstanding, Kevlar line offers approximately a 75 percent weight savings over wire rope with comparable mechanical attributes and therefore is widely used aboard contemporary racing boats.

Cordage containing Spectra fiber has only been available for about four years at the time of this writing, but it would appear to be a significant improvement over Kevlar for many applications. Even

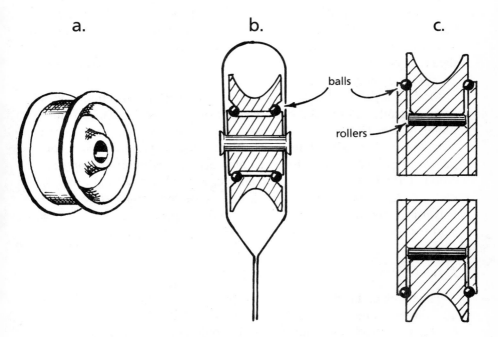

Fig. 16–4. Details of modern blocks: (a) Kevlar-scored sheave. (b) Cross section showing design of a typical small-boat low-friction block in which the same ball bearings sustain both radial and side loads. (c) Typical low-friction block for big boats with a separate race of roller bearings to handle the high-radial loads.

lighter than Kevlar of corresponding strength, it has proven more resistant to chafe and sharp bending. Its propensity to "creep" or gradually elongate with long-term loading is unlikely to pose a serious problem with running rigging because these lines are ordinarily adjusted quite often while under way. High cost aside, Spectra is an excellent choice for halyards, particularly when the alternative is wire rope, as well as for spinnaker sheets and guys.

Cam cleats and jam cleats are really too old by now to be considered new sailing technology, although significant improvements in the design of these standbys continue to be made from time to time. On the other hand, a derivative of the cam cleat—the rope clutches and lock-offs mentioned earlier—are a recent and important development. The simplest lock-offs are nothing more than a large, single-cam cleat that can be opened with a lever under load (fig. 16-5). Sophisticated designs (fig. 16-1) use a more complex mechanism to obtain three advantages. First, they allow a highly loaded line to be eased out without having to take up the strain first with a winch. Second, with the control lever in the "closed" position they behave like one-way valves for a rope, allowing the line to be winched in, but holding it fast when the tail is eased with virtually no backsliding. Most up-to-date designs also treat the line quite gently, which was not always the case with earlier versions.

Modern rope clutches used in combination with low-friction blocks have radically altered the deck layouts of many sailboats. Offshore racing yachts that might once have had a dozen winches now need only four to six. **Multiline cheek blocks** are frequently used to organize lines leading from the mast area back along the cabin top (fig. 16-1). Larger racing boats sometimes also employ a second array of cheek blocks "downstream" of a battery of rope clutches so that a halyard or control line can be tensioned using either a port-side or starboard-side winch depending upon which is more convenient.

Low-Friction Blocks and Travelers

The block and tackle is still a basic rigging element aboard virtually all sailboats, and in the case of most small craft, the primary means of obtaining mechanical advantage. The ball- and roller-bearing blocks developed over the past two decades have played a starring role in the evolution of modern sail-handling systems. Peter and Olaf Harken deserve recognition as pioneers in the development of practical low-

Fig. 16–5. "Jammers" such as these are less costly than cam-action rope clutches, but require that a highly loaded line be pretensioned by the winch for release.

friction blocks, and their well-known Wisconsin-based company continues to break new ground in the area of sailing-system development.

Before good low-friction blocks became available, it was typical to experience frictional losses of 10 to 20 percent for each sheave in a tackle system. As a consequence, multipart tackles were often grossly inefficient. Substituting ball-bearing blocks, it was often feasible to eliminate several parts in the tackle system for a substantial gain in handling speed and no loss of force. In addition, because there is almost no frictional penalty associated with adding extra turning blocks to a ball-bearing system, many control setups can now be designed to maximize crewing convenience in ways that would have been impractical with earlier equipment.

Small and medium-sized ball-bearing blocks typically have twin ball-races recessed into the side of the sheave and shaped so that the same balls can sustain both radial and lateral loads (fig. 16–4b). The balls are usually made of plastic rather than metal to avoid corrosion problems and minimize the need for lubrication. **Torlon**™ is the trade name of a mustard-yellow plastic developed by Amoco that is particularly prized for bearings because of its great strength and hardness. In most designs, the balls are contained by some sort of open cage, so that the dirt and salt can be flushed out easily.

Load-bearing capability in a ball-bearing block is directly related to the area of contact between the balls and their races. Bearing surface can be dramatically increased by substituting rollers for balls to handle the radial loads (fig. 16–4c), but friction, too, rises more or less in proportion. Because the stresses on hardware climb exponentially with increasing boat size, low-friction blocks were surprisingly slow to find their way onto big boats. However, during the mid-1980s a number of manufacturers resolved the engineering problems associated with very high loads, and now low-friction big-boat systems are finding widespread use. As usual, racing machines lead the way, but an increasing number of cruising sailors and cruising yacht builders are favoring this equipment simply because it can make sailing a lot easier.

Nowhere is the improvement in handling more evident than in mainsheet travelers. Until recently, most traveler cars ran on several pairs of small wheels that rolled on the underside of a flanged metal track. Such traveler cars are inherently poor at handling nonvertical loads, and they impose very high point loads on both their wheels and the track.

The **recirculating ball traveler**, again initially introduced by Harken, has gained wide acceptance of late because it represents a genuinely better solution (fig. 16–6). In a traveler system of this type, two continuous lines of plastic balls bear directly against the underside of twin V-shaped grooves in the side of the aluminum traveler track. As the car rolls down the track, each ball in turn reaches the end of the car where it is deflected outward along a curved tunnel which guides it back to begin the cycle again.

Recirculating ball travelers spread the load quite evenly over a large number of balls and a substantial length of track. They are also very effective at handling nonvertical loads. Thanks largely to this second advantage, they are being used effectively in unusual ways, such as for genoa sheet lead tracks that can be adjusted fore and aft while under load. Even more novel is their use aboard huge ocean-racing multihulls as a means of attaching the mainsail luff, headboard, and inboard batten ends to the aft edge of enormous wing masts.

It would be impossible, in one chapter, to mention all the clever hardware innovations that have found a place aboard contemporary sailboats. However, one gear item—the **ratchet block**—has quite quickly come into nearly universal use on performance-oriented small craft. Ratchet blocks are low-friction blocks that incorporate an internal mechanism very similar to the pawl arrangement used in winches. When engaged, this ratchet prevents the sheave from rotat-

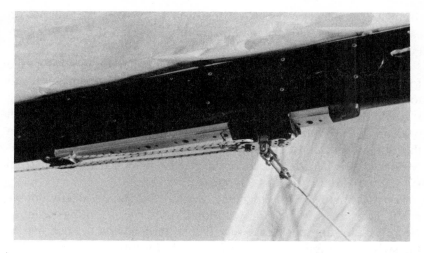

Fig. 16–6. Versatile recirculating ball-type travelers are finding many applications aboard modern sailboats. This is a simple but powerful boom vang.

ing in one direction. The sheave itself is textured or grooved so that it will grip the line tenaciously, just as a winch drum holds a line as long as a little tension is maintained on the tail of that line. This allows the sailor to easily hand-hold a sheet or guy for long periods, ready to make instantaneous adjustments without uncleating.

Luff Foils and Reefing/Furling Systems

Twin-groove luff foils are invaluable aboard offshore-racing yachts because they allow a replacement headsail to be run up and sheeted while the old one is still at work. However, streamlined headstay foils have failed to gain any significant following among cruising sailors. Early claims of dramatically improved pointing ability could not be substantiated, and it is vastly more difficult to control a lowered head-sail on a windy foredeck when the luff is not hanked to the forestay.

On the other hand, during the 1970s and 1980s, roller reefing and furling for headsails truly came of age. Well-engineered systems have, by now, completed countless long ocean voyages without difficulties, and only an exceptionally closed-minded sailor can continue to dis-miss the breed as inherently unseaworthy. As for a skipper who both races and cruises, many systems are now designed so that the furling drum and upper swivel can be removed to convert the unit into a twin-groove headfoil capable of accommodating full-hoist racing genoas.

The difference between **roller reefing** and **roller furling** is that the former can only be used for sail storage while the latter enables a sail to be rolled up partially to reduce its area for heavy weather. Furling systems can frequently get away with wrapping the sail around an ordinary 1 × 19 wire, often the forestay itself. Reefable systems, on the other hand, must be capable of handling much higher top-to-bottom twisting loads and therefore need luff foils constructed from substantial alloy extrusions (fig. 16–7).

For maximum weight efficiency, the luff foil should ideally double as the forestay as is the case with units from Sterns Sailing Systems. However, this approach puts very high axial loads on the bearings in the swivel assemblies at each end. Largely for this reason, most reefing/furling gear features an extrusion that envelops the forestay and sustains only torsional loads. Typically the gear is assembled from 6- to 8-foot segments which are slid over the forestay one at a time and locked together.

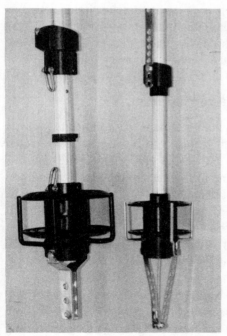

Fig. 16–7. Most headsail roller reefing/ furling systems utilize a substantial aluminum extrusion to resist the torsional loads that occur while reefed.

One common problem with roller reefing is that the shape of the reefed (partially rolled) sail can leave a lot to be desired. Furling headsails are usually designed to get much of their camber from positive luff around and only a little from broadseaming (see Chapter 15), because a sail that had too much built-in shaping would wrinkle excessively when furled. Unfortunately, when a sail is rolled up evenly from head to tack, the shape of the convex luff curve remains unchanged while the sail gets smaller, so camber naturally increases. More fabric stretch and headstay sag associated with the building wind only makes matters worse.

In the search for a reefable headsail that will get flatter rather than fuller as it is rolled in, sailmakers and hardware manufacturers have been experimenting with several interesting approaches. One is to sew a tapered foam pad just behind the luff rope of the sail so that each turn of the furling gear will remove more material from near the center of the luff than at each end. Another is to add a second ball-bearing swivel to the tack fitting (similar to the one on the head slider of all roller-reefing systems). In theory, when neither the head nor the tack of the sail is attached directly to the luff foil extrusion, the furling action will begin by removing only the "excess luff round" near the center of the luff. In practice, this arrangement only seems to work on headsails that have fairly full (convex) luff curves. It also helps if several feet of boltrope are cut away above the tack and below the head.

For mainsail reefing it has been difficult to improve upon conventional jiffy or slab reefing, although numerous alternatives have been tried. Rigging systems for jiffy reefing have been gradually improved so that now it is often feasible for one person to quickly put in or shake out a reef without leaving the safety of the cockpit. A solid, spring-loaded vang will eliminate the need to adjust a topping lift or lower the boom into a boom crotch while reefing.

Until recently, the only successful roller furling/reefing mainsails have been in-the-mast installations. These work nicely, when properly designed, but require a special mast extrusion capable of housing the furled sail and roller foil mechanism. In addition a specially rigged boom is required, and the mainsail itself must be cut (or recut) with a concave leech and no battens. Lately, a number of rigging firms, lead by Hood Sailing Systems, have come out with in-the-boom mainsailing furling/reefing systems. Unlike the rather unsatisfactory roller-reefing booms of the 1960s, the new gear operates by rotating a spindle that is housed within a large but conventionally shaped boom. The sail itself passes through a slot in the top of the boom. With in-the-boom reefing, a conventional vang or mid-boom mainsheet can be fitted. Reefed sail shape is usually quite satisfactory so long as the mainsail used doesn't have too much built-in camber. Mainsails with battens and a normal roach can be accommodated, and, of course, there is no need to replace an existing mast.

A Hydraulic Edge

As a method of power transfer, hydraulics offers unparalleled versatility and controllability. There are two types of hydraulics used in modern sailboats. The first are the relatively simple hand-pumped systems used much like winches or tackles as a means of boosting mechanical advantage and as a method of remote control. The second, found most often on large cruising yachts, employ power-driven pumps to operate a wide variety of hydraulic functions, often at the touch of a button. This new technology of automated sailing will be discussed in more detail a bit later, but both kinds of hydraulics work in much the same way.

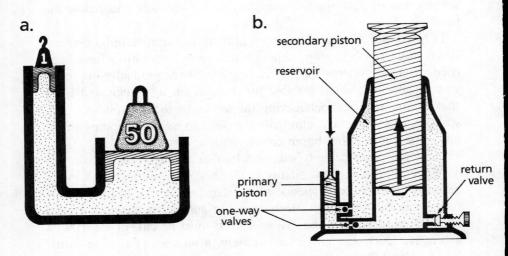

Fig. 16–8. Basic hydraulic systems: (a) With the ratio of piston areas being 50 to 1, this simple system is in equilibrium as shown. (b) Even a $10 hydraulic jack contains all five of the elements found in the most complex hydraulic controls.

Although most sailors still regard them as complex, the basic operating principles of hydraulics are amazingly simple.

Figure 16–8a shows a simple hydraulic lifting device involving two interconnected cylinders with pistons of different sizes. This system can be used to generate a mechanical advantage in direct proportion to the ratio of piston areas. The 1-ton hydraulic jacks available in auto parts stores for about $10 are barely more complicated, and work in precisely this way (fig. 16–8b).

There are five components found in all hydraulic systems: The **driver** is the engine, motor, or muscle that powers the **hydraulic pump**. This pump boosts fluid pressure and moves liquid within the system. **Valves** are used to regulate the flow rate of the hydraulic fluid, thus stopping, starting, and adjusting the action of the system. They are frequently also used to admit or release some fluid from an external reservoir to allow for volume changes in the system as it works. The **hydraulic motor** or **actuator** applies force to the load. Finally, of course, there is the **load** itself that must be moved to accomplish useful work.

Hydraulic pumps can be piston types, as described above, or rotary-action pumps. The former are simpler, but the later provide a continuous stream of pressurized hydraulic fluid rather than an intermittent flow (fig. 16–9a, b). For this reason, they are preferred for hydraulic systems that incorporate several actuators driven by a single pump. Actuators are nothing more than pumps operating in reverse. Linear actuators are the familiar hydraulic cylinders often used for sailboat-rigging controls. Rotary actuators designed to produce continuous rotation are often called hydraulic motors, although technically the term motor can be correctly applied to any type of hydraulic actuator. They are very compact and quiet running considering the torque and power they produce.

Steering is a common application of hydraulics aboard cruising yachts, because it offers great mechanical advantage with no need for connections between wheel and stern gear save some slender, flexible hoses. Manual hydraulic steerers use a pump connected to the steering wheel shaft and either a rotary actuator on the rudder shaft or, more commonly, a double-acting linear ram connected to the rudder shaft by a crank arm (fig. 16–9c).

Very large yachts sometimes have power-assisted hydraulic steering fundamentally similar to the arrangements found on most trucks and larger automobiles. Power-assisted hydraulic steerers not only in-

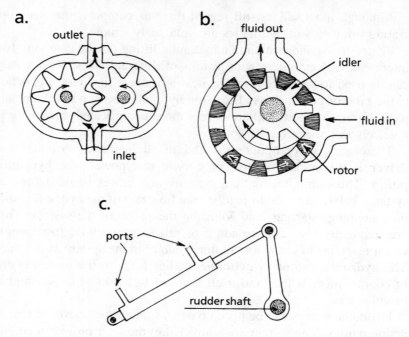

Fig. 16-9. Rotary hydraulic pumps provide a continuous supply of pressurized fluid. Geared pumps *(a)* and rotor/vane pumps *(b)* are two common types. Hydraulic steering in most sailboats is accomplished by a double-acting hydraulic cylinder acting through a crank arm.

crease response speed and reduce steering effort but make it easy to incorporate an autopilot into the steering system. With mechanical steering, the autopilot must incorporate a powerful servomechanism to drive the mechanical steering linkage, but with power-assisted hydraulic steering, the autopilot control needs only to open and close the appropriate valves.

Racing sailors discovered hydraulic rig controls in the early 1970s, and for a while they were the latest high-tech status symbol. It is perhaps unfortunate that the early association of hydraulic controls with Grand Prix offshore racing was made so strongly, because in many cases, a hydraulic device is both simpler and cheaper than its mechanical equivalent. Any time a mechanical advantage of twenty to one or more is called for and the operating range of the control is fairly short, there is a good chance the hydraulics is worth considering. Hydraulic boom vangs were the first of the "solid" vangs, although mechanical versions are now widely used aboard smaller

Fig. 16–10. Hydraulic jumper struts on a 12-meter mast *(a)* are a straightforward, lightweight system for adjusting top mast bend. Two powerful hydraulic jacks at the base of the mast *(b)* are used to tension the rig prior to sailing.

yachts. Hydraulics is also used regularly for backstays, outhauls, and the fine control features of double-ended main sheets and runner systems. A **hydraulic load cell** (nothing more than a very short hydraulic ram connected to a pressure gauge in the cockpit) is often placed in series with the forestay of a contemporary fractional rigged boat in order to measure forestay tension and reset the running backstays properly after each tack.

Big, elaborate racing boats also employ hydraulics for a myriad of other functions. **Jumper struts** may incorporate hydraulic rams as a means of adjusting top mast bend while under way (fig. 16–10 top). When it becomes difficult to tension the shrouds sufficiently using conventional turnbuckles (because the threads are likely to be damaged), a hydraulic ram at the mast base can be used to jack up the whole rig (fig. 16–10 bottom). With this arrangement, once the proper shroud tension is achieved, metal wedges are slipped under the mast butt to lock everything into place.

Push-Button Sailing

The late 1980s have brought a worldwide population explosion of really big sailboats ranging upward from 60-foot performance cruisers to mega-yachts of 120 feet or more. While to some extent this is obviously an indication of sociological and cultural changes, it could not have happened without dependable equipment enabling small crews to readily manage thousands of square feet of sail.

Of course, for every mega-yacht, there are a hundred more modest cruisers in the 40-to-60-foot range, and the owners of these vessels, too, are quickly coming to appreciate the virtues of power-assisted sail (and anchor) handling. One result is that the average size of cruising boats is on the rise. Another is that sail cruising is attracting more participants and older ones now that physical strength and a durable back are no longer the limitations that they once were. Indeed, for the first time in history, sailing has largely ceased to be an activity that appeals primarily to tough and perhaps slightly masochistic young males.

Most powered windlasses, chain gypsies and winches for sailboats are electric, using either 120-watt or 24-volt direct current from the ship's batteries. The motors used are similar (and occasionally identical) to automotive starter motors because they need to produce lots of torque, but generally only in short bursts.

On the positive side, electric winches are simple and reasonably inexpensive to manufacture. Most consist of an electric drive unit, mounted below deck, that is coupled to the gear train of a standard manual winch. Most electric winches can be hand cranked for racing

Fig. 16–11. A Lewmar hydraulic powerpack and its microprocessor control unit designed to handle nine separate functions aboard a large yacht.

or as a backup, and incorporate a safety switch to prevent the electric drive from being operated with a winch handle in place.

On the debit side, electric winches draw a lot of current, especially when heavily loaded and approaching stall. They are also almost totally allergic to water, and may burn out if used hard for extended periods. Furthermore, to minimize voltage drop, long runs of expensive, very heavy gauge cable must be used whenever a high-output electric motor is located a significant distance from the main batteries.

To overcome these shortcomings, hydraulically driven winches and other powered accessories are an increasingly viable alternative. Lewmar in the U.K. has been a leader in developing efficient hydraulic systems of this type. Interestingly, Lewmar has elected to retain electric power at the heart of their systems by chosing electric motors to drive the central hydraulic pumps. At first glance, this might appear to represent a step backward in terms of overall efficiency, because an extra energy transfer step is introduced between burning the diesel fuel and spinning the winch drum. In practice, however, net efficiency is somewhat improved in most cases, partly because the electric motor(s) can be located adjacent to the batteries for minimal current loss, and partly because the hydraulic system can be regulated to keep the pump motors running at near optimum speed.

Perhaps the greatest advantage of these centralized hydraulic power packs (fig. 16–11) is their ability to manage complex systems with several winches, furler drives, a windlass, and with perhaps a few linear hydraulic cylinders for rigging or centerboard control. A battery of electronically controlled valves directs hydraulic fluid to whichever winch or other actuator is currently selected with feedback from pressure sensors in the system to avert overloading. If too many functions are simultaneously selected, some will automatically be put on "hold" until hydraulic capacity is available. To avoid potentially vulnerable wiring, commands to the central power pack in a Lewmar system are sent via plastic air lines using pneumatic squeeze bulbs.

Push-button sailing is a wide-open field, and so far the focus has been upon "automatic brawn" as represented by the new generation of powered winches and windlasses just discussed. On the other hand, rapid advances are also being made in the area of "automatic sailing brains"—computerized sailing aids and navigation functions. This area—perhaps the fastest changing in all of sailing—is the subject of the next chapter.

17

Electronics for Sailing

Although knotmeters, wind sensors, and radios have been a part of big-boat sailing for over twenty years now, the microchip revolution has provided previously undreamed-of capabilities at remarkably modest prices. Consequently, recreational sailors are using marine electronics far more widely than ever before. Whether this trend has eroded the basic simplicity and "naturalness" of our sport is open to debate, but by and large it appears that sailors are enthusiastic about this new technology.

An in-depth treatment of sailing electronics would require a substantial book rather than a single chapter. Accordingly, the discussion here aims only to introduce some of the ways electronics can assist the recreational sailor. I have decided to further narrow the field of view for this chapter by emphasizing those electronic aids that are linked specifically to sailing applications. For this reason, most "general-purpose" marine electronics like depthsounders, radar, and radio telephones will be mentioned only in passing, despite the fact that these tools are every bit as valuable aboard sailboats as on power craft. For those readers who want to know more about marine electronics in general, several good, down-to-earth reference books are listed under Further Reading.

Electronic Informants

To sail a boat efficiently, a sailor needs a great deal of information. Under favorable conditions, much of this information can be gathered simply by examining the water ahead, the behavior of yarn tell-tales, and so forth. Important clues also come from the sound of the water flowing past the hull, the feel of the wind on one's face, and the movements of the boat transmitted, quite literally, through the seat of one's pants. However, invaluable though all this may be, it is far from being an exhaustive list of the clues that can be of real assistance to the sailor. Electronics can be a great help in filling gaps in the information spectrum, particularly during darkness or periods of poor visibility. Furthermore, today's instrumentation can, in some cases, supply information that is unavailable to the human senses.

Speed through the water is, of course, the fundamental measuring stick for sailing performance, and is routinely evaluated by a marine speedometer, or **knotmeter**. The transducer for most modern knotmeters is a small propeller or paddle wheel which is exposed to the water flow and wired to produce a series of tiny electrical pulses. Circuitry housed within the knotmeter essentially counts the number of pulses per unit of time and offers up this information in the form of a visual display. Some knotmeters still employ a swinging-needle analog gauge, but an increasingly high proportion use digital electronic displays. For sailing instrumentation, liquid crystal displays (LCDs) are increasingly favored over light-emitting diodes (LEDs) because the latter consume much more current. The "cone of visability" for many early LCDs was annoyingly narrow, but recent designs such as the new "super-twist" types are much improved in this respect.

Rotating-speed transducers are generally reliable and inexpensive, but they are not infallibly accurate. Water flow is often substantially retarded in the boundary layer close to the hull, and the spinning transducer can be slowed by marine fouling or deterioration of its bearings. For this reason, there has been considerable interest in developing speed transducers that have no moving parts. The most promising so far is a device developed by Brooks and Gatehouse of the U.K. and marketed under the trade name SonicSpeed™. It consists of two tiny sonar units, one mounted on the bottom of the hull near the bow and the other on the leading edge of the keel. Sound pulses traveling from the bow transducer are received by the keel-

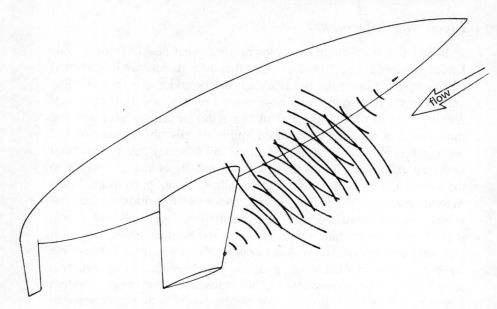

Fig. 17-1. The Brooks and Gatehouse SonicSpeed™ knotmeter works by comparing the transit time of sound signals traveling with the flow to signals traveling against it.

mounted one and vice versa. The device works because when the boat is moving, it takes a little longer for sound to travel against the flow than with it (fig. 17-1). By electronically measuring the difference between the transit times for simultaneous sound signals traveling in opposite directions, the central processing unit of the SonicSpeed knotmeter can measure speed with an accuracy of a hundredth of a knot or so, even when the boat is barely moving.

Along with boat speed, information on the velocity and direction of the apparent wind is of enormous importance to sailors. Almost all wind speed indicators are very similar in principle to paddle-wheel knotmeters. Wind direction indicators can use one of several types of transducers to translate the angular position of a carefully balanced wind vane into an electrical signal. In all cases this information is electronically converted into either a digital or an analog display of apparent wind angle. Both wind speed and wind direction transducers are normally mounted on an arm that slopes upward and forward from the masthead in order to minimize aerodynamic disturbances from the sails. Unfortunately, masthead transducers are subjected to violent pitching and swinging movements, making it difficult to design a unit that will give steady yet reliable readings in rough seas. This obstacle is generally attacked through a combination of lightweight construction and electronic averaging or "damping" techniques. However, even the most advanced masthead transducers are rarely able to compensate fully for variations in the aerodynamic upwash from the sails and fluctuations in heel angle. Users of sailing instrumentation should be aware that these transducers continue to be the weakest links in most systems. For this reason, the accuracy of the computer-processed information supplied by such systems may well be less reliable than the impressive two-decimal digital displays would lead us to believe.

Accuracy is less of a problem with the positional information provided by Loran C, the similar Decca Navigator system used in Europe, and the various types of satellite navigation. The basic operating principles of these navigational systems, while not particularly complicated, are outside the province of this discussion. Nevertheless, it should be noted that fixes provided by a Loran or SatNav receiver are commonly used in conjunction with boat performance data nowadays to determine the influence of tidal currents and to help select a course that will maximize progress toward a destination. This topic is discussed further in the following sections on integrated functions and autopilots.

Microcomputers and Integrated Functions

Boat speed, apparent wind speed and apparent wind direction are still the "big three" of sailing instrumentation, but thanks to the advent of the microcomputer, it has become feasible to evaluate sailing performance in new ways. Linked or integrated functions are derived from the combined inputs from two or more basic instruments. For example, **upwind velocity made good (VMG)** is the speed at which a sailboat gains upwind distance when in fact it is progressing on a course that is approximately 40 degrees from the true upwind direction.

To compute VMG, a microcomputer very quickly solves a series of vector problems using basic trigonometric principles. First it works out the speed and direction of the true wind by "subtracting" the effect of the boat's speed from the apparent wind to determine true wind speed and direction. Ideally, leeway, too, should be measured and used in determining true wind direction, but it almost never is.

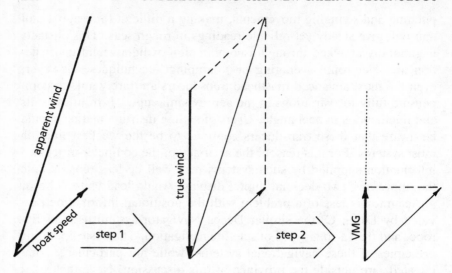

Fig. 17–2. Velocity Made Good (VMG) is computed by a two-step process. Onboard instrumentation supplies two vectors representing the velocity and direction of the apparent wind and the boat itself. These vectors are first resolved to determine the speed and direction of the true wind *(step 1)*. Then the true wind and boat speed vectors are resolved to provide VMG *(step 2)*.

VMG is then computed by resolving the vector of boat speed vs. true wind direction (fig. 17–2).

Upwind VMG is valuable information because it can aid in finding out how to sail a particular boat to windward most efficiently. Typically the best upwind VMG is achieved by pinching in flat water and footing off when it gets choppy. By referring to a VMG meter occasionally, a helmsman can get an idea of how high to point on the average. However, an attempt to steer by the VMG display will prove disastrous because the instrument has a significant, built-in time delay. Upwind, what typically happens is that the helmsman starts to pinch because the momentum of the boat is sufficient to temporarily increase the VMG reading as the boat is turned into the wind. The improvement is short-lived, however, because the luffing boat soon slows dramatically, causing VMG to plummet, and the only way to recover is to foot off substantially before gradually bringing the boat up hard on the wind again.

Downwind VMG is probably more valuable than upwind VMG because it is often extremely difficult to estimate the most efficient downwind tacking (actually gybing) angles, particularly in light air.

All the same, any attempt to steer directly by the VMG readout will be no more successful downwind than upwind. VMG information is a great tool for assisting a crew in zeroing in upon the optimum combination of boat speed and apparent wind angle for the particular conditions, but it doesn't get updated quickly enough to be much help with the moment-by-moment decisions involved in trimming and steering.

VMG readouts (along with the related true wind speed and true wind direction functions) are commonly available these days as a feature of instrumentation packages that include boat speed and apparent wind speed/direction. The "computer" in a typical instrument package is a type known as a **microprocessor**—a microchip that is permanently preprogrammed to perform a few specific tasks. Compact units typically house the central processing unit in a single small cabinet which has a multifunction digital display on its front face. By pressing waterproof switch pads, the functions can be viewed one at a time. More elaborate systems offer multiple display heads so that it is possible to view different functions simultaneously from different sites on deck and in the cockpit.

The state of the art in sailing instrumentation today has advanced far beyond simple VMG readouts. On serious offshore-racing boats today it is common practice to use the detailed performance predictions such as those obtained through the IMS handicapping program (see Chapter 6) as a means of establishing a performance baseline for the crew to try to match. This performance prediction data is loaded into an onboard microcomputer which is **interfaced** (electronically linked) with the transducers for boat speed and apparent wind speed/direction. Later, while sailing, the computer will display the performance for the particular true wind speed and angle currently being experienced and make a comparison to the performance that is actually being achieved. For example, the performance prediction for a 40-foot offshore yacht might be 7.2 knots on a 90 degree beam reach in 11 knots true wind, but, in reality, the boat is only making 6.7 knots. In this case, the computer will point out that the boat is performing at just 93 percent of her potential, and the crew should experiment with some trim adjustments in order to work up toward that target speed of 7.2.

This concept of **target speed** has become a very important one in contemporary performance sailing because it has proven easier to sail a boat to the knotmeter than to any other instrument. Beating to windward, a popular approach is to drive off to accelerate to the target boat speed before shifting attention to pointing high. Indeed, in most cases, if an effort is made to point before the target speed is reached, the boat speed may remain too low indefinitely. Downwind, a similar approach is used except that the boat is headed up slightly to reach the target speed before the crew shift their focus to sailing as low as possible.

Thanks to the growing popularity of the IMS and other performance prediction services, it is no longer necessary to install an on-board computer to take advantage of performance prediction and the target speed concept. Using target speeds taken from either an IMS certificate or a full-length performance prediction printout, a yacht owner can determine appropriate target speeds without the intervention of a computer. Often this information is presented in the form of a **polar plot**, which graphically depicts the boat speed that can be anticipated on each point of sail at a particular true wind speed. While it is easy enough to pick target speeds off a polar plot, it is just as easy and more accurate to obtain them from the numerical data printout of wind speed/direction vs. predicted boat speed upon which the polar plot is based. Approximately 500 types of yachts have been rated under IMS at the time of writing. Therefore it is often unnecessary to obtain a new IMS rating to make use of IMS performance prediction data; the certificate for a sister ship will do as well. Certificates and performance printouts are available from the United States Yacht Racing Union for a nominal fee. Good use can be made of this IMS data even if the only instrumentation aboard is a knotmeter (although the addition of a hand-held anemometer will usually improve the accuracy of wind speed estimates considerably).

In the last few years, the use of performance prediction data and target speeds has even changed sailboat racing techniques in some small but fundamental ways. Whereas conventional wisdom would have us bear away slightly with the arrival of each gust on a downwind leg of the course, performance prediction work has shown that it is more effective to delay bearing away until the higher target speed for the newly increased wind velocity has been achieved (fig. 17–3 left). The reason is that the boat accelerates much better when the apparent wind remains forward and as a result gets to spend more time at the higher target speed before the gust falters. Similarly, at the end of a gust, performance predictions show that it pays to sail extra low for a little while in order to convert the remaining ''speed surplus'' into

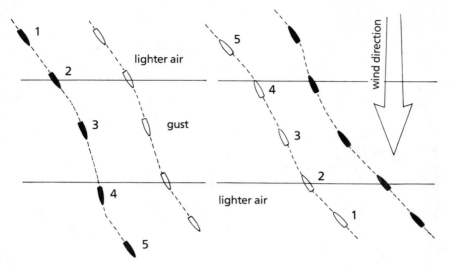

Fig. 17–3. Racing sailors have learned techniques to improve the efficiency of downwind and upwind sailing as a result of experience with modern instrumentation. In each illustration, the black boat makes use of the procedures described in the text to gain downwind or upwind distance on a competitor using "seat of the pants" sailing.

extra downwind distance. Sailing upwind in puffy conditions, the same principles apply in reverse (fig. 17–3 right).

Course Planning and Wind Shifts

The principle of VMG can be raised to a higher plane with the introduction of actual positional data as provided by Loran C or SatNav. True VMG can be defined as progress toward an actual destination as opposed to progress in the upwind or downwind directions. In the case of a long-distance passage or race that spans a period of days or weeks, it is highly improbable that the wind will fail to shift. Therefore, the best strategy is often to select the course that will cause the boat to close in upon the desired destination at the maximum possible rate (fig. 17–4). Later, when the wind changes, a new course is selected that again will result in the greatest true VMG.

Naturally, when it is possible to correctly predict the next wind shift, this strategy can be modified to further reduce the time required to complete a passage. For several years now, this approach has been used with spectacular results by top transoceanic racers. The record

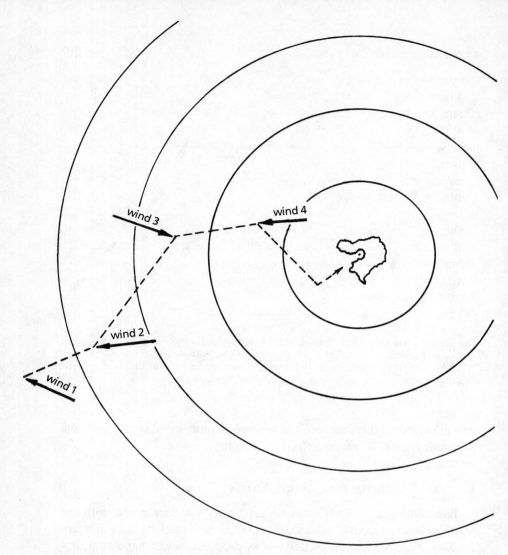

Fig. 17–4. On long passages during which major windshifts will probably occur, it usually pays to select the course and point of sail that will provide the best VMG toward the destination given the conditions of the moment. As the illustration shows, this does not necessarily mean "tacking on the headers."

crossings that have been broken and rebroken over the past few years by big sponsored multihulls are as much the result of space age weather forecasting (used in conjunction with computerized performance analysis) as they are a consequence of superior sailing performance. The trick in course selection is to find the ideal compromise between maximizing true VMG at the given moment and positioning the yacht where she will best be able to benefit from the next major windshift. Satellite weather data transmitted to an onboard weather facsimile receiver is an enormous help in making these predictions, as is sophisticated computer modeling of possible scenarios. Ultimately, of course, human judgment remains an important factor. However, in many of the prestigious single-handed and shorthanded races, as well as most record crossing attempts, skippers and navigators are permitted to receive advice radioed to them by shore-based analysts.

During the 1987 America's Cup in Perth, Australia—the last to be held in 12-meters—somewhat similar techniques were developed to improve upwind and downwind performance over much smaller distances. Like the majority of sailboat races everywhere, most races in Perth were conducted in oscillating winds which shifted from right to left and back again over a time scale of minutes. Working with wind data and performance instrumentation, the top competitors figured out how to boost VMG toward the next mark by sailing faster toward the side of the course that would benefit during the next wind shift. Racing upwind, for example, it was common practice to foot off until the VMG readings obtained were up to half a knot below those that the same 12-meter could have achieved by pointing higher and sailing slower. However, because the yacht was sailing faster, it moved farther away from the center of the course and realized a greater gain when it tacked on the next header (fig. 17–5). Computer modeling using wind and performance data made it feasible to determine the optimal sailing angles and target speeds that would maximize true VMG toward the windward or leeward mark in these oscillating breezes. Of course, trying to apply these techniques will only magnify the losses if the boat's tacks and gybes get out of phase with the wind shifts, so it is crucial to have a pretty good idea of what the wind will do next.

It should be noted that contemporary performance and tactical instrumentation, good as it is, has limitations, particularly in terms of response time. Like the basic VMG meter, it can only evaluate what has already happened. This can erode its usefulness aboard extremely fast boats like high-performance multihulls. Formula 40 catamarans, for example, change speed so abruptly and drag their apparent wind around so radically that the current generation of performance electronics developed for ballasted monohulls has proven of very little value.

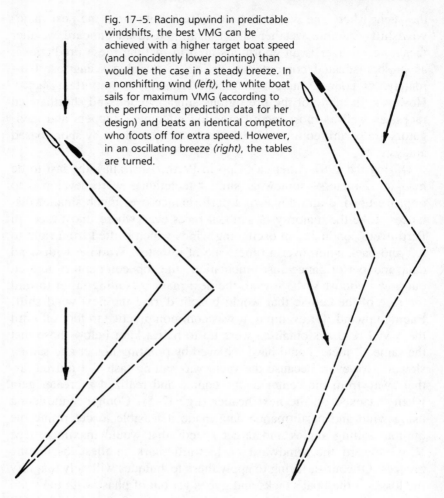

Fig. 17–5. Racing upwind in predictable windshifts, the best VMG can be achieved with a higher target boat speed (and coincidently lower pointing) than would be the case in a steady breeze. In a nonshifting wind *(left)*, the white boat sails for maximum VMG (according to the performance prediction data for her design) and beats an identical competitor who foots off for extra speed. However, in an oscillating breeze *(right)*, the tables are turned.

Autopilots and Electronic Compasses

Sailing is mostly fun, but steering hour after hour can get pretty tedious. This is particularly true, of course, when the wind fails and the cruiser is forced to resort to auxiliary power. Therefore it's not surprising that the potent yet modestly priced autopilots available today are extremely popular. Mechanical wind vane self-steering systems, while by no means extinct, are clearly losing ground to the electronic alternative and will probably become still rarer in years to come as more autopilots with optional wind-angle sensors become available.

As things stand, a typical sailing autopilot is fundamentally very similar to one for a power vessel. The unit consists of three components: a magnetic compass to detect changes in heading, a control unit to process heading information and send steering instructions, and a mechanical steering actuator that turns the rudder each time the boat must be brought back onto course. Primitive autopilots reacted to every detectable error in heading and as a result "hunted" for the correct course almost continually, gobbling lots of electric power in the process. Today, however, most units have a **deadband** with an adjustable range of perhaps 2 to 8 degrees. Automatic helm corrections are applied only when the boat's heading strays outside this preset null zone on the principle that a small course deviation will, as often as not, be rectified by the next wave. Alternatively, the electronics of the autopilot may incorporate a time-delay filter that prevents small course deviations from triggering the steering drive unless the boat remains off course for a short, predetermined time period.

The more advanced units may offer **proportional response**, so that larger heading errors are corrected by more vigorous rudder action than smaller ones. A **counter rudder** feature provides still greater refinement in automatic steering by reversing the helm as the boat swings back onto course to minimize oversteering. Finally, many autopilots offer a **trim** feature which permits the rudder to be set to an off-center position to compensate for an unbalanced helm. The automatic trim capabilities provided by some advanced units work by comparing the amount of time the controller signals for port helm vs. starboard helm, then adjusting the neutral position until both corrections are being used equally.

Regardless of the sophistication of their microprocessors, virtually all of today's small-craft autopilots rely primarily upon a magnetic compass to determine whether the vessel is on course or not. Conventional, rotating card compasses can be electronically "read" by either a simple electromagnetic device or a photocell arrangement. Increasingly often, however, a **fluxgate**, or electronic compass, is used to obtain better directional sensitivity and improved damping in rough weather.

A typical fluxgate compass consists of two small wire coils (weak electromagnets) that are set at right angles to each other. The strength of the electric current flowing through each coil is influenced by its orientation with respect to the earth's magnetic field and is maximum when that coil is aligned north-south. The relative strength of the signals from each coil provides a microprocessor with the raw data needed to derive the orientation of the fluxgate with respect to the earth's magnetic field and to display this information in degrees. Because the fluxgate compass provides an instantaneous and continuous readout, the microprocessor is generally programmed to average out the minor, short-term fluctuations in heading that are caused by waves or steering action.

Fluxgate compasses designed for tactical racing applications may be programmed to detect and identify trends in boat heading which can then be graphically displayed as, for example a "port tack lift." Those intended for autopilot and general use are frequently designed to perform other neat tricks such as compensating automatically for the deviation caused by onboard magnetic influences. Automatic compass correction requires that the vessel be powered through one or more full circles at a steady rate of turning. While this is going on, the microprocessor in the compass notes irregularities in the rate of swing that show up in the stream of data from the fluxgate, and subsequently applies corrections. There is even a fluxgate hand-bearing compass on the market now that can store a series of readings in its electronic memory. However, in this application, as well as for portable, self-contained autopilots, the fluxgate compass suffers somewhat because it is less tolerant of pitch and heel than a conventional compass. For this reason, it is generally desirable to mount the fluxgate unit below decks and as centrally as possible.

The day may be approaching when most autopilots will no longer be controlled primarily by magnetic compasses. Many already can be interfaced to a Loran C or SatNav receiver to permit automatic correction of the **cross-track errors** caused by currents or leeway. The next step is to use detailed positional information as the sole input for triggering course corrections. This is already possible in areas where Loran or Decca coverage is good, but it will not be feasible on a world scale until all the satellites that make up the NavStar Global Positioning System are in orbit, probably in the mid-1990s.

Sometimes it is desirable to steer to a particular apparent wind angle rather than to a set course. This is the case while beating to windward, or while running before the wind when an accidental gybe could be dangerous. Surprisingly few sailboat autopilots currently on the market offer wind vane inputs as an option to compass control.

Part of the problem is that high-performance sailboats tend to "make their own wind," especially while broad reaching in light-to-moderate conditions. Very likely, this stumbling block will be resolved in the next few years by a new generation of "smarter" autopilot controllers that will accept input from several sources simultaneously, much as a human helmsman can.

The Trend toward Integrated Functions

The electronics found aboard many yachts today often contains a great many redundancies, with separate microprocessors even in those instruments or subunits that perform largely overlapping functions. More and more, however, complex systems are being built around a single, general-purpose microcomputer similar (or identical) to those found on desktops everywhere. Using a mass-produced microcomputer as a centralized processor to digest the information from a bunch of transducers, electronic position finders, and so forth offers the advantage of more bang for the buck. Indeed, with the help of the navigation and performance evaluation programs now available, a stock portable computer can outperform the dedicated custom-built systems found on the America's Cup competitors of just a few years back and play amusing games on the side! The chief drawback is that a single component failure in a highly integrated setup is more likely to bring down the entire system. This is the reason why, marvelous as marine electronics has become, the traditional compass, sextant, and paper chart will doubtlessly be going to sea for a long time to come.

18

Where Next?
Sailing into the Twenty-first Century

Change is nothing new in sailing. During the 1950s and 1960s, the sport became egalitarian with the widespread acceptance of simple, mass-produced boats such as the Sunfish, O'Day Daysailer, and Catalina 22. The 1960s and 1970s brought increased diversity and rapid growth with numerous larger keelboats on the one hand and sailboards and Hobie cats on the other.

Recreational sailing was a bit like a gangly teenager during those boom years—full of energy and enthusiasm, but rough around the edges. During the 1980s, it grew up and became sophisticated, but perhaps lost something along the way. There is little question that advanced technology—the subject of this book—is having both positive and negative influences upon pleasure sailing. Although boats that perform better and superior sailing equipment should, in theory, be nothing but assets to the sport, more than a few sailors have been turned off by experiences with less-than-perfect innovations or by the high costs of keeping abreast of the state of the art. Nevertheless, for better or worse, there is no chance of returning to the more primitive sailing technology of earlier eras. Technological progress is by and large a one-way street.

Of course, there are other forces changing the character of contemporary sailing, and some of these may well have more short-term impact than any new technology. In many sailing centers, the cost and scarcity of wet-berth moorage, in conjunction with a generous supply of attractively priced used boats, have sharply curtailed the market for new sailboats. The numerous fiberglass sailboats built during the 1970s and 1980s won't be going away in any great hurry, particularly with the fiberglass maintenance and repair procedures that are now available. During their extended lives, these boats will continue to occupy a lion's share of the available moorage space—probably until well into the next century.

With a substantial number of yacht owners electing to maintain or upgrade existing vessels rather than acquire new ones, it is likely that the demand for up-to-date equipment such as new sails, rigging, sail-handling systems, electronics—even retrofitted keels and rudders—is likely to remain brisk. Another trend, directly linked to the escalating costs of maintaining a wet-berthed boat, is the growing popularity of trailerables. Because it is so difficult to design and build a small, lightweight boat that can fulfill the same roles as a large one, there is enormous scope for inventiveness in this area. The next few decades should bring numerous and exciting developments in the small sailboat field.

Mankind has been sailing for thousands of years, flying in airplanes for less than a hundred, and using computers extensively for barely thirty. It therefore seems paradoxical that much of the recent progress made in sailing technology stems directly from these upstart newcomers. The difference, of course, is that both aircraft and electronics are generally regarded as economic and military essentials, while sailboats today are viewed primarily as recreational equipment.

There is, however, reason to believe that sailing is on the verge of acquiring a new and less "frivolous" image. As fossil fuels get scarcer and the future of nuclear industry becomes increasingly uncertain, wind-propelled commercial shipping may soon become economically viable once again. Advanced windship propulsion systems are currently under development in many parts of the world. Should commercial wind-powered (or, more likely, wind-assisted) shipping become at all common, some of the technology from this new industry will probably trickle down to the pleasure-boating field. The chief benefactors are most likely to be those fortunate cruising sailors who can afford exceptionally large, highly automated yachts. However, spin-offs with more widespread applicability to recreational sailing cannot be ruled out. At the same time, commercial windships would probably provide additional opportunities for sailing technologists such as riggers, sailmakers and gear manufacturers who at present are struggling to make a living from the recreational sector.

For the time being, the chief motivation for research and development in sailing continues to be mankind's innate competitive urge, with a smattering of economic incentives thrown in for good measure. The great majority of sailors who race still do so entirely for pleasure, and often spend a good bit of their own money in the process. On the other hand, there is a growing subclass of racing sailors at the forefront of the sport who profit either directly as professional competitors or indirectly through the promotion of their sailing-related businesses. If sail racing continues to develop as a spectator and mass-media sport, there is every reason to believe that the pace of performance-related technological development will accelerate through the 1990s and into the next century. While it is virtually certain that professional racers will eventually be excluded from the amateur arena, this segregation is unlikely to prevent the spread of these innovations throughout the sport.

Most innovations in cruising sailboat technology in the twentieth century have been developed through racing and subsequently adopted for cruising, but this one-way flow may not be so apparent during the twenty-first. Examples of important sailing developments that have, in recent times, originated outside of racing include roller furling gear, compact autopilots, and self-tailing winches. The first two innovations on this list have become an accepted part of transoceanic racing, while the third is now used extensively on all sorts of larger racing yachts.

In the same vein, the gap between big racing yachts and their cruising brethren is starting to close after yawning widest during the late 1980s. The fast-declining IOR may well be the last of the type-forming rating rules. If, as seems likely, the evolving International Measurement System (or perhaps a successor to the IMS) proves capable of equitably handicapping a great diversity of cruisable boats, most future yachts will probably be designed, first and foremost, as fine cruisers. At the same time, existing cruising and racing/cruising designs will potentially be able to compete with new yachts on an equal footing, while many older racing machines will, no doubt, be fitted with heavier keels and nicer accommodations. After all, it makes no sense to sail an uncomfortable or unseaworthy boat if one that is free of these vices can compete with equal success!

There currently appears to be more room for improvement in the design of sailing rigs than in almost any other aspect of yacht design, and the next few decades should see major advances in this area. The present generation of stayed rigs setting triangular sails is highly refined, but inherently quite inefficient. Look forward to more widespread use of rotating rigs, both stayed and otherwise; and to nonrotating masts with vertical slats or other aerodynamic devices that will minimize turbulence along the leading edge of the mainsail. Rigid rigs too will no doubt become more sophisticated, but unless ways can be devised to reliably douse or reef them, they are unlikely to become very common.

Electronic navigation, while already impressive, is slated to advance much further in the near future. Electronic chart displays, for example, are still in their infancy. However, eventually, they are almost certain to become the norm, if only because the continued use of paper charts will become too difficult to integrate into what will otherwise be all-electronic navigation systems. In the early 1990s, as the aging Transat system of navigation satellites is superseded by the new Global Positioning System, the price of GPS receivers can be expected to drop even more precipitously than the price of Loran C receivers fell during the 1980s. This is expected because GPS, unlike Loran, will be of value to large numbers of land-based users.

Hand in hand with the improvements in navigation technology will be further advances in automated sailing. Theoretically it is already possible to build a robotic sailing yacht capable of trimming its sails efficiently and making its own way to a preselected waypoint or destination, even when upwind work is required. However, the development work involved in making such a system operate smoothly would be enormous, and it is highly questionable whether the exercise would be worthwhile. On the other hand, many of the individual ingredients that might go into a fully automated sailing system are certain to find widespread use. In addition to autopilots, which are clearly of enormous value to many sailors, powered sail-handling equipment is likely to become increasingly popular. After all, there is no inherent reason why sailing should be an athletic endeavor. Considering that autopilots are already allowed in some racing events, it would be surprising if powered sail trimming gear is not eventually permitted as well.

In small-boat sailing, the most successful and best-established one-design classes will no doubt carry on into the twenty-first century as islands of relative stability in a river of change. On the other hand, as in the past, amateur experimenters will continue to explore the outer limits of sailing technology using small and hence reasonably affordable boats as their test vehicles. Sailboarding is currently enticing many newcomers onto the water, but whether a significant proportion of these new converts will ever make the transition to other types of sailing craft remains to be seen. If there is much of a crossover effect, the next few decades could be a Golden Age for new varieties of radical beach-launched sailboats and lightweight, yet safe and comfortable trailerables. For the open-minded sailor, it promises to be an exciting time.

Further Reading

The books mentioned here should prove particularly useful (and interesting) to the recreational sailor who wants to learn more about various aspects of sailing technology. However, new technology, whether in sailing or any other area, seldom remains new for very long. For this reason, those who wish to remain reasonably up-to-date in what has become a fast-moving field must read periodicals as well. For this reason, I've included a list of six magazines which I feel will quite regularly be of interest to technically minded sailors.

BOOKS:
Sailboat Design and Function

Brewer, Ted. *Ted Brewer Explains Sailboat Design.* Camden, Maine: International Marine Publishing Co., 1985. A layman's introduction to yacht design. Should prove smooth sailing for most readers, while at the same time offering a strong grounding in fundamental principles. Stresses conventional knowledge and accepted practices rather than the latest thinking.

Gutelle, Pierre. *The Design of Sailing Yachts.* Camden, Maine: International Marine Publishing Co., 1979 (English translation, 1984). An interesting and, for the most part, lucid discussion of many aspects of modern sailboat design that aims at a considerably higher level than Brewer's book. Particularly good sections on waves and the dynamic behavior of sailing craft.

Marchai, C.A. *Aero-hydrodynamics of Sailing*. New York: Dodd, Mead & Co., 1979. Still the most detailed, comprehensive book on sailing theory available. Written on a level that a technically minded reader lacking formal training in engineering or advanced mathematics can understand, although certain sections are likely to take time and patience.

Seaworthiness

Marchai, C.A. *Seaworthiness: The Forgotten Factor*, Camden, Maine: International Marine Publishing Co.; 1987. A critique of many contemporary sailing and yacht design practices. While not everyone will agree wholeheartedly with the views Marchai expresses here, it would be difficult to disregard them in light of his credentials as a leading sailing theorist.

Rousmaniere, John, ed. *Desirable and Undesirable Characteristics of Offshore Yachts*. New York: W.W. Norton & Co., 1987. Written by members of the Technical Committee of the Cruising Club of America, this book presents a detailed analysis of the design characteristics and equipment requirements for safe offshore sailing in conventional ballasted monohulls. Recent research on breaking wave capsize phenomena is emphasized.

Offshore Racing Overview

Van Rietschoten, Cornelius, and Pickthall, Barry. *Blue Water Racing*. London: Nautical Books, 1985. An excellent handbook for offshore sailing and racing that covers almost everything from boat construction to emergency procedures. Very much up-to-date in most respects at the time of this writing.

Yacht Structures and Boatbuilding Technology

Gordon, J.E. *The New Science of Strong Materials, Or Why You Don't Fall Through the Floor*. 2d ed. London and New York: Penguin Books, 1976.

Gordon, J.E. *Structures, Or Why Things Don't Fall Down*. London and New York: Penguin Books, 1978. James Edward Gordon is a noted Professor of Materials Technology, and the two books he has written to introduce this fascinating field to the lay audience are real gems. Together they offer a highly entertaining, yet informative introduction to materials science and structural engineering. Gordon even discusses sailboats from time to time.

Gougeon, Meade, Joe, and Jan. *The Gougeon Brothers on Boat Construc-*

tion: Wood and the WEST System Materials. Bay City, Michigan: Gougeon Brothers, Inc., 1979. Although obviously slanted toward
contemporary wood boatbuilding techniques, this book is also one of
the best available on boatbuilding and yacht structures in general. Interesting reading even for sailors who have no interest in building their
own boats.

Nicolson, Ian. *Surveying Small Craft.* Camden, Maine: International Marine Publishing Co., 1974. Excellent guide for sailors who want a fundamental grounding in sound conventional boatbuilding practices.

Rigs and Sails

Donaldson, Sven. *A Sailor's Guide to Sails.* New York: Dodd, Mead &
Co., 1984. A basic handbook covering the design, construction, and
use of modern sails. Chapter 15 of *Understanding the New Sailing
Technology,* focuses on developments that have taken place since 1984
and represents an extension of this earlier book.

Henderson, Richard. *Understanding Rigs and Rigging.* Camden, Maine:
International Marine Publishing Co., 1985. A good, pragmatic treatment of conventional stayed rigs and their rigging. Basically conservative, with little discussion of advanced and unusual rigs.

Ross, Wallace. *Sail Power.* New York: Alfred A. Knopf, Inc., 1984. A
popular 1973 book that received minor revisions in 1984, *Sail Power*
is becoming fairly dated in some respects. Nevertheless, it remains an
encyclopedic source of information on sails, sail-handling gear, and
trimming techniques.

Marine Electronics

Pike, Dag. *Electronics Afloat.* London: Nautical Books, 1986. A clearly
written, up-to-date discussion of contemporary marine electronics. This
book is geared primarily to the needs of pleasure craft owners, although it covers all aspects of the field quite well.

West, Gordon, and Pittman, Freeman. *The Straightshooter's Guide to Marine Electronics.* Camden, Maine: International Marine Publishing Co.,
1985. Just what the title suggests—a no-nonsense, user's guide to buying, installing, and using modern electronics.

PERIODICALS

Multihulls. Sometimes funky, but basically a good source of information on
multihull sailing developments. Published monthly. May be difficult to
obtain except by subscription: 421 Hancock St., Quincy (Boston), MA
02171.

Sail. Well-known monthly that offers frequent analytical articles and good news coverage of late-breaking advances.

Sailing World. A monthly magazine of interest primarily to racing sailors although recent years have seen it broaden its targeting to include "performance sailors" in general. Regularly publishes informative articles on new technological developments.

Seahorse, International Yacht Racing. Until recently a bimonthly house publication of Britain's Royal Ocean Racing Club, this flamboyant magazine has now been purchased by the Observer and changed to a monthly, all-color publication. Routinely provides a remarkable assortment of worthwhile news and technical information that is pretty much unavailable elsewhere. Essential reading to any racing sailor who wants to keep abreast of developments in Europe. Subscription only: Lavender Ave., Mitcham Surrey, U.K. CR4 3HP.

Wooden Boat. Along with the nostalgia, this glossy bimonthly provides quite a bit of worthwhile information of modern boat design and construction.

Yachting. Established monthly which provides some fairly high level technical coverage, although not on a particularly regular basis.

Glossary

Added Drag—The extra resistance to motion through the water that is caused by rough sea conditions.

Airfoil—An object, typically streamlined in cross section, that is designed to produce lift when properly oriented with respect to a stream of moving air.

Ama—One of the outboard hulls of a trimaran or the smaller hull of a proa.

Angle of Attack—The angle made by the chord of a foil and the approaching flow.

Apparent Wind—The wind produced by the combination of the true wind blowing over the water and the "induced wind" created by the forward motion of the boat. The apparent wind is the wind felt by the crew whenever a sailboat is underway, as well as the wind to which the sails react.

Aspect Ratio—The ratio of height to girth in a sail, keel, centerboard, or rudder. A high-aspect foil has a long span and a short chord.

Autopilot—An electrical/mechanical device that automatically steers a boat on a preselected course or maintains a constant orientation with respect to the apparent wind.

Backstay—A rigging element extending from the mast to the stern that helps to prevent the rig from falling forward.

Batten—A stiff, narrow strip or rod used to support the leech of a sail and, in some cases, to control its draft.

Bernoulli's Principle—The pressure within a mass of moving fluid is inversely proportional to its velocity (a fundamental law of fluid dynamics which was first expressed by Daniel Bernoulli in 1738).

Bias—At an orientation of about 45 degrees to the threadlines of a woven fabric.

Bilge Boards—Paired centerboards situated on either side of the hull centerline and used primarily by the inland lake scow classes. Except while tacking, only one bilge board is extended at a time.

Block—A sheave or pulley contained in a housing and used to turn or deflect a line or rope with a minimum of frictional resistance.

Boom—A more-or-less horizontal spar which pivots athwartships and is used to hold the clew of a sail outboard.

Boundary Layer—The region close to the surface of an object immersed in a moving fluid where frictional forces retard the flow to some extent.

Brazier Buckling—Compression failure of a hollow structure such as a tubular mast that is initiated by sudden creasing and crumpling of its load-bearing walls while the structure itself remains "in column."

Broadseam—An overlapping seam whose width varies to create the effect of slightly tapering two adjacent panels in a sail. Broadseams are used to increase or, occasionally, to reduce the camber of sails.

Bulb Keel—A keel in which a substantial portion of the ballast is housed in a streamlined swelling at the keel tip in order to achieve a lower center of gravity.

Bulkhead—An internal structured panel that extends transversely across a hull to provide local support of the outer skin and overall torsional stiffness, as well as to subdivide the interior into compartments.

Buttocks—A series of longitudinal cross sections through a hull in the vertical plane that are parallel to the boat's centerline.

Camber—The curvature of a foil such as a sail, or of a hull/deck panel.

Carbon Fiber—A strong, extremely stiff material made by baking certain organic fibers at high temperatures under conditions that will not allow combustion.

Catamaran—A sailboat (or other vessel) consisting of two similar hulls connected in parallel.

Centerboard—An underwater foil which pivots aft to retract into an elongated trunk in the boat's bottom when it is not needed for resisting leeway.

Center of Buoyancy—A point at which all the buoyant forces acting upon a floating body may be considered to be concentrated so that, in effect, the combination of these forces behaves as a single greater force.

Center of Effort—The "balancing point" where all the forces acting upon a sail, fin, or other lift-generating foil have the net effect of a single combined force.

Center of Gravity—The point within (or near) an object around which all the parts of the object exactly counterbalance one another.

Checkstay—A backstay extending partway up the mast whose primary purpose is to prevent the mast from bowing forward excessively.

Chord—A direct line from the leading edge to the trailing edge of a foil.

Cold Molding—Building a laminated wooden hull by bending thin planks over a male mold and bonding them in place with an adhesive that cures at room temperature.

Composites—See *Fiber Composites.*

Compressive Strength—Ability of a material or structure to withstand inwardly directed end-to-end forces.

Crimp—The zigzag paths taken by the yarns comprising a woven material as they alternately pass over and under one another.

Critical Crack Length—The maximum length that a crack can attain in a piece of stressed material without precipitating rapid and complete fracture.

Crossbeams—The transverse structural members than link together the hulls of a multihull.

Cross Flow—The passage of air or water diagonally across a foil or around the tip of a foil.

Daggerboard—An underwater foil that retracts and extends by sliding more or less vertically through a short slot in the bottom of the boat.

Deadband—A range of a few degrees in vessel heading which an autopilot is programmed to ignore so as to reduce its running time and power consumption.

Doubler—An additional layer of aluminum alloy that is riveted or bonded to a spar to reinforce a highly stressed area.

Downwash—The deflection of flow that takes place downstream of a lift-generating foil. Downwash is so named because the air flowing past the trailing edge of an airplane wing is deflected toward the earth below.

Draft—The camber or curvature of a sail.

Drag—The retarding forces that act upon a sailboat as it passes through the air and water.

Ductility—A property of many metals, similar to plasticity, which enables them to be drawn out, bent, and formed without being appreciably weakened.

E-glass—The lowest grade of glass fiber commonly used in reinforcements for boatbuilding. Initially intended for making electrical insulators.

End Plate—A flat, perpendicular flow barrier affixed to one end of a fin or other foil that reduces tip vortex formation and induced drag.

Epoxies—A family of thermosetting plastic resins which are widely used in coating and adhesives.

Euler Buckling—A mode of compression failure that occurs when a slender structure bows out of column to the point that it can no longer sustain the load it is bearing.

Extrusion—Shaping heat-softened metal or unpolymerized plastic by forcing it through a die.

Fair—A curved line or surface that is free from localized undulations and irregularities.

Fatigue—Structural failure that eventually results from gradual changes which take place in a material when it is stressed repeatedly at relatively low levels.

Fiber Composites—Structural materials composed of a dense array of load-bearing fibers embedded in a plastic resin matrix.

Fillet—A strip of reinforcing material forming a rounded, concave junction where two surfaces meet.

Fin—The keel, centerboard, or rudder or a sailboat.

Finite Element Analysis—A computerized technique for modeling the stresses within a complex structure which involves subdividing the structure into a very large number of small, discrete units. In this way, the forces acting upon each portion of the structure can be more easily resolved and the design of structure optimized.

Flow Separation—See *Stall*.

Fluid—A substance, either gas or liquid, that has no fixed shape.

Fluxgate Compass—A popular type of electronic compass which detects the earth's magnet lines of force by measuring minor differences in electric current flow in two weak electromagnets oriented at right angles to each other.

Flying Shape—The three-dimensional shape a sail assumes when bent on the rig and pressurized by the wind.

Foil—An object, ordinarily streamlined in cross section, that is designed to produce substantial lift and only modest drag when correctly oriented in a stream of moving fluid.

Forestay—A rigging element extending from the foredeck to the mast whose primary role is to prevent the mast from falling or bowing backward, but which is often used to support the luff of a sail as well.

Form Drag—Drag resulting from the lateral deflection of fluid as it streams around a body.

Fractional Rig—A rig in which the forestay intersects the mast significantly below the masthead.

Global Positioning System—The highly sophisticated, second-generation satellite navigation system currently being deployed by the U.S. space shuttle and other launch vehicles. When fully operational sometime in the mid-1990s GPS will be capable of providing continuous positional information accurate to a few meters almost everywhere on earth.

Head—Pressure measured in terms of height of a column of fluid. (See *Hydrostatic Pressure*.) Also the intersection of the luff and the leech at the top of a sail.

Headstay—The forestay closest to the stem of a sailboat.

Honeycomb—A lightweight structural core material composed of thin sheets of paperlike material arranged to resemble the hexagonal cells of a natural honeycomb.

Hounds—The point where the headstay of a fractional rig attaches to the front of the mast.

Hydrofoil—A foil, functionally analogous to an airfoil, but optimized for the creation of lift in water. Most sailboat hydrofoils are vertical fins used to generate lateral resistance or steering forces. A few, however, are oriented more or less horizontally to provide vertical lift and support for advanced high-speed craft.

Hydrostatic Pressure—The pressure created at depth by the weight of the water above.

Induced Drag—Drag created as a direct consequence of the generation of lift.

Inertia—The tendency for an object to remain at rest, or if already in motion, to continue at a uniform speed in a straight-line path unless acted upon by an external force.

Interference Drag—Drag created by interaction of diverse flow patterns in an area where dissimilarly shaped objects ajoin one another. Interference drag occurs where the wings of an airplane adjoin its fuselage or where the fins of a sailboat attach to the underside of the hull.

Jumpers—A pair of stays used on many fractional rigs to support the portion of the mast that extends above the hounds. Jumpers pass over short spreaders called jumper struts which are ordinarily raked forward to some extent.

Kevlar—Trade name for plastics belonging to the aramid group that were developed by DuPont for use in automobile tire cords, but which have since found favor for many other applications requiring high strength and low weight.

Kinetic energy—The energy that a moving body possesses by virtue of its motion.

Lateral Resistance—The lift force created by the fins and immersed hull(s) of a sailboat which counteracts the lateral forces generated by the rig while closehauled or reaching.

Leading edge—The upsteam edge of a foil.

Leeway—The tendency of most boats to sideslip slightly while sailing upwind or crosswind courses.

Lift—A force acting at right angles to the axis of flow that is produced when moving fluid is diverted in an asymmetrical pattern by a body in its path.

Loran C—An electronic position-finding system for vessels that functions by measuring the tiny differences in arrival times of simultaneously transmitted radio signals from widely separated shore-based beacons. Loran C is popular in North America, while the fundamentally similar Decca system fulfills the same role in Europe.

Luff foil—A grooved plastic or aluminium extrusion that accepts the bolt rope of a headsail and becomes the actual leading edge of the flying sail.

Masthead Rig—A rig characterized by a headsail that extends to the very top of the mast.

Mechanical Advantage—The ratio of the force generated by a machine to the force that is applied to operate the machine.

Microprocessor—A computer memory-processing unit that is preprogrammed to perform a particular role and miniaturized on an integrated circuit chip.

Monocoque—A type of construction used in some boats and aircraft in which the outer skin sustains all or most of the stresses.

Mylar—DuPont trade name for polyester in sheet or film form.

Neutral Axis/Neutral Plane—The areas within a beam or panel that sustain neither tensile nor compressive stresses when these structures are subjected to bending loads.

Oil Canning—Undesirable in-and-out movements of inadequately stiffened hull panels.

Overhangs—The portions of the bow and/or stern of a boat's hull that extend beyond the resting waterline.

Pan—A molded fiberglass inner hull liner, often incorporating channels and corrugations, that is bonded inside the hull of a series-built fiberglass yacht to provide added strength, stiffness, and a finished look.

Panels—1) The areas of hull or deck that span the distance between internal supporting members such as stringers or bulkheads; 2) sections of a stayed mast between the shroud insertions; 3) individual pieces of sailcloth which are sewn together to make a sail.

Parasitic Drag—Extra drag caused by superficial bumps and protrusions that stand out from the overall smooth surface of a boat or other vehicle.

Pitching—Vigorous up-and-down motions of the bow and stern of a vessel caused by the passage of waves.

Pitchpoling—Literally a forward capsize usually initiated by burying the bow while sailing rapidly downwind in large waves.

Planform—The outline of a fin, sail, or other foil as viewed directly from the side.

Planing—In general terms, skimming across the surface of the water. In sailing, the term is used specifically to describe a situation where dynamic lift created by water deflected downward from the underside of the hull supports a major proportion of the boat's weight.

Plotter—A computer-controlled machine that traces patterns on flat sheet stock.

Polar Plot—A radial graph of sailboat performance for various wind speeds and directions.

Polyester—A family of plastics consisting of long chains of ester subunits. Polyesters are widely used in fiber manufacture and as thermosetting resins for fiberglass laminating.

Potential Energy—Latent energy possessed by something as a consequence of its position, internal stresses, or its capability of undergoing an energy-yielding chemical reaction.

Pre-pregs—Short for pre-impregnated reinforcing materials; fiber composite laminating materials that come from the manufacturer already coated with resin and ready to apply.

Pressure Gradient—A progressive increase or decrease in pressure over a distance.

Proa—A two-hulled vessel consisting of a main hull and a smaller stabilizing hull mounted off to one side.

Radial—Sail layout pattern in which a series of more-or-less triangular panels radiate from a head, tack, or clew.

Rake—The front-to-back inclination of a rig, fin, or other foil.

Range of Positive Stability—Heel angles up the critical angle at which a particular boat's self-righting tendency shifts to a capsizing tendency.

Ratchet Block—A sailboat block equipped with a mechanism that permits the sheave to rotate in only one direction. Attempts to pull the line through in the opposite direction must overcome the friction of the line sliding over the stationary sheave.

Resistance—In the language of naval architecture, drag associated specifically with the passage of a vessel through the water.

Ring Frame—A bulkhead that has been "trimmed back" extensively to save weight and provide a more open interior. (See *Bulkhead.*)

Rocker—The extent to which the bottom of a boat curves up at the bow and stern as viewed in profile.

Rod Rigging—Standing rigging made of individual metal rods instead of multistrand wire or fiber ropes.

Rotational Inertia—The tendency of an object to resist intermittent forces that cause rotation about a central axis. High rotational inertia is usually associated with shapes in which a high proportion of the total mass is situated far from the central axis.

Roving—Reinforcing materials using composite construction that are composed of relatively large bundles or bands of untwisted fibers.

Running Backstays (Runners)—Paired port and starboard backstays extending from the hounds of a fractional rig to the stern of the boat. Underway, the windward runner is tensioned to provide headstay support while the leeward runner is eased to prevent interference with mainsail shape.

Sandwich Construction—Common method for building a stiff, weight-efficient panel by bonding two high-strength skins to the opposite faces of a relatively thick, low-density core.

Scantlings—The specifications for the materials, configuration, and assembly of a yacht's structures.

Scow—A flat-bottomed sailboat with a wide bow that is designed to be sailed upwind at a substantial angle of heel.

S-Glass—A type of fiberglass developed specifically for structural applications that has mechanical properties superior to the less costly and more widely used E-glass.

Shear Strength—The ability of a material to withstand forces which tend to cause contiguous portions of an object to slide past one another.

Sheer—The curved shape of the line formed by the intersection of the hull topsides and the deck.

Shrouds—Standing rigging elements whose primary role is to support a mast from side to side.

Skeg—1) A small fixed fin near the stern of a boat that is intended to improve tracking ability and directional control; 2) the fixed fin that supports the movable rudder blade in a skeg-mounted rudder installation.

Skin Friction—See *Viscous Drag*.

Solid Rig—A sailing rig consisting of a relatively thick, rigid airfoil as opposed to flexible, two-dimensional sails. The term is something of a misnomer because solid rigs are almost always hollow, lightweight structures.

Space Frame—In boatbuilding, the incorporation of a lattice-like internal skeleton to reinforce a lightweight hull/deck shell.

Spade Rudder—A rudder whose entire blade area is cantilevered from a sturdy shaft that projects downward from the stern of the boat.

Span—In aeronautics, the distance from wing tip to wing tip of an airplane. Now used for the corresponding dimension of any foil as measured perpendicular to the direction of flow.

Spectra—Allied Chemical's brand name for a high-strength plastic fiber related to polyethelene.

Spreaders—Struts used primarily to hold shrouds away from a mast so that they intersect at a more favorable angle.

Stall—Stoppage or detachment of flow along the low-pressure face of a foil that results in a dramatic loss of lift along with an increase in turbulence and drag.

Stays—Rigging elements that support a mast fore and aft.

Stiffness—The ability of a solid material to resist deformation under load. (See *Young's Modulus.*)

Straddle Stability—A term that graphically describes the exceptionally high lateral stability of multihulls. (In fact, both monohulls and multihulls achieve their stability by the same mechanism.)

Strain—The deformation that results when a solid object is subjected to stress.

Stress—A force that tends to deform a solid object in one way or another.

Stress Concentration—A site within a part or structure where stress levels are particularly high as a consequence of design and construction features.

Stress Trajectories—Hypothetical curved pathways followed by the stresses within a structure or part.

Stringers—Longitudinal structural members that back up the outer skin and ordinarily pass through notches in the bulkheads or ring frames.

Surfing—In sailing, a temporary planing action down the face of a wave that is assisted by gravitational forces.

Target Speed—The boat speed known to provide the best VMG for a given wind speed and wind angle.

Tensile Strength—The ability of a material sample or part to withstand end-to-end pulling loads.

Time Allowance—The amount of time that a faster-handicapped boat must finish ahead of a slower-handicapped one in order to tie it in a race.

Tip Vortex—A swirling pattern of turbulence that trails continuously from the open end(s) of most lift-generating foils as a consequence of the pressure differential between one face of the foil to the other.

Toggle—An articulating linkage designed to avert cyclical bending that would otherwise cause fatigue in standing rigging.

Torlon—The trade name for an exceptionally hard, strong plastic manufactured by Amoco.

Toughness—The ability of some materials to withstand impacts and other physical abuse without fracturing.

Trimaran—A boat with a central hull and two smaller outboard hulls.

True Wind—Wind speed and direction as perceived by an observer who is motionless with respect to the earth.

Upwash—The deflection of approaching fluid toward the low-pressure side of an airfoil situated farther downstream.

Velocity Made Good (VMG)—The rate at which a sailboat makes upwind or downwind progress while sailing obliquely with respect to the true wind on either a closehauled or a broad-reaching course. Similarly, the rate a vessel approaches a geograpical goal while sailing a course other than the direct one to the destination.

Velocity Ratio—The ratio between the speed at which a crew member spins a winch handle to the speed at which the line moves over the drum. Velocity ratio is identical to the theoretical mechanical advantage of a winch, but the actual mechanical advantage after frictional losses is always lower.

Ventilation—Partial loss of lift in a hydrofoil caused by surface air being sucked down to the low-pressure side of the foil.

Viscous Drag—Drag associated with frictional sheer forces within the boundary layer. Frequently, but less accurately called skin friction.

Wake—A turbulent zone downstream of an object immersed in moving fluid.

Wetted Surface—The total surface area of the immersed portion of a sailboat including its fins.

Wings—Lateral extensions of the topsides and decks used on some high-performance boats to position crew weight farther to windward.

Yield—Permanent deformation of a material or object as a result of excessive stress.

Young's Modulus—The stiffness of a solid material expressed as the ratio of stress to strain.

Index